Contemporary Issues in Islamic Law, Economics and Finance

A Multidisciplinary Approach

Giappichelli-Routledge Religions, Laws and Economies in the Mediterranean Space

Book Series Direction

The Director of the Book Series is appointed by the Scientific Council of the Research Center REDESM of the University of Insubria.
The Editorial Board is composed of academics belonging to different scientific and disciplinary sectors of the macro-area involved by the Book Series approved by the Scientific Council of the Research Center REDESM.

The Mediterranean was the cradle of many religious and political models, which transformed themselves into universal paradigms. Much has been written about this geopolitical space and its peoples, within the context of their religious and political institutions and their commercial and cultural exchanges. However it seems that this unitary vision, predominant in the past, has recently been replaced by a fragmented and partial approach; that one focuses on the individual regional actors only, neglecting the overall picture and the connections between the different parts.

This *Book Series* aims to promote an interdisciplinary analysis of the connection between the religious, social, economic, and legal aspects of the Mediterranean world. It emphasizes the role of religious beliefs and institutions as a "discursive heritage", pragmatically used in the construction of political and economic systems. Religious phenomenology will be analysed from a diachronic and dynamic perspective to highlight the interdependence between the diversified cultural forms of the Mediterranean area. The core idea is that contemporary globalization, by re-proposing old questions in new scenarios, deepens and reveals forms of osmosis between different social systems. Globalization, and the pluralism it entails, challenges the post Second World War constitutional and democratic model, which was based on the universality of human rights, with the difficulty of realizing its promises; such a challenge reactivates tensions between contemporary universalistic claims and modern nationalistic reactions. Religion, economy, state politics, international and religious rights, and soft rules are all part of this transformation, which combines in a new way modern and contemporary paradigms.
To achieve these objectives, this *Book Series* is committed to publish works produced in languages different than the English one. Exchanging methods and knowledge in one of the most important languages of globalization, along with a comparative study of the relationships between the two shores of the Mediterranean, shall constitute a further step towards the overcoming of unilateral interpretations and culturally rooted stereotypes. Moreover, the *Series* will be linked to a web platform, created to stimulate a dialogue between researchers, but also to gather and share documents.

The *Book Series* "Laws and Economies in the Mediterranean Space" is an integrated academic project, organized by the *Research Centre for Religion, Law and Economy in the Mediterranean Area* of the Insubria University, together with other Italian and foreign academic and research institutions (among others, three Universities of Milan, the Universities of Rome III, Padua, Turin, the Oriental Piedmont and, abroad, the Universities of Carthage, Tunis and Saint-Joseph, Beirut); furthermore, it is also an educational project, aimed at stimulating a cultural exchange between students, teachers, and researchers, on the one hand, and religious, social, economic and institutional actors, on the other hand.

Contemporary Issues in Islamic Law, Economics and Finance

A Multidisciplinary Approach

Edited by
Flavia Cortelezzi and Alessandro Ferrari

ROUTLEDGE
Routledge
Taylor & Francis Group

IUSTITIAM COLIMUS
G. Giappichelli Editore

First published 2023
by Routledge
2 Park Square, Milton Park, Abingdon, Oxon OX14 4RN

and by Routledge
605 Third Avenue, New York, NY 10158

Routledge is an imprint of the Taylor & Francis Group, an informa business

British Library Cataloguing-in-Publication Data
A catalogue record for this book is available from the British Library

Library of Congress Cataloging-in-Publication Data
A catalogue record for this book has been requested

ISBN: 978-0-367-72508-2 (hbk-Routledge)
ISBN: 978-1-003-15521-8 (ebk-Routledge)
ISBN: 978-0-367-72542-6 (pbk-Routledge)
ISBN: 978-88-921-3707-3 (hbk-Giappichelli)

Typeset in Simoncini Garamond
by G. Giappichelli Editore, Turin, Italy

The manuscript has been subjected to a double blind review process prior to publication.

This book has been published in the frame of the project PRIMED - Prevenzione e interazione nello spazio trans-mediterraneo *thanks to the financing of the Italian Ministry of University and Research*.

RELEMS PriMED Ministero dell'Università e della Ricerca

CONTENTS

LIST OF FIGURES AND TABLES

INTRODUCTION

Flavia Cortelezzi and Alessandro Ferrari

SUMMARY: 1. Premise. – 2. Contemporary Issues in Islamic Law, Economics and Finance: The Analysis. – 2.1. Part 1: Fundamentals and Comparative Perspectives. – 2.2. Part 2: Fundamentals of Mediterranean Economics and Finance. – 2.3. Part 3: Banking, Finance, and Business Opportunities. – About the Authors/Editors.

1. Premise

It is possible to say that the roots of Islamic finance and Islamic banking are at the beginning – and at the core – of the Islamic revelation. It was also the appeal for justice and the human voluntarism in this direction promoted by the revelation of a merciful God that pushed the Prophet from the merchant's Mecca to Yathrib-Madinah legitimizing, with time, the economic thinking of Islam. It is for this reason, and because Islamic finance and banking genetically express a foundational link between revelation and human earthly well-being, that they occupy a very special place in the contemporary global market. If it is already arguable to define this latter as a real "secularised" space, Islamic finance and banking, with their direct link with at least one of the five Islamic pillars, have a very complex relationship with secularisation. In fact, they not only openly recall the inevitable moral tensions between means and purposes but raise the question about their role as real factors of "economic pluralism" able to interact with other economic "justice-oriented" economic approaches. Today, Islamic finance and Islamic banking are mostly found in the Middle East, Asia, and Africa, where they provide financial services to individual Muslims and to several governments and central banks in countries that often give Islamic finance an official or semi-official status. However, globalisation is also spreading Islamic banks and financial services across the so-called "Western world". In this way, Islamic finance is one of the instruments that aims, at the same time, to answer and to cause Muslim identity, revealing how thin is the thread on which walk those who really want to be instruments of divine justice and, at the same time, aspire to well-being as a reward for their commitment. For this reason, the Islamic finance industry today represents an important reality not only because of the oil wealth of the Gulf states, which have fuelled demand for such financial services, but also for an increased demand from a growing Muslim population in the West that aspires to express a full and all-inclusive religious identity. The increased demand for Muslim financial institutions in the West has also prompted Western non-Muslim firms to begin providing these services in an interesting effort of "acculturation" to the new plural scenario. HSBC, Lloyds Bank, Deutsche Bank and Citigroup are among the most notable examples of Western firms adapting to tap into these new Islamic, religiously oriented funds.

2. Contemporary Issues in Islamic Law, Economics, and Finance: The Analysis

By adopting a multidisciplinary approach, which will also take into account theological, legal and geopolitical frameworks, this book will offer a comprehensive picture of Islamic financial tools, contracts and business opportunities. These topics were at the centre of the training in Islamic finance and banking offered to businesspeople and market operators organised in the academic year 2020–2021 by the Research Centre RELEMS (Religion, Law and Economy in the Mediterranean Space) of the University of Insubria in the frame of PRIMED (Prevenzione e Interazione nello spazio Trans-Mediterraneo), a research grant funded by the Italian Ministry of University and devoted to foster the cooperation between Italian and OCI universities and from which this book has taken its inspiration.

The book explores how the interaction among religious principles, (different kinds of) laws, economics and finance, through different institutions and dynamics shape the evolution of instruments such as funds and contracts and their impacts in fostering business opportunities. In particular, the book will provide a complete and extensive overview of the practice of Islamic finance and banking through the lenses offered by studies of economics and management.

The book is organised into three Parts. The first Part explores how ethics and religious laws, legal system(s) of state(s) and economics interact in an integrated approach, generating sustained economic growth. Part 2 analyses some general principles related to the Economics and Finance of MENA Regions, the role of the EU's Cooperation Policy with the MENA and the capacity of Islamic Finance and banking to cope with a plural and democratic societal landscape. The third Part of the book focuses on Islamic Banking and Financial systems as a generator of Business Opportunities.

2.1. Part 1: Fundamentals and Comparative Perspectives

In the first chapter, Murat Cokgezen, going to the core of the issue, analyses the problem of how to reconcile Islam and Finance, and integrate Muslims into a universalistic and self-grounded Financial Market. According to Cokgezen, if there is a consensus among economics about the crucial role of financial markets in economic development and if it is possible for Muslims to allocate savings into investment channels, some of the allocation mechanisms of these markets conflict with basic Islamic teachings. A traditional example is interest, which remains one of the major prices in financial markets that allocates resources but also remains banned in Islam. These conflicts raise dilemmas for Muslims who want both to improve their economic status and live in accordance with the teachings of Islam. Scholars and practitioners from various disciplines have discussed different aspects of the tensions between market rules and Islam prescriptions. In order to find an accommodation and facilitate the inclusion of Muslims in the global financial markets – within this "osmotic frame", where different normative orders interact – practitioners and scholars have experienced and proposed financial instruments aimed at answering the claims of an Islamic orthopraxis. Obviously, the debate on the effective compliance of these financial instruments with "Islam" is still not over.

Deborah Scolart, in Chapter 2, highlights the relationships between Islamic Ethics, Law and Economics. In particular, she explores the conditions of the "islamicity" of a social or/and legal institution. To answer this question it is necessary to take into account not only the specific borders and contents of the so-called religious law, sharia in this case, but also the way in which the rules are formulated and how they translate the values generated by religious experiences. In the light of these methodological principles, according to Scolart, Islamic finance is not only the answer to the prohibition of *riba* and *gharar* but a broader expression of ethics and morality whose institutions share with others sharia-governed institutions the same orthopratic ambition towards the building of an effective justice-oriented society.

Murat Çizakça, in Chapter 3, examines the pre-conditions for Islamic finance to generate sustained economic growth. In this chapter he argues that the current obsession of Muslims with Islamic finance obscures the fact that unless certain pre-conditions are fulfilled, Islamic finance cannot trigger sustained economic growth in the Islamic world. The chapter identifies these pre-conditions and examine whether they can be "imported" from the West through an osmosis with Islam.

2.2. Part 2: Fundamentals of Mediterranean Economics and Finance

The first chapter of this section, written by Jamus Jerom Lim, offers a retrospective on the economics and finance of MENA regions. Lim examines the economic geography and history of the region, and then proceeds to sketch out the current political-economic structure of MENA economies, with a focus on intra-region commonalities and interrelationships. He then examines the region in a comparative perspective, with attention to future prospects. The paper then zooms in on one important aspect of finance in the MENA region: Sovereign Wealth Funds (SWF). SWF are here analysed in their main features, taking into account their both regional and global spread, with a particular focus on the role of macroeconomic assumptions.

Chapter 5, written by Giuseppe Colangelo, examines the EU Cooperation Policy with the Northern African Mediterranean and the Middle East Countries. The chapter analyses the recent developments of the European neighbourhood policy, starting from the pivotal Barcelona declaration, to illustrate the major changes, developments and results obtained since then. The chapter also evaluates the importance and the effectiveness of the aids granted by the European Union to these countries on their way to both economic improvement and the democratic transition after the Arab Spring turmoil.

2.3. Part 3: Banking, Finance, and Business Opportunities

In the first chapter of Part 3, Flavia Cortelezzi briefly presents the main principles and instruments used by Islamic finance, its diffusion and the opportunities and challenges of development of Islamic Financial System. After analysing the diffusion of this financial system in Mediterranean countries, she focuses on its main instruments, in particular stressing its distinctive features. Estimating the value of any asset on the basis of its "real" value, entering into contract and clearly defining the prices of goods/services and the share of each partner in profit/loss seem the more important assets of this financial system today by traditional firms and banks when considering promising business opportunities.

In Chapter 7, Paolo Biancone and Silvana Secinaro describe the framework and functioning of the Islamic Bank, analysing its differences from conventional banks. In particular, they emphasise the parallelism between the universality of the religious roots of this system and the universality of the possible replication of the latter at the international level. In fact, the goal of the chapter is to analyse the characteristics and functions that can guarantee the replicability of the Islamic banking in the global market as a catalyser of ethical-social oriented investments.

In Chapter 8, Cedomir Nestorovic, focuses on the marketing of Islamic banks and Takaful companies. The concept of marketing is considered a novelty for the Islamic banking industry, which used to rely mainly on "natural" Muslim, Islamic sentiments. This chapter explores how banks promote the performative effect *marketing* strategies to Islamise their financial products and services through articulated plans based on principles, policies and practices.

Michael J.T. Mcmillen, in Chapters 9 and 10, examines how Islamic finance enhances business opportunities in becoming a global industry and providing financial services to Muslim populations across the world. Some of these services, primarily Islamic banking, serve local Muslim populations. Others serve the needs of Middle Eastern investors who have sought to diversify and expand their investment portfolios – this is the case of services assisting the investments of Middle Eastern investors in real estate and private equity in the United States and Europe. The growth pattern of Islamic finance leaves the impression that Islamic finance is for Muslims and those relatively few North American and European entities that serve Muslim investors. Nevertheless, these chapters urge a broader view. In fact, they suggest a counterintuitive view that includes the perspective of the use of Islamic financing techniques to enhance the economic opportunities and interests of non-Muslim businesses in predominantly non-Muslim areas. Among the benefits of this approach, the chapters suggest the capacity of Islamic financing in facilitating the access to a large pool of otherwise unavailable investment capital and the related advantages of risk diversification in capital sourcing affording, at the same time, the benefits of ethical financing. Lack of familiarity with Islamic finance is an impediment to the use its techniques in jurisdictions where Muslims are the minority. For the other, various preconceptions attend that lack of familiarity. In fact, Islamic finance transactions are thought to be based upon mysterious and uncertain principles and to be more complicated in terms of documentation and implementation. These two chapters address those preconceptions and attempt to dispel some of the related misconceptions. A few of the most common transactional structures are discussed and compared to their interest-based financing equivalents in the "traditional" market. Within this general frame, the first paper addresses the realm of private investment and the second that of capital markets financings.

Finally, Fabrizio Vismara concludes Part 3 with Chapter 11 which provides some insight specifically from the Italian financial market. In fact, this chapter examines some aspects related to the application of Islamic finance principles in the Italian legal system, comparing the possibility of accommodation between the principles of Islamic finance and national rules. The most relevant aspects of Islamic finance products are examined in the light of Italian internal regulations, with particular reference to the Consolidated Financial Act (Legislative Decree no. 58 of 24 February 1998) and the practice of the National Commission for Companies and the Stock Exchange.

About the Authors/Editors

Paolo Biancone, is Full Professor of Islamic Finance at the Department of Management, University of Turin – Italy. He attended the Business Case Study Programme at Harvard University and the ITP International Teacher Programme at the London Business School. He is the Editor in Chief of the European Journal of Islamic Finance, and President of HalalTo, University of Turin Spin off. He is the Scientific Director of the Islamic Finance Observatory of the University of Turin, which deals with topics related to international finance and the attraction of investments TO the area.

Murat Cizakca is a professor of comparative economic and financial history as well as Islamic economics at the KTO Karatay University in Konya, Turkey. He received his B.A. degree from the University of Leicester and his Ph.D. from the University of Pennsylvania. After retiring from Bogazici University in Istanbul he taught at the University of Luxembourg, the Ludwig Maximillian's University in Munich and at INCEIF University in Kuala Lumpur. He is a former fellow of Wissenschaftskolleg zu Berlin, Institut d'Etudes Avancées de Nantes, and Istituto di Storia Economica (Datini), Prato. In 2016 he has been awarded memberships by Academia Europaea and European Science Foundation.

Murat Çokgezen is a Professor in economics at Marmara University, Turkey. He received his Ph.D. in Economic Development and international Economics from Marmara University in 1995. He has published extensively in leading academic and policy-oriented journals on a wide range of topics in the area of Islamic economics, empirical issues in microeconomics, economics education, and business association.

Flavia Cortelezzi is Associate Professor of Political Economy in the Department of Law, Economics and Culture, at Insubria University Como (Italy) and Deputy Director of the Research Center "Religions, Rights and Economies in the Mediterranean Space" (REDESM) at the same university. Besides Insubria University, she is currently teaching at the Catholic University of Milan. She graduated at the Catholic University of Milan and she obtained a Master of Arts in Economics at the Université Catholique de Louvain la Neuve. She received her Ph.D. degree in Economics from the

University of Bologna. Her research focuses on innovation, capital structure and strategies of firms in local economic systems. Her research has been published in journals such as *Oxford Economic Papers*, *Review of Quantitative Finance and Accounting*, *Industry and Innovation*, and other leading journals in Economics and Finance.

Giuseppe Colangelo is Full Professor of Economics in the Department of Law, Economics and Cultures at the Insubria University in Como, Italy. He has an M.Sc. in Economics from the London School of Economics and a Ph.D. in Economics from Birkbeck College, University of London. Besides Insubria University, he has taught at the Catholic University of Milan, at the Institute for Advanced Studies of Vienna and at the Franklin University Switzerland. He has research interests in the field of Industrial Organization, Economics of European Integration and Public Economics. He has authored many articles and essays, also published in international reviews and journals like the *Journal of Industrial Economics*, *International Tax and Public Finance*, *Journal of Agricultural & Food Industrial Organization*, *Economia Politica*, *Metroeconomica*, *Public Finance and the Manchester School.* He has written several essays published in printed books. He was Vice-Rector of Insubria University from 2012 to 2018.

Alessandro Ferrari is Full Professor of Law and Religion at the University of Insubria (Varese and Como) and Director of the Research Center "Religions, Rights and Economies in the Mediterranean Space" (REDESM) at the same university. His research focuses on the transformation of the right to religious freedom in Europe and in the countries of the MENA area. Since 2019 he has been Visiting Fellow at the Islamic Legal Studies Programme of the Harvard Law School (Law and Social Change). In 2018 he was Directeur d'Etudes invité at the Ecole des Hautes Etudes Pratiques. In 2014–2015 he was Roberta Buffett Visiting Scholar at Northwestern University, Evanston (IL).

Jamus Jerome Lim is an associate Professor of Economics at ESSEC Business School. Previously, he was the chief economist of the ThirdRock Group, an investment management and wealth advisory, a lead economist at the Abu Dhabi Investment Authority – where he oversaw economic inputs underlying tactical and strategic asset allocation for the sovereign fund's multi-hundred-billion dollar portfolio – and before that, a senior economist with the World Bank, where he led a number of initiatives on macroeconomic forecasts, along with analysis of trade, finance, and governance issues in East Asia, the Middle East, and Africa. His research expertise and interests lie at the intersection of international macro-finance, political economy, and development economics, and his work has appeared in leading academic journals such as the *Journal of Monetary Economics* and

Journal of Money, Credit, and Banking, along with policy flagships such as the World Bank's *Global Economic Prospects* and the joint IMF-World Bank *Global Monitoring Report.* A seasoned communicator, his ideas have been featured in print media such as the *Financial Times* and *Straits Times*, and he also regularly shares his views on radio and television outlets such as *CNA*. An old Rafflesian, he graduated with first-class honours in economics from the University of Southern Queensland, and went on to graduate work at the London School of Economics, the University of California, and Harvard University.

Michael J.T. Mcmillen is a partner of the international law firm of Curtis, Mallet-Prevost, Colt & Mosle LLP and an Adjunct Professor at the University of Pennsylvania Law School, teaching Islamic finance at the Law School and The Wharton School. His principal areas of practice are Islamic finance and project and infrastructure finance. Among his many honours, Michael has twice been the recipient of Euromoney's award for Best Legal Advisor in Islamic Finance and the Sheikh Mohammad bin Rashid al Maktoum award in Special Recognition for Regional Continuing Contributions to Islamic finance. Michael was the founding chair, and twice chair, of the Islamic Finance Section of the American Bar Association. Euromoney magazine identified Michael as one of the 16 pioneers of modern Islamic finance and he is identified as one of ten global leaders in Islamic finance, and the sole lawyer, in Emmy Abdul Amin's book (*Global Leaders in Islamic Finance*). Michael received a Doctor of Medicine degree from the Albert Einstein College of Medicine, a Juris Doctor degree from the University of Wisconsin Law School, and a Bachelor of Business Administration from the University of Wisconsin. Michael has published extensively on both Islamic finance and project and infrastructure finance, including a leading book (*Islamic Finance and the Shari'ah*). He is currently completing a two-volume book and a series of papers on the historical origins and early development of equipment finance, including lease finance.

Cedomir Nestorovic is a Professor of Geopolitics and Islamic Business at ESSEC Business School. He is also the Academic Director of the ESSEC & Mannheim Executive MBA Asia-Pacific. He has taught at ESSEC Business School for more than 20 years and is also the Academic Co-Director of the MBA programme at the Arabian Gulf University, Manama, Bahrain. Prof. Nestorovic's research interests include the Geopolitics of Asia, International Marketing and Commerce, and Islamic Business and Management. He regularly teaches in Paris, Mannheim, Tokyo, Seoul, Singapore, Kuala Lumpur, Bahrain, Amman, and Casablanca either for students or companies such as Takeda, Danone, Delphi or Thales. Prof. Nestorovic is based on the ESSEC campus in Singapore and is a regular guest on news and current affairs programmes providing expert commentary on geopolitical issues, especially on the relationship between the US and China. He appears on TV channels such as CNBC, CNA, and in newspapers such as *Le Monde*, *Liberation*, *La Tribune*, *The National* (Abu Dhabi), *Jakarta Post*, *Bangkok Post*, *The Business Times* (Singapore), *The Edge* (Singapore).

Silvana Secinaro is associate professor in Business administration and accounting at University of Turin. She, is member of several groups of study and author of papers focused on accounting and Islamic finance. She is included as an external expert to support the implementation of structural reforms in Member States in European Commission.

Deborah Scolart is researcher in Islamic law at the Law Department of University of Roma Tor Vergata. Her research topics are mainly focused on criminal law and women's rights. Among her recent publications is *L'islam, il reato, la pena. Dal fiqh alla codificazione del diritto penale*, second revised edition, Roma, 2018.

Fabrizio Vismara is Full Professor of International Law and Director of the Center on Customs and International trade law at the Insubria University. He is admitted as attorney to the Supreme Court of Italy. He has published numerous books and articles on international law, trade law and European Union law. His most recent books include: *L'obbligazione doganale nel diritto dell'Unione europea* (Customs obligation in European Union Law) (2020); *Clausole di eccezione nel diritto internazionale privato* (Escape clauses in private international law), 2017; *Lineamenti di diritto doganale dell'Unione europea* (Fundamental features of European Union Customs law), 2016. He has published articles in major Italian law journals such as *Rivista di diritto internazionale* (International Law Review), *Il diritto dell'Unione europea* (The European Union Law), *Rivista di diritto internazionale privato e processuale* (Private and Procedural International Law Review).

Part 1

FUNDAMENTALS AND COMPARATIVE PERSPECTIVES

Chapter 1

RECONCILING ISLAM AND FINANCE:

CHALLENGES IN INTEGRATING MUSLIMS INTO FINANCIAL MARKETS

Murat Çokgezen

1. Introduction

Islam is an earthly religion which regulates all aspects of life, and a Muslim should organise their life in harmony with these rules, the Islamic law (*Sharia*). The basic sources of Islamic law are the Quran (words of *Allah*) and the *Hadiths* (sayings of the Islamic prophet Muhammad). In addition to the Quran and the *Sunnah*, Muslim jurists developed secondary sources [1] which provide principles to interpret these primary sources in the event they are silent or unclear on an issue. As every single jurist has interpreted the primary sources in their own way, [2] no uniform rules have been laid down on issues that are not clearly regulated by the primary sources. Each interpretation is binding only on the one who makes the interpretation and on those who have bound themselves to the interpreter. This means that in practice, on issues where primary sources are silent or unclear, Muslims themselves decide what is Islamic-compliant and act accordingly.

Islam also governs the financial activities of Muslims and imposes restrictions on them. Some of these restrictions have raised questions regarding the compatibility of the conventional financial instruments commonly used in markets with Islamic regulations. Primary sources did not provide definitive answers to these questions. Muslims then turned to Islamic jurists

---

[1] The main secondary sources are *Qiyas* (analogy), *Ijma* (consensus) and *Ijtihad* (reasoning).

[2] Since the creation of Islam in the 7th century various schools of jurisprudence have emerged, each with its own interpretation and application of the *Sharia*. There are two main schools of thought within Islam: Sunni and Shia. Sunnis are further divided into four surviving schools of law (Hanafi, Hanbali, Maliki, Shafi'i).

for an answer. However, their answers were not uniform. Whereas one group of Islamic jurists allowed the use of conventional financial products, another group did not. Of these answers, whereas some were satisfied with the those of the first group of jurists, for the followers of the second a new question was raised: If the conventional instruments are not permissible, how could they borrow and lend money without breaching Islamic regulations? This problem has been solved with the creation of Islamic-compliant financial tools that have been developed with the cooperation of financial professionals, lawyers, and Islamic jurists (El-Gamal, 2006, p. 12). The issuance of new Islamic financial instruments has once again divided Islamic scholars and triggered another discussion on the compliancy of these products with Islam.

This chapter provides an overview of the restrictions imposed by Islam on financial activities, the different interpretations of these restrictions, the Islamic financial products developed as a response to such Islamic restrictions, the discussions of these products, and Muslims' responses to these discussions. It is intended as a guide for a Muslim who aims to involve themselves in an Islamic compliant (*Halal*) financial transaction, and does not claim to be a detailed jurisprudential analysis of Islam restrictions. [3] As is shown in the following sections, involvement in a *Halal* transaction is not an easy task for an inquisitive Muslim who wants to live a life in harmony with Islamic principles. Our analysis is limited to two restrictions (*Riba* and *Gharar*) and two financial transactions (borrowing/lending and insurance), but the results can also be extended to other restrictions and transactions.

2. Islamic Restrictions on Financial Deals

Involvement in a financial activity that is compatible with Islam requires adopting some principles and attitudes, and avoiding certain prohibitions prescribed in Islamic teachings. Some of these principles, such as enunciating justice, mutual help, honesty, avoiding fraud, the promotion of transparency and disclosures, etc., are no different from the norms of other faiths or the formal rules of the secular world (Ayub, 2007, 64–70). The distinguishing feature of Islam in the field of finance is prohibitions. Islamic teachings identify two major elements [4] that should be avoided in finan-

---

[3] Detailed analyses can be found in AYUB (2007), EL-GAMAL (2006), USMANI (1998) and VISSER (2009).

[4] AYUB (2007) also mentions a third element: Maisir and Qimar (gambling). Since Maisir and Qimar are closely related to Gharar, this chapter concentrates on Gharar only.

cial transactions (El-Gamal, 2006; Visser, 2009): *Riba* (interest) and *Gharar* (excessive uncertainty). The presence of these elements in financial transactions will make them Islamically void.

Riba

Riba is an Arabic word which means "increase" or "addition". It refers to an addition to the principal and is the equivalent of the term "interest" in modern finance. The *Riba* ban is mentioned in a number of verses in the Quran (Al-Baqarah 2:275, 276, 278 and 279, Al-Imran 3:130, Al-Room 30:39). For instance, in Al-Baqarah 2:275, it is stated that "*Allah* has permitted trading and forbidden usury".[5] *Riba* is unlawful not only for the lenders but also the borrowers and other parties involved. It is only permissible for the borrowers in the case of desperate need (Aransyub, 2007, p. 47). Therefore, there is no discussion among Islamic scholars regarding whether *Riba* is banned in Islam.

Although the *Riba* ban is clearly stated, it is not clearly defined in the Quran and no consensus exists in this regard. For the definition of *Riba*, Islamic scholars refer to *Hadiths*. In a *Hadith*, an Islamic compliant financial transaction is defined by the prophet Mohammed as:

> Gold for gold, silver for silver, wheat for wheat, barley for barley, dates for dates, and salt for salt, like for like, equal for equal, hand to hand, if the commodities differ, then you may sell as you wish provided the exchange is hand to hand.... Whoever gives more or ask for more has engaged in *Riba*.
>
> (Sunan an-Nasa'i 4560)

According to this *Hadith*, to be Islamically permissible, the exchange of the same item needs to be conducted simultaneously and with the same value or amount. Any increase or delay in this exchange is considered *Riba*. Accordingly, two broad categories of *Riba* are defined: *Riba al-nasi'ah* and *Riba al-fadl*. The first refers to conditional excess for delay of payment, whereas the second refers to the exchange of the same item, on the spot, but in excess.

Why *Riba* is prohibited in Islam is not explained in the Islamic texts. It is believed that if it is forbidden by God, its harm is greater than its benefits.[6] Detailed harms of *Riba* and the socioeconomic justification for the

---

[5] Riba is usually translated as usury, not interest.

[6] "In them is great sin and (yet, some) benefit for people. But their sin is greater than their benefit" (AL-BAQARAH 2:219).

Riba ban are provided by Islamic jurists, who interpret and analyze the Quran and the sayings and actions of the prophet Muhammad (El-Gamal, p. 50). The arguments made to defend the *Riba* ban are based on a mixture of jurists' subjective evaluations on interest by using socioeconomic concepts such as fair income distribution, efficient use of resources, uncertainty and unemployment as well as related Islamic concepts such as brotherhood and *Tawhid*, none of which is peculiar to either an Islamic or any religious worldview.

Gharar

Gharar is a word in Arabic like *Riba* but its meaning is less clear. The term is associated with concepts such as risk, uncertainty, unknown and deception (Waemustafa & Sukri, 2016). In Islamic finance literature, *Gharar*

> is the sale of a thing which is not present at hand or the sale of a thing whose "*Aqibah*" (consequence) is not known or a sale involving hazard in which one does not know whether it will come to be or not.
>
> (Ayub, 2007, p. 58).

More broadly, the concept refers to contracts and transactions that contain excessive uncertainty, which are banned in Islam.

The *Gharar* ban is not specifically mentioned in Quran; rather, scholars usually refer to the following verse which condemns transactions and contracts which cause injustice for the contracting parties: "O you who have believed, do not consume one another's wealth unjustly but only [in lawful] business by mutual consent". (Al-Nisa 4:29). As seen, in this verse there is no specific reference to uncertainty. However, the issue of *Gharar* is more explicitly addressed in the sayings of the prophet Mohammed. Abu Hurairah – one of the *Sahabah* (companions) of Muhammad – narrates that "Prophet prohibited the pebble sale and *Gharar* sale". Classical examples of *Gharar* – sale of fish in the sea, the birds in the sky, an unborn calf in its mother's womb – are also provided explicitly in a *Hadith*.

Each financial transaction involves a decision based on a choice between present and future rewards. Almost all of these financial transactions contain some amount of uncertainty – as the future is unknown to all of us – and interest – because of the time value of money – and therefore are potentially subject to Islamic restrictions. Consider borrowing money from a bank to buy a property, with interest charged on the loan at a floating rate, payable every month. This financial transaction, which takes place every day in many parts of the world, is prohibited in Islam because the transaction contains *Riba* (interest). Similarly, buying insurance, as millions of people do, to protect yourself from a potential loss is also prohibited in Islam because the transaction contains *Gharar* (uncertainty).[7] One may count many other financial transactions, which are carried out frequently in markets worldwide, as suffering from one or both of the prohibitions mentioned above. If this is the case, would a Muslim really borrow/lend money or buy insurance at all?

3. Continuing with Conventional Instruments

The restrictions imposed on financial transactions by Islamic canonical texts have raised questions about the permissibility of conventional products. That, in turn, has triggered a discussion among jurists and divided them into two main groups: Those who allow the use of conventional financial instruments and those who do not. The first group of jurists claims that *Riba* and *Gharar* forbidden in Islamic teachings refer not to the interest and uncertainty inherent in conventional transactions, but something different. Accordingly, the followers of the first group continue to use conventional instruments.

Some Interpretations Allowing Conventional Interest-Bearing Instruments

Although there is no question that *Riba* is prohibited in Islam, the meaning of *Riba* is unclear. It is not clearly defined neither in the Quran nor in the *Hadiths*. The ambiguity in the definition of *Riba* is also reported by the second *Caliph*,[8] Umar, who states that the Quranic verses on *Riba* were revealed in the last days of the prophet Mohammed's life, and he did not have an opportunity to interpret them properly (Rahman, 1964). The task of defining *Riba* therefore fell on Islamic scholars' shoulders. They have been fulfilling this task ever since. Therefore, today, the *Riba* definitions available in the Islamic literature are based on the interpretations of Islamic scholars by using secondary sources, and the number of definitions is as many as the number of scholars.

---

[7] In insurance, the price of insurance (insurance premium) is certain, but its compensation (insurance payment) is not certain (EL-GAMAL, 2006, 62).

[8] The supreme religious and political leader and successor to the Islamic prophet Muhammad.

At the one extreme lies those who claim that present-day interest and *Riba* are not the same. According to some scholars, what is prohibited in Islam is *Riba al-Jahiliyyah*, that was practiced in the Arab world in the pre-Islam era, or other specific forms of *Riba* that were available in the prophet Mohammed's time, and these cannot be applied to the forms of interest practice of modern times. For instance, unlike the loan transactions of the modern financial system in which the interest is added to the loan in the beginning, in *Riba al-Jahiliyyah*, the amount of debt is doubled in the event of default only (Farooq, 2009).

By referring to the verse "do not consume usurious interest, doubled and redoubled" in the Quran (3:130), some scholars have argued that only excessively high amounts of interest, usury, is banned in Islam. Another group have claimed that at the time of the revelation of the Quran, money was borrowed mainly for consumption needs, not for productive purposes and, therefore, for them the *Riba* ban is limited to consumption loans and does not cover interest over productive or commercial loans. Again, some jurists have legalised charging interest indexed to the inflation rate to a loan on the grounds that in an economy with inflation, the amount borrowed will not be the equivalent of the amount paid back in real terms, if no interest is charged (Ayub, 2007; Farooq, 2009).

Islamic jurists disagree over the interpretation of the abovementioned *Hadith*, which is also considered to define Islamic compliant financial transactions. For example, as noted earlier, the hadith identifies six commodities: Gold, silver, wheat, barley, date, and salt. Does the prohibition of *Riba* apply only to these six commodities or are they given as examples only? Some scholars take the literal meaning and conclude that *Riba* applies only to the six commodities specified in the *Hadith*, whereas others consider the six commodities as examples and claim that coverage of the *Riba* ban is wider. There is no unanimity of opinion on the range of coverage.

All of these interpretations and alike imply that what is prohibited in the Quran is either *Riba al-Jahiliyyah*, or usury or interest on consumption, or the interest imposed on the six goods mentioned in the *Hadith* etc. – but not the interest charged in conventional financial markets. Hence, there is no harm in using conventional financial instruments.

Some Interpretations which Allow Conventional Insurance

All transactions which involve *Riba* are unquestionably forbidden in Islam. However, some degree of *Gharar* (uncertainty) is acceptable in the Islamic framework; what is forbidden is excessive uncertainty. Next comes the question, "What is excessive?" No consensus exists among scholars regarding this question. In many cases, some scholars find the level of uncertainty in a contract acceptable and render the contract permissible, whereas others consider the opposite.

Take, for instance, insurance. Islamic scholars classify insurance into three categories with respect to their organisational structures:

1) Mutual insurance, in which a group of individuals or associations set up a fund to compensate the potential losses of group members;
2) Social insurance, in which the state compensates the potential losses of group members (citizens);
3) Commercial insurance, in which profit-oriented companies compensate losses of their customers in exchange for a premium.

Most Islamic jurists conclude that whereas mutual and social insurance is permissible, commercial insurance is unacceptable in Islam on the grounds that it contains excessive *Gharar*.[9] Insurance is said to contain *Gharar* as the insured person is unsure whether or not they will receive the compensation they are paying for. If the risk does not occur, they have paid an insurance premium but received nothing in return. Similarly, the insurer does not know how much they will pay to the insured if the risk occurs (Anwar & Hussain, 1994; Ahmad, 2002; Shalim, 2016).

However, some Islamic scholars hold that conventional insurance is compatible with Islam. They argue that an insurance contract has a definitive objective in the beginning; the contractual parties do not rely upon something that is uncertain. The incident insured is not vague and is identified in the policy. Moreover, insurance companies can accurately predict the likelihood of the occurrence of insured risks simply by collecting and analysing data from past events (Anwar & Hussain, 1994; Ahmad, 2002).

Proponents of the view that Islam allows conventional insurance also refer to similarities between the logic of insurance and some allowed practices mentioned in Islamic teachings to support their argument. For instance, some scholars argue that insurance is similar to the practice of *Diyyah* – compensation paid to the victim or heirs of a victim in the cases of murder, bodily harm or property damage – and the insurance company is the *Aqilah*, the party responsible for the payment of the *Diyyah*. Another ancient type of contract similar to insurance is *Wala al-Muwalat*. In this contract, one party agrees to leave their estate after their death to the latter, on the understanding that the benefactor will pay compensation in case the former commits any wrongful act. These and other permissible practices of

[9] It is also considered a form of gambling and is based on the concept and practice of charging interest.

early Islamic societies are used by the scholars who permit conventional insurance to support their views.

Some jurists justify the use of conventional insurance by referring to two concepts of traditional Islamic law: *Al-Maslaha* (public interest) and *Darurah* (necessity). In Islam, Muslims may disregard aspects of Islamic laws if it is necessary (to save lives or preserve the Islamic community) or if it serves the public interest of the Muslim community. Based on these notions, jurists deem conventional insurance permissible, because insurance preserves the wealth of the insured and their dependents, and improves the welfare of Muslims (Anwar & Hussain, 1994; Shalim, 2016).

4. Creating Islamic Alternatives

The strict restrictions on financial contracts imposed by Islam have not discouraged Muslims from financial activities. They have continued to be involved in financial transactions since the early stages of Islam yet have not been able to create efficient financial institutions such as a conventional banking system until the mid-20th century. Although the forerunners appeared beforehand, the emergence of Islamic financial institutions coincides with the oil shock of the 1970s. The influx of petro-dollars first helped the development of Islamic banks in oil-rich Arabic countries and then their spread to the world. More recently, conventional financial institutions have opened Islamic subsidiaries. The development of Islamic financial institutions, accompanied by the growth of financial instruments specifically designed with respect to Islamic restrictions and as a substitute for conventional financial tools, were created with the cooperation of financial professionals, lawyers and Islamic jurists. Muslims who are not convinced by the views of jurists who allow the use of conventional financial products prefer these "Islamic" alternatives.

Lending/Borrowing without Interest

Inspired by their modern counterparts, Islamic financial instruments can be grouped under two broad categories: Equity-like and debt-like products. [10]

One form of equity-like financial instrument is *Mudaraba*. This is a partnership contract where one party (lender) provides capital and acts like a passive investor and the other party (borrower) provides labour and skills

[10] On may also add a third category, charitable lending (*Quard Hassan*).

and manages the use of capital. Profits are shared between the two parties as a per agreed upon ratio, but losses are absorbed by the financier, who does not have the right to interfere in the management of the financed operation except if it is due to negligence, misconduct, or breach of contract. *Musharaka*, the second form of equity-like financial instrument, is also a partnership contract. Unlike *Mudaraba*, both parties inject capital and participate in the management. Profits are shared as a per pre-agreed ratio, but losses are borne proportionally to the invested capital.

Murabaha, also known as mark up or cost plus financing, is the most prevalent mode of debt-like Islamic financing. In a *Murabaha* agreement, the asset a client wants to purchase is bought by a financer and sold to the client at a pre-agreed markup. The asset is delivered immediately, but the repayment is made in instalments over a set period. The financer also bears the risk of default on repayment, because they are not allowed to charge any additional late fees.

Based on the principle of prohibition of *Gharar*, Islamic law prohibits the sale of a commodity that is not in the possession of the seller. *Salam* and *Istisna'a*, two other forms of debt-like instruments, are the exceptions to the rule. They are the Islamic counterparts of conventional futures contracts. In a *Salam* contract, the financer makes an advance payment to the producer for the future delivery of the good. The borrower pays the pre-agreed price to the financier when the good is delivered and acquires the ownership of the good. *Istisna'a* is a contract similar to *Salam* with several differences. First, in *Salam* the price must be paid in full in the beginning, whereas it can be paid in full, or instalments, or upon delivery of the product in *Istisna'a*. Second, the subject of *Istisna'a* is always a thing that needs manufacturing and is tailormade, whereas the subject of *Salam* is a fungible good. Third, the time of delivery need not be fixed and subject to the completion of product in *Istisna'a,* whereas the time of delivery is an essential part of the sale contract in *Salam*. Fourth, the *Istisna'a* contract can be cancelled before the manufacturer starts working, yet the *Salam* contract cannot be rescinded unilaterally (Ayub, 2007).

Ijara is the Islamic counterpart of a conventional leasing contract. In an *Ijara* contract, the financier purchases an asset or equipment for the borrower. The borrower then pays a rental fee until the total cost (price of the asset or equipment plus management costs) has been paid off. The duration of the rental and the fee are agreed in advance and at the end of the leasing tenure, the possession of the asset or equipment is transferred to the customer.

Another Islamic financial instrument is *Sukuk*. This is similar to a conventional bond. However, unlike bonds that indicate a debt obligation,

Sukuk indicates ownership an asset or its usufruct. Therefore, the bond holder earns interest, whereas the *Sukuk* holder receives a share of profit/loss from the underlying assets.

Insurance without *Gharar*

Islamic scholars' declaration of conventional insurance as contrary to Islam[11] raised the need for an alternative financial instrument that acts as a substitute for it and is compatible with the religion. The *Takaful* system is the product of efforts to meet these needs. It is a form of mutual insurance wherein members contribute money into a pool system (fund) to protect each other against risks that would be devastating if faced individually. The amount of contribution deducted is determined by the type of coverage and the individual risks of the participants. Any claims made by participants are paid out of the *Takaful* fund and any remaining surpluses resulting from the operation of the fund are distributed among the participants (policy holders). A *Takaful* company, as a trustee, manages the fund on behalf of the participants and charges an agreed-upon management fee or earns a share of the profits derived from *Takaful* funds.

The operation of *Takaful* companies is far from uniform. Essentially there are four types of *Takaful* models – *Tawuni*, *Wakalah*, *Mudarabah*, and *Wakf* (*Wakalah-Mudarabah*) – identified with respect to the ownership of the *Takaful* fund, the earning sources of a *Takaful* company and the ownership of the surplus. For instance, a *Takaful* company earns nothing in the *Tawuni* model, a *Wakalah* fee in the *Wakalah* model, a share of the surplus in the *Mudarabah* model, and a fee plus a share of the surplus in the *Wakf* model. Similarly, the fund is owned by participants in the *Tawuni* and *Wakalah* models, both participants and the *Takaful* company in the *Mudarabah* model and, accordingly, the surplus of the fund shared among the owners. In the *Wakf* model, the ownership is held by the *Wakf* and distribution of the surplus is determined by the *Wakf* administration (Malik & Ullah, 2019, s. 53–74).

Takaful is considered to be different from conventional insurance in many ways. First, in conventional insurance, risk is transferred from insured to insurer. In the case of loss, the insurance company promises the insured that they will cover all the losses. *Takaful*, however, is a risk sharing model where the risks are shared among the participants. A *Takaful* company provides an interest-free loan enabling the fund to pay *Takaful* bene-

---

[11] The Fiqh Academy of the Organisation of Islamic Cooperation ruled that conventional commercial insurance is forbidden (EL-GAMAL, 2006, p. 147).

fit(s) to eligible participants in the case of a deficit arising in the fund only. These loans are repaid from the future surpluses that arise from the fund. Second, whereas the conventional insurance companies are free to invest in any legal instrument, all investments managed by the *Takaful* companies should be *Sharia* compliant. Finally, whereas the profits of *Takaful* funds are shared among the participants, the profits of insurance companies belong to shareholders.

Takaful is considered a financial product which performs the same functions as insurance but, unlike conventional insurance, it does not contain the aspects prohibited in Islam, for several reasons. First, whereas insurance is a bilateral commercial transaction, *Takaful* is a "solidarity scheme" in which a group of people pool money to help participants of the pool in cases of need or loss, as per the predetermined rules. In Islam, the uncertainty is only prohibited in transactions that involve the exchange of money. The issue of *Gharar* is eliminated in *Takaful* because it is based on voluntary contributions. Second, as a *Takaful* company is obliged to invest insurance contributions in line with Islamic principles, the issue of *Riba* is also eliminated.

Before leaving this section, one final point should be noted regarding "Islamic" financial products. In the above, only the basic definitions and features of Islamic financial products are given. In practice, these products are far from uniform because of the lack of universally accepted Islamic principles applicable to the financial system. In the absence of uniform rules and a central authority to enforce these rules, Islamic banks have formed their own religious (*Sharia*) boards, consisting of eminent scholars, for guidance. They have to consult these boards, or *Sharia* advisors, to ensure their products or procedures are compliant with Islam. Due to the differences in interpretation of Islamic principles by different scholars, no consensus has yet been reached on the religious compliance of certain products and transaction structures. A financial instrument or procedure that is rejected by one board might be accepted by another. Therefore, differences and sometimes conflicting applications among Islamic financial tools even within the same country are very common. [12]

5. How Islamic are "Islamic" Financial Instruments?

As mentioned in the previous section, for those who are not convinced by the view that conventional financial instruments are allowed, Islamic finance institutions, with the approval of Islamic scholars, offer "more Islam-

[12] See for instance (ÇOKGEZEN & KURAN, 2015) for Islamic credit cards in Turkey.

ic" substitutes. However, many religious scholars and researchers are not convinced by the adherence of these new, so-called "Islamic" products and processes to Islamic teachings and claim that they are cosmetically different from their conventional counterparts.

El-Gamal (2006) criticises the current practice of Islamic finance for being inefficient, arguing that the system is essentially driven by Islamic scholars. First, they identify a financial product that inhibits the non-Islamic elements in it, then they develop an "Islamic analog" that is very similar to that product. The basic elements of developing a new "Islamic" product are finding an Arabic name that is extensively used in Islamic text for the product and adding unnecessary transactions to differentiate the new product from its conventional counterpart. These spurious transactions increase its legitimacy and marketing opportunities but reduce the economic efficiency of the new product. El-Gamal also implies that increasing competition from conventional banking increases the risk of deviation from Islamic principles.

In his critical study, Kuran (2004) argues that the principles and practices of Islamic banks are different, and Islamic financial instruments differ only cosmetically from the interest-based financing practices. Although they claim to be operating on a profit and loss sharing basis, Islamic banks channel their deposits mostly into bonds and other interest-bearing instruments, and therefore the "profit shares" received by their depositors follow the movements of market interest rates. Similarly, Khan (2010) states that the operations of Islamic banks are indistinguishable from their conventional counterparts. He also asserts that Islamic banks are simply replacing conventional banking terminology with terms from classical Arabic and offering near-identical services to their clients but at a higher cost.

Each Islamic bank has a *Sharia* Supervisory Board consisting of prominent Muslim jurists. They judge the compatibility of a new Islamic instrument, and no instrument is released without their approval. However, approval of a product by a board does not exempt it from criticism, and all financial products receive their share of critics. One of the criticisms concerns the capabilities of jurists. Making a decision about the Islamic compliancy of a financial product or a process requires not only a good command of Islamic teachings but also a command of economics, finance etc. The number of scholars who meet these requirements is very limited. The second criticism concentrates on the issue of independence. Jurists receive a considerable amount of money for the opinions (*Fatwas*) they provide from the banks they are working for. Critics claim that the jurists do not hesitate to stretch the rules of Islam or use legal tricks (*Hiyal*) to justify the products and processes of their "bosses". These issues raise concerns about reliability of the jurists' decisions.

Even though jurists' approval of Islamic products shows that they theoretically meet the requirements of Islamic law, some claim that these products contradict Islamic regulations in practice. Some of the issues raised regarding the "Islamic" instruments discussed in the previous section are as follows. [13]

Murabaha transactions of Islamic banks have been criticised by scholars in many aspects (Usmani, 1998). First, mark-ups are related to the maturity of repayment (the longer the maturity, the higher the mark-up) like interest, and many banks use current interest rates as a benchmark to determine their mark-ups. Second, the subject matter of *Murabaha* is not owned by the bank when the client seeks financing. Before the Islamic Bank purchases this commodity, the client has to sign a promise to purchase the commodity from the Bank. Whether this promise is binding or permissible is subject to discussion. Third, unlike conventional transactions, in *Murabaha* financing if the client defaults in payment when due, the price cannot be increased. To protect themselves against dishonest clients who might exploit this restriction, Islamic Banks charge a compensation fee, given to charity, to the clients who do not make their payments on time. The permissibility of charging such a fee is, again, questionable.

The compatibility of current Sukuk practices have also been questioned by scholars. For instance, Muhammad Taqi Usmani (2007) a well-known Islamic scholar, addresses several issues in this regard. First, having ownership shares in assets, i.e., the presence of ownership rights in *Sukuk* structures, is one of the features of *Sukuk* which distinguishes it from conventional bonds. However, he asserts that some *Sukuks* offer *Sukuk* holders merely the right to return the assets rather than ownership rights. For him, such a practice is no more than the purchase of returns from shares, and it is unlawful from an Islamic perspective. Second, in most cases the distributed "profits" are fixed at current interest rates. This practice is justified simply by transferring the amount exceeding the interest to the enterprise manager (*Mudarib*, or a partner, or an investment agent) as an "incentive premium" and getting back the difference if the actual profits are less than the prescribed percentage based on interest rates. Third, like conventional bonds, almost all of the *Sukuk* issued today guarantee the return of principal to the *Sukuk* holders at maturity.

Similar questions have been raised concerning Islamic insurance, *Takaful*. As mentioned above, *Takaful* is an alternative to the conventional form of insurance that involves excessive uncertainty, which is prohibited in Is-

---

[13] Compliancy issues are not limited to the abovementioned practices. Studies in this realm demonstrate that similar issues are available for other financial tools such as credit cards (ÇOKGEZEN & KURAN, 2015), Tawarruq (NAGAOKA, 2012) etc.

lam. Khan (2013) states that *Takaful* has a similar nature to conventional insurance, and a *Takaful* holder is entitled to similar risks to those a conventional insurance holder is entitled. He draws attention to an additional dimension of *Gharar* available in *Takaful*. In the *Takaful* system, in the case where the losses are more than available in the *Takaful* fund and the *Takaful* company is unable to provide an interest-free loan to bridge the gap, the deficits are passed on to the *Takaful* holders. This means that *Takaful* holders face higher uncertainty than conventional insurance holders because they do not know what their liabilities will ultimately be. Moreover, Khan also describes how, in practice, the operation of the *Takaful* system is no different from conventional insurance.

Whereas many Islamic scholars and researchers are dubious about the *Sharia* compliance of debt-like Islamic instruments, they almost unanimously agree on the permissibility of the profit-sharing instruments *Mudaraba* and *Musharaka*. However, the vast majority of financial instruments on the asset side of Islamic banks have been debt-like since the Islamic banking system was begun in the 1970s (Nagaoka, 2012). A focus on the more Islamically controversial products by Islamic banks has been interpreted as sacrificing Islamic ideals for the sake of more profit, or the defeat of *HomoIslamicus* in favor of *Homoeconomicus* (Asutay, 2007).

6. Muslims and Islamic Financial Instruments

Despite all the efforts of the Islamic finance industry, Muslims' interest in Islamic financial products remains limited. The share of Islamic finance in the world's financial market is approximately 1%, whereas Muslims account for 24% of the world's population and produced 15.6% of the global output in 2016 (Kuran, 2018, p. 1328). Even in countries where the vast majority of the population is Muslim, the share of Islamic banking in total banking assets is less than 20% (Islamic Financial Services Board, 2019). These low rates indicate that the Islamic financial system has not been sufficiently adopted by Muslims.

Some studies (Marimuthu, Jing, Gie, Mun, & Ping, 2010; Islam & Rahman, 2017; Hati, Wibowo, & Safira, 2020) ascribe the low willingness of Muslims to patronise Islamic products to their low levels of awareness and understanding of Islamic financial products and services. However, when the resources Islamic banks have, and the level of information technology is considered, the inadequacy of Islamic banks in informing potential customers about Islamic instruments does not necessarily offer an adequate explanation for the unwillingness of Muslims to work with Islamic banks. Other studies may offer further explanations.

One possible explanation might be that Muslims are comfortable with conventional instruments – either they are convinced of their compliance with Islam or they do not care about the prohibition against interest. Some studies provide findings which support this explanation. For instance, the results of a survey conducted among a sample of pious Muslim businessmen in Turkey (Savaşan, Saraç, & Gürdal, 2013) show that only 14.7% of the participants preferred Islamic banks in their financing activities. For more than half of those surveyed, the cost of the loan was the only criterion in their financing decisions, regardless of the bank type, which implies that they prefer a cheaper interest-bearing loan of the conventional bank to a high-cost loan of an Islamic bank. Another study (Ireland, 2018), based on a survey administered to 300 UAE Islamic banking customers, reveals that the customers of Islamic banks consider conventional and Islamic banks as substitutes, and if a conventional bank offers 1% better rates, 44% of the respondents would switch to the conventional bank. The ratio of "switchers" reaches 62% when the advantage is increased to 2%.

Another explanation might be that Muslims are dubious about Islamic compliance with "Islamic" financial instruments/institutions. Some studies support this argument. For instance, Samreen, Robson, and Sekhon (2015) find that Muslim customers of Islamic banks in Pakistan were unsure whether Islamic banks adhere to Islamic principles. In this study, the interviewed customers stated that even the bank personnel were unsure if the best practices in terms of Islamic rules were being followed by their banks. One-third of the pious Muslim businessmen in Turkey think that Islamic banks do not operate in compliance with Islamic principles (Savaşan, Saraç, & Gürdal, 2013). Another study of Gulf countries finds that only half (52%) of existing Islamic Bank customers agreed with the statement that their provider was 'an Islamic bank and followed Islamic *Sharia*' (PWC, 2014).

The abovementioned studies demonstrate that Muslims are also confused about the *Riba* ban and the Islamic alternatives. They have not come to a consensus on the definition of *Riba*. Therefore, many Muslims see no wrong in involving in earning-bearing transactions in conventional financial markets. However, those who wants to avoid interest in the conventional manner are not confident about the Islamic compliancy of Islamic financial products issued by Islamic financial institutions.

7. Conclusion

Islam prohibits the payment and receipt of interest and involvement in financial transactions that contain excessive uncertainty. However, it is obvious that interest and uncertainty are integral parts of all financial transactions, because financial decisions can only be made about the future. This has raised doubts about the compliance of conventional financial products with Islam. Primary sources are either silent or unclear in this regard; therefore, Muslims turned to Islamic scholars to dispel their doubts. However, their opinions, which were derived from canonical texts and other references, were not uniform. Whereas one group of Islamic jurists allowed the use of conventional financial products, another group did not. The second group later contributed to the development of new products that they claim to be "genuinely" Islamic and advised Muslims to use these products. Muslims then chose the opinion they most agree with: either preferring new products developed by the scholars or opting to continue with conventional financial instruments.

These developments in Islamic finance show that even though the literal sources for Islamic compliance of a product are the words of Allah and the sayings of Mohammad, in practice, the decisions of Muslims are based on the opinions of jurists. Consulting Islamic scholars on every controversial issue, while increasing their power in the system, has exposed them to more criticism. Every single viewpoint of jurists and their relations with financial institutions are questioned from an Islamic and ethical perspective by Islamic scholars and academics. They have even been accused of being merely a rubber stamp for the financial institutions which pay their salaries.

Developments in Islamic finance also demonstrate the futility of debates regarding the Islamic compliance of financial products and/or the distinction between Islamic and non-Islamic financial products. As discussed above, all financial instruments have the potential to be "Islamic" depending on where you stand. In other words, for each financial instrument it is possible to find an Islamic scholar who will approve its compliance with Islam. The wide range of interpretations of financial instruments by Islamic scholars might be comforting for many, but it is surely confusing for the more inquisitive Muslim.

For some reasons, Muslims do not patronise enough of the "Islamic" financial products developed cooperatively by Islamic scholars, finance professionals, and lawyers, even in Muslim majority countries. Even though studies explain this phenomenon by referring to low levels of awareness and understanding of Islamic finance products and services among Muslims, other studies imply that being comfortable with the conventional instruments, ignoring the interest ban, and not being convinced by the so-called "Islamic" products are other possible explanations worth considering, though so far ignored by researchers in this field.

References

AHMAD, W.W., *Some issues of Gharar (Uncertainty) in insurance*, in Journal Syariah, 10(2), 2002, 61–80.

ANWAR, M., & HUSSAIN, M., *Comparative study of insurance and "Takafol" (Islamic Insurance)*, in The Pakistan Development Review, 33(4), 1994, 1315–1330.

ASUTAY, M., *Conceptualisation of the second best solution in overcoming the social failure of Islamic finance: Examining the overpowering of homoislamicus by homoeconomicus*, in IIUM Journal in Economics and Management, 15(2), 2007, 167–195.

AYUB, M., *Understanding Islamic Finance*, USA: John Wiley & Sons Ltd., 2007.

ÇOKGEZEN, M., & KURAN, T., *Between consumer demand and Islamic law: The evolution of Islamic credit cards in Turkey*, in Journal of Comparative Economics, 43(4), 2015, 862–882.

EL-GAMAL, M.A., *Islamic Finance: Law, Economics and Practice*, Cambridge, UK: Cambridge University Press, 2006.

FAROOQ, M.O., *Riba, interest and six hadiths: Do we have a definition or a conundrum?* in Review of Islamic Economics, 13(1), 2009, 105–141.

HATI, S.R., WIBOWO, S.S., & SAFIRA, A., *The antecedents of Muslim customers' intention to invest in an Islamic bank's term deposits: Evidence from a Muslim majority country*, in Journal of Islamic Marketing, 2020, https://doi.org/10.1108/JIMA-01-2020-0007.

IRELAND, J., *Just How loyal are Islamic banking customers?*, in International Journal of Bank Marketing, 36(1), 2018, 410–421.

ISLAM, J.U., & RAHMAN, Z., *Awareness and willingness towards Islamic banking among Muslims: An Indian perspective*, in International Journal of Islamic and Middle Eastern Finance and Management, 10(1), 2017, 92–101.

ISLAMIC FINANCIAL SERVICES BOARD, *Islamic Financial Services Industry Stability Report 2019*, Kuala Lumpur: Islamic Financial Services Board, 2019.

KHAN, F., *How 'Islamic' is Islamic banking?*, in Journal of Economic Behavior & Organization, 76(3), 2010, 805–820.

KHAN, M.A., *What is Wrong with Islamic Economics? Analysing the Present State and Future Agenda*, Cheltenham, UK; Northampton, MA: Edward Elgar, 2013.

KURAN, T., *Islam and Mammon: The Economic Predicaments of Islamism*, Princeton and Oxford: Princeton University Press, 2004.

KURAN, T., *Islam and economic performance: Historical and contemporary links*, in Journal of Economic Literature, 56(4), 2018, 1292–1359.

MALIK, A., & ULLAH, K., *Introduction to Takaful*, Singapore: Palgrave Pivot, 2019.

MARIMUTHU, M., JING, C.W., GIE, L.P., MUN, L.P., & PING, T.Y., *Islamic banking: Selection criteria and implications*, in Global Journal of Human Social Science, 10(4), 2010, 52–62.

NAGAOKA, S., *Critical overview of the history of Islamic economics*, in Asian and African Area Studies, 11(2), 2012, 114–136.

PWC, *What customers want: Customer insights to inform growth strategies of Islamic banks in the Middle East*, PWC, 2014.

RAHMAN, F., *Riba and interest*, in Islamic Studies, 3(1), 1964, 1–43.

SAMREEN, A., ROBSON, J., & SEKHON, Y., *Consumer trust and confidence in the compliance of Islamic banks*, in Journal of Financial Services Marketing (20), 2015, 133–144.

SAVAŞAN, F., SARAÇ, M., & GÜRDAL, T., *Exploring the demand side issues in participation banking in Turkey: Questionnaire survey on current issues*, in Afro Eurasian Studies, 2(1-2), 2013, 111–125.

SHALIM, Z.H., (2016), *Revisiting life insurance in Islamic law*, in Turkish Journal of Islamic Economics, 3(2), 2016, 39–62.

USMANI, M.T., *An Introduction to Islamic Finance*, 1998.

USMANI, M.T., *Sukuk and their Contemporary Applications*, AAOIFI, 2007.

VISSER, H., *Islamic Finance: Principles and Practice*, Cheltenham, UK: Edward Elgar, 2009.

WAEMUSTAFA, W., & SUKRI, S., *Theory of Gharar and its interpretation of risk and uncertainty from the perspectives of authentic hadith and the Holy Quran: Review of literatures*, in Journal of Islamic Economics, Banking and Finance, 10(2), 2016, 1–27.

Chapter 2

WHEN CAN FINANCE BE CALLED "ISLAMIC"? REFLECTIONS ON THE RELATION BETWEEN ISLAMIC ETHICS, LAW AND ECONOMICS

Deborah Scolart

SUMMARY: 1. Law as a Guide for the Believer. – 2. Homo Economicus Islamicus. – 3. Unlawful Gains *v.* Lawful Contracts. – References.

1. Law as a Guide for the Believer

The adjective "Islamic" concerning economy and finance which are the subject of this volume refers, intuitively, to a set of values and principles expression of a religion, Islam, which in its universal vocation tends to govern, through the law, every area of human life.

Islamic law, *šarīʿa*, is a divine law, a set of ethical, moral and legal rules that guide the action and behaviour of every Muslim believer. What is called in English Islamic law refers to the Arab word *šarīʿa*: this term, although it has its own specific meaning, is normally used to indicate both the *šarīʿa* in technical sense, as the rules and principles issued by the will of the divine Legislator; and *fiqh*, i.e., the result of the hermeneutic activity (*iğtihād*) exercised by the jurists (*fuqahā'*) on the sources of law (*uṣūl al-fiqh*).

Šarīʿa is the straight path given by God to humankind to regulate their lives. As a sacred law, it is also a confessional law, intended to be followed and applied by all those who profess the Islamic religion. A *šarīʿa* law has also been given to Jews (*šarīʿa yahūdiyya* or *šarīʿa Mūsā*, the (sacred) law of Moses), to Christians (*šarīʿa masīḥiyya* or *šarīʿa al-Masīḥ*, the (sacred) law of Messiah), to Zoroastrians (*šarīʿa al-Mağūs*); as such, it is an expression of the monotheistic message given by God to humanity. When referred to Muslims only, *šarīʿa* regulates the *ʿibadāt*, acts of worship which concern the relationship between God and man: "Now We have set you [O Prophet] on the [clear] Way of faith (*šarīʿa*). So follow you that, and follow not the desires of those who know not" (XLV, 18).[1] It also regulates the

[1] All the English quotes from the Quran are taken from The Noble Quran, www.quran.com.

muʿāmalāt, *negotia*, relating to relations between human beings: personal status (marriage, divorce, filiation, succession), contracts and obligations, even criminal law.

On the other hand, *fiqh* represents the human element of a right of divine origin; since *fiqh* retains the connotation of human, it cannot be ascribed to God and while *šarīʿa* can be specified by the name of a religion (*islāmiyya*, *yahūdiyya*), *fiqh* is usually accompanied with the name of a scholar: the *fiqh* of Mālik, the *fiqh* of Abū Hanīfa, or Jaʿfarī *fiqh* or Ismāʿīlī *fiqh*. This is why Antonio d'Emilia[2] used to say that Islamic law has a divine origin but is also a *juristenrecht*, the product of a doctrine initially linked to geographical factors,[3] that has subsequently developed in various addresses (*maḏāhib*) or school of thought that, despite their multiplicity, have not affected the unity of the legal system. The roots of *fiqh*, Quran and Sunna[4] above all, but also *iǧmāʿ* (doctrinal consensus) and *qiyās* (analogy), were the basis on which jurists have exercised the *iǧtihād*, the interpretative effort aimed at qualifying – according to *šarīʿa* – human actions into five distinct categories: forbidden (*ḥarām*), obligatory (*wāǧib*), recommended (*mandūb*), disapproved (*makrūh*) and neutral or free (*mubāḥ*).

Fiqh, as a human interpretation of divine law, is fallible or at least perfectible: in this weakness lies the source of its strength, since interpretation can change over time in the light of new circumstances, and develop new rules or adapt old ones to new context. The modern interpretation of *šarīʿa* consists in this: a new approach to the sources, the possibility of questioning interpretations that could be correct in a given era because they reflected the culture and sensibility of the time, but that today are no longer current, the rediscovery and use of institutes belonging to classical law to fulfil new purposes or functions. Therefore, it is possible today to give a new life to contracts developed by Islamic legal tradition and bend them to the needs of contemporary finance; in this perspective, for example, *ṣukūk* have become an important financial instrument also known as "*šarīʿa* compliant bond" and an old medieval contract like *muḍāraba* has become a key instrument at the service of Islamic banking.

The purpose and function of *šarīʿa* is to satisfy the interests and well-

---

[2] D'Emilia, A., *Scritti di diritto islamico*, raccolti a cura di F. Castro, Istituto per l'Oriente, Roma, 1976, 8.

[3] Legal schools originated in Arabian Peninsula, but they ended up establishing themselves on a geographical basis following the routes of merchants and warriors.

[4] *Sunna* refers to the behaviour of the Prophet as preserved in eyewitness records of his words, actions, approbations and even silence (*ḥadīṯ*); it is considered an authoritative source in Islamic law because the Quran ordered Muslims to "obey Allah and His Messenger if you are true believers" (VIII,1).

being of people in both earthly and otherworldly life (*taḥqīq maṣāliḥ al-ʿibād fī l-maʿāš wa-l-maʿād*). In the legal context, the instrument of analogy, *qiyās*, allows the development of the doctrine of *maqāṣid* (aim, purpose): if the solution given as true for one situation can be applied to another, the law must necessarily be consistent, and if it is consistent this is because it expresses the will of the Legislator. The question of whether or not the divine will can be known is still open: some, like Zāhirī jurist ibn Ḥazm (d. 1064), openly rejects it. This has not prevented al-Ġazālī (d. 1111) from stating with authority that one way to know the rationale (*ʿilla*) of a decision is to compare it to the general aim (*maqṣūd*) of the law, identified in the promotion of good (*maʿrūf*) and the reduction of evil (*munkar*). On these basis, Mālikī jurist Abū Isḥaq al-Šaṭibī (who lived in Granada during XIV cent. a.C.) took up al-Ġazālī and, analysing the benefits of *šarīʿa* in light of the notions of *qiyās* (analogy), *istiḥsān* (often translated into English as 'juristic preference', literally means to consider something good and just) and *istiṣlāḥ* (to deem proper), argues that the whole of *šarīʿa* is aimed at promoting the well-being of believers. Therefore, the objectives of the law can be distinguished in three different categories: in the first group there are elements indispensable (*maṣāliḥ ḍarūriyya*, necessities) for human development: the preservation of life, property, progeny, intellect and religion. To the second group belong those things that are necessary (*maṣāliḥ ḥağiyya*, needs) to make obedience to God less burdensome; so it is, for example, when the law allows the sick not to observe the obligation of ritual prayer; a more stringent example is the prohibition of speculation (*iḥtikār*). Finally, there are elements aimed at improving (*maṣāliḥ taḥsīniyya*, luxuries, embellishments) the lives of believers (for example, the prescription to choose a clean place for prayer, or the invitation to be discreet and not to insult others).[5]

The constant attention Islamic law dedicates to the guidance to a fair conduct of life can be seen also in that the dominant idea of Muslim jurists is that law, an eminently social fact, although divine in its origins, finds in human coexistence its raison d'être, its own subject matter and the connection of the various institutions it is composed of. The legal rules are therefore dictated in view of the social man. As Santillana[6] highlights, private law, as Islamic jurists conceive it, is not a mere matter of mine and yours,

---

[5] The literature on the subject is wide. See among the many GLEAVE, R.M., *s.v.* "maḳāṣid al-sharīʿa", in *Encyclopédie de l'Islam*, Vol. XII, 2007, 580–581; KHADDURI, M., *s.v.* "maṣlaḥa", in *Encyclopédie de l'Islam*, Vol. VI, 1991, 727–729; ABU SAHLIEH, S. A.A., *Il diritto islamico. Fondamenti, fonti, istituzioni*, Carocci, Roma, 2008, 357–359.

[6] SANTILLANA, D., *Istituzioni di diritto musulmano malichita con riguardo anche al sistema sciafiita*, Istituto per l'Oriente, Roma, Vol. II, 1938, 53.

between strangers interested only in their own well-being; it has as its subject the relationships between members of the same family, between brothers and sisters by faith, who must help each other or at least offer each other loyalty and good advice. The Quranic foundation of this principle can be traced in the repeated invitation to facilitate good (*maʿrūf*) and forbid evil (*munkar*): "Let there be a group among you who call [others] to goodness, encourage what is good, and forbid what is evil, it is they who will be successful" (III, 104); "You are the best community ever raised for humanity, you encourage good, forbid evil, and believe in Allah" (III, 110). Within *šarīʿa*, ethics, morals and law overlap and merge: the rule is juridical in that it is also moral, aimed at defining the spiritual element of man's behaviour, especially in relation to the criterion of judgment with regard to the two antithetical concepts of "good" and "evil" that represent one of the fundamental canons to distinguish the action of the good Muslim. As Hallaq underlines, "Islam – both as a worldview and as an intellectual system – made no real distinction between the legal and the moral on the grounds that morality and ethics were never perceived as anything less than integral to the law." [7] In this perspective it becomes clear why *iṯm*, the sin, can be seen not only in case of a flagrant violation of an order given by God (i.e., not to kill) but also when, for example, the seller does not inform the buyer of the defects of the goods sold.

2. Homo Economicus Islamicus

The social context at the time of Islamic revelation was based on the idea of group: an individual was not relevant *per se* but as a member of the community to which he belonged; the family – which was an extended, tribal

---

[7] HALLAQ, W.B., *Sharīʿa. Theory, practice, transformations*, Cambridge University Press, Cambridge, 2010, 85. In a different perspective, that moves from a linguistic analysis of the Quran dedicated to the study of the virtues of the good Muslim believer, Zilio-Grandi underlines how in the Quran the moral and legal components seem to be clearly separated. The actions that have legal relevance concern what God orders or commands (*amara*), what is prescribed or determined (*kataba*: retribution/retaliation, fasting, emancipation of slaves, determination of Quranic hereditary quotas, etc) and what is legislate (*šaraʿa*, same root of *šarīʿa*). The field of morality is marked by divine love (*aḥabba*); God loves goodness (*iḥsān*), pity (*taqwā*), equity, the right measure, equanimity (*qisṭ*, *iqsāṭ*), repentance (*tawba*): certainly God does not love pride, vanity, avarice ("Surely Allah does not like whoever is arrogant, boastful – those who are stingy, promote stinginess among people, and withhold Allah's bounties" Quran, IV, 36–37) and does not love excess ("Eat of the fruit they bear and pay the dues at harvest, but do not waste. Surely He does not like the wasteful" VI, 141). ZILIO-GRANDI, I., *Le virtù del buon musulmano*, Einaudi, Torino, 2020, 5.

family – claimed the rights of individuals, avenged offenses against members of the clan, was responsible for their crimes. Islam preserves the general lines of this model while substituting the blood ties with brotherhood in the faith:[8] *lā ḥilfa fī-l-islām*, no longer tribal alliance in Islam, is the new principle, even if the severance of kin ties concerned only the Meccans who migrated to Medina during the *hiğra* and blood ties continued to coexist alongside the brotherhood of faith throughout Islamic history. The person becomes autonomous and draws his rights and duties not from the group he belongs to but from his quality of believer.[9] The union of Muslim believers constitutes the community of Islam (*umma islāmiyya*), destined to promote good and repress evil, being the depository of true faith and justice on earth. Although a real political unity of the Islamic community was nothing more than an ephemeral event in the story of Islam, its ideal lies behind the construction of the theoretical model of Islamic society. Since believers are brothers in faith, the Islamic legal-ethical system dictates the legal duty of mutual assistance, the precept that makes every Muslim the auxiliary and protector of other Muslim in case of need; obedience to divine law is a social duty and a religious precept and who violates the law commits a sin (*ma ʿṣiya*, rebellion against God).

As a consequence of the ethical-religious foundation of the law. and also of the Quranic principle of the brotherhood of believers, before Islamic law Muslims are equal, without distinction of race or social class, the measure of rights and duties being calibrated only on the brother's duty to his brother. The modern jurists make reference to the *ḥadīṯ* of the Prophet Muhammad: "He who sleeps on a full stomach whilst his neighbour goes

[8] Quran III, 103: "Remember Allah's favour upon you when you were enemies, then He united your hearts, so you – by His grace – became brothers (*iḫwān*)"; IX, 11: "but if they repent, perform prayer, and pay alms-tax, then they are your brothers in faith (*iḫwān fī-l-dīn*)".

[9] Some verses of the Quran highlight the duty to distance from the family if its members insist on rejecting the true faith: IX, 23: "O believers! Do not take your parents and siblings as trusted allies if they choose disbelief over belief. And whoever of you does so, they are the true wrongdoers"; 115: "Allah would never consider a people deviant after He has guided them, until He makes clear to them what they must avoid. Surely Allah has full knowledge of everything"; LVIII, 22: "You will never find a people who truly believe in Allah and the Last Day loyal to those who defy Allah and His Messenger, even if they were their parents, children, siblings, or extended family"; LX, 1–4, where the concept is evident in "neither your relatives nor children will benefit you on Judgment Day – He will decide between you all. For Allah is All-Seeing of what you do"; LXIV, 14–15: "O believers! Indeed, some of your spouses and children are enemies to you, so beware of them. But if you pardon, overlook, and forgive their faults, then Allah is truly All-Forgiving, Most Merciful – Your wealth and children are only a test, but Allah alone has a great reward."

hungry is not one of us" [10] to underline the duty of assistance and aid that ties together the believer. The fundamental principle that inspires the *šarīʿa* is the freedom (*ibāha*) of actions (*umur*), but for the usefulness (*maṣlaḥa*, public interest) of humankind the law sets limits (*ḥadd*) to man who – left free to be himself – would be greedy and ungrateful, avid of the goods of others, stingy with his own, alien from fatigue, unaware of the benefits bestowed by God. [11] Ethical concept of assistance leads the need to protect fair reciprocity in the legal transactions [12] and prevent one party from gaining an unjustified profit at the expense of the other. The respect of these limits can be seen in every part of the system of contracts elaborated by the jurists: contractual autonomy, formation of consensus, good faith, ethical dimension of contracts. [13] "As for the sky, He raised it [high], and set the balance [of justice] – so that you do not defraud the scales – Weigh with justice (*wazana bi-l-qisṭ*), and do not give short measure" (Quran LV, 7–9): the whole system of contracts under Islamic law is pervaded by the doctrine of undue enrichment from which derive the prohibition of *ġarar* (risk, uncertainty) and the prohibition of *ribā* (unjust gains, often translated as usury).

In Islamic culture, *homo oeconomicus* [14] and believer (*mu'min*) are not

---

[10] Other references are usually made to the so-called "Last Sermon" where the Prophet affirmed: "Verily your blood, your property are as sacred and inviolable as the sacredness of this day of yours, in this month of yours, in this town of yours. Behold! Everything pertaining to the Days of Ignorance is under my feet completely abolished. Abolished are also the blood-revenges of the Days of Ignorance. [...] And the usury of the pre-Islamic period is abolished, and the first of our usury I abolish is that of al-ʿAbbās b. ʿAbd al-Muṭṭalib, for it is all abolished" Muslim, *Ṣaḥīḥ*, Book 15, *ḥadīṯ* 159, https://sunnah.com/muslim/15/159.

[11] Quran LXX 19–21: "Indeed, humankind was created impatient; distressed when touched with evil; – and withholding when touched with good"; XXII, 38: "Allah does not like whoever is deceitful, ungrateful"; XX, 121: "so Adam disobeyed his Lord and lost his way" XLII, 47: "Respond to your Lord before the coming of a Day from Allah that cannot be averted. There will be no refuge for you then, nor [grounds for] denial [of sins]"; XVI, 55: "only returning Our favours with ingratitude"; XXII, 66 "surely humankind is ever ungrateful"; C, 6 and 8: "surely humankind is ungrateful to their Lord – and they are truly extreme in their love for [worldly] gains."

[12] SANTILLANA, D., *Istituzioni di diritto musulmano malichita con riguardo anche al sistema sciafiita*, Istituto per l'Oriente, Roma, Vol. II, 1938, 54.

[13] PAPA, M., *La definizione di contratto e l'autonomia contrattuale in diritto musulmano: dai principi della shari'a alle legislazioni contemporanee*, in Roma e America. Diritto romano comune, 7, 1999, 277–297.

[14] *Homo economicus* is here used as a mere Latinism to indicate a subject in his capacity to carry out an activity with economic content. In economic theory the expression *Homo economicus* has, instead, a technical meaning referring to a subject while

two distinct and separate entities, but a single whole: Islamic economic theories are at the same time philosophy of life and regulation of relationships between men inspired by the redistribution of wealth and the correct use of money and goods. The prohibitions of *ribā* (literally: growth; in modern economic language: interest, usury) and *ġarar* (uncertainty) respond to the need to protect the weaker contracting party in view of the criteria of solidarity and equity that must inspire patrimonial relationships.

The principles of the Islamic economic model date back to the dawn of Muslim religious and juridical history, but the current model of Islamic finance and banking occurs in a rather recent era, as a reaction to an excessive recourse to economic and juridical instruments peculiar to the western legal tradition. The principles underlying the Islamic economy are justice and fairness, mercy, brotherhood, solidarity, cooperation; the Muslim believer is an individual who is integrated into a more complex reality, the *umma* (Islamic community), with respect to which he can even be called to sacrifice himself if this is in the general interest (*maṣlaḥa*) of the society.

Hard work and participation in economically creative activity is a duty for the Muslim believer; together with fairness, honesty in trade and fair competition, prohibition of hoarding wealth and worshipping it, these are the pillars of a moral Islamic economy.[15] As a member of a faith-based

---

pursuing a certain number of objectives trying to achieve them as satisfactorily as possible and at the lowest costs. The *homo economicus* theory is based on the assumption of his rationality (to be understood with reference to the calculation capability and precision with respect to the objective – whatever it may be, useful or useless – pursued) and of preeminent interest toward his own benefit. In Warde opinion "the most important difference between *Homo islamicus* and *Homo economicus* is the assumption of altruism. As with other pre-capitalist systems, Islam is preoccupied with the welfare of a community where every individual behaves altruistically and according to religious norms" (WARDE I., *Islamic Finance in the Global Economy*, Edinburgh University Press, Edinburgh 2010 (second edition), 41). Furthermore, in the Islamic perspective every human action can be conceptually framed in one of the five *al-aḥkām al-ḫamsa*; as a consequence, a behaviour is religiously worthy as far as it is also respectful of Islamic principles and precepts. Even though Islam recognises that every human being aims at maximizing his material well-being, the Islamic system requires that this happens while maximizing the *maṣlaḥa*, the general interest of the *umma*, therefore avoiding the selfishness which is, on contrary, a characteristic of *homo economicus*. On the theory of *homo economicus*, CARUSO, S., *Homo oeconomicus. Paradigma, critiche, revisioni*, Firenze University Press, Firenze, 2012; PARETO, V., *Manuale di Economia Politica*, Edizione Critica, A. Montesano, A. Zanni, L. Bruni (eds), EGEA-Università Bocconi Editore, Milano, 2006; see also FAROOQ, M.O., *Self-Interest, Homo Islamicus and Some Behavioural Assumptions in Islamic Economics and Finance*, in International Journal of Excellence in Islamic Banking and Finance, 1, 1, 2011, 52–79.

[15] WARDE, I., *Islamic Finance in the Global Economy*, Edinburgh University Press, Edinburgh, (second edition), 2010 60. The application of these moral and ethical rules

group, the believer is asked to act with trust and loyalty towards his fellow human beings; he is a member of a society that, obeying the divine will, intends to eliminate the need and redistribute wealth (an example is the *zakāt*, ritual almsgiving and fundamental pillar of faith [16]) without mortifying economic initiative. In this context, the prohibition of *ribā* and *ġarar* expresses the prohibitions of abuse of one's position of strength; of unjustified enrichment (i.e., not based on a real entrepreneurial risk); and of excessive onerousness of the obligation of one party with respect to the other.

3. Unlawful Gains *v.* Lawful Contracts

Man is body and soul and must provide for the needs of earthly life. He is a political (*madanī*) animal and needs the cooperation of his fellow men, each according to his own abilities and capacities. The relationships arising from social interaction are the cause and subject of law, but some of them regard what is considered right of God (*ḥaqq Allāh*), i.e., what goes beyond private interest and concerns the community. Examples can be traced in the rules on *status libertatis*, marriage, legitimate filiation (*nasab*), penal law and the prohibition of risk (*ġarar*) and usury (*ribā*); these rules cannot be disregarded or waived because they refer to the public interest (*al-maṣlaḥa al-ʿāmma*) while all other personal relationships are rights of man (*ḥaqq al-ādamī*) since they refer to private interests of individuals.

Islamic law does not prohibit commerce or lawful gain ("Allah has permitted trade (*bayʿ*) and has forbidden usury (*ribā*)" Q. II, 275), it is only hostile to the idea of wealth producing wealth merely thanks to the passing of time. In the Quran, the initial disapproval of the loan at interest (XXX, 39: "Whatever loans you give, only seeking interest at the expense of peo-

---

is clear in al-Ġazālī when, in his *Iḥyāʾ ʿulūm al-dīn* (the revival of religious sciences), he lays down seven fundamental principles for a Muslim merchant in his pursuit of profit: a merchant should (1) begin his transactions with good faith and intention; (2) conceive of trade as a social duty; (3) not be the first to enter and the last to leave the market; (4) avoid forbidden and all doubtful and suspicious business; (5) carefully watch his words and deeds in business; (6) not be distracted from fulfilling his religious duties and rituals; and (7) not travel by sea. KHALILEH, H., *Merchant, Muslim*, in *Medieval Islamic Civilization. An Encyclopaedia*, Routledge, New York, 2006, 498–499.

[16] It is said in the Quran to "take from their wealth charity to purify and bless them" (IX, 103) and it is the Quran that gives the first instructions on how to use proceeds from alms: "Alms-tax is only for the poor and the needy, for those employed to administer it, for those whose hearts are attracted to the faith, for freeing slaves, for those in debt, for Allah's cause, and for needy travellers" (IX, 60).

ple's wealth will not increase with Allah. But whatever charity you give, only seeking the pleasure of Allah – it is they whose reward will be multiplied") is followed by a decisive divine condemnation of the *ribā* (III, 130: "O believers! Do not consume interest, multiplying it many times over. And be mindful of Allah, so you may prosper"). *Ribā* is a monetary advantage without a countervalue;[17] in the classical Islamic theory, *ribā* applies to payment or collection of interest on a money loan while the liberal theory restricts its meaning to usurious interest only, thus allowing all the transactions where the gain or profit cannot be considered usurious.[18] The Quranic ban is to be read together with the traditions on *ribāwī* goods; the rule, based on the *ḥadīṯ*, is as follows: gold for gold (*al-ḏahabi bi-l-ḏahabi*), silver for silver (*al-wariqi bi-l-wariqi*), wheat for wheat (*al-burri bi-l-burri*), barley for barley (*al-ša'īri bi-l-ša'īri*), date for date (*al-tamri bi-l-tamri*) and salt for salt (*al-milḥi bi-l-milḥi*), the same thing for the same thing (*miṯl*^{an} *bi-miṯl*^{an}) and hand to hand (*yad*^{an} *bi-yad*^{an}).[19] The ancient jurists (*fuqahā'*) agree on considering these as mere examples and they all accept the extension to other goods via analogical reasoning (*qiyās*). In the logic of early Islam economics, gold and silver represent precious metals, while wheat, barley and dates are food products; in a different perspective, gold and silver are examples of goods sold by weight, while wheat, barley and date represent goods sold by measure. Today the question is whether or not money is a *ribāwī* good; the affirmative answer is based on the fact that at the time of the Prophet gold and silver were used to determine the value and price of a good, exactly the same function performed today by money.

Fuqahā' also distinguished *ribā al-nasī'a* (when the creditor's profit comes from a monetary obligation) from *ribā al-fadl*, where the exchange or sale transactions effectively result in the charging of "interest" through the exchange of the same commodity, but of a different quality or quantity. To this distinction is connected the one between obligation *dayn* and obligation *'ayn*: the former has a pecuniary nature and is surrounded by extreme attention due to the obvious risk of falling into usury; the latter regards goods, commodities and, due to the presence of a *res* (real goods such as merchandise or raw material), it can better guarantee the lawfulness

---

[17] SCHACHT, J., *An Introduction to Islamic Law*, Clarendon Press, Oxford, 1964, 145.

[18] On this basis 'Abd al-Razzāq al-Sanhūrī, author of the 1948 Egyptian civil code, allows simple interests binding it to specific circumstances generally linked to necessity (*ḍarūra*); the liberal theory is also followed by the majority of civil and commercial codes in the Arab world.

[19] *Sunan* al-Nasā'ī, Book 44, Hadith 112, https://sunnah.com/urn/1085445.

of the transaction and of the gain obtained.[20] This explain why jurists prefer contract of exchange (*'uqūd mu'āwaḍa*) where the object of the contract can be immediately delivered, especially when the assets are susceptible to change in quality or quantity due to the passing of time.

Islamic *favour* toward concomitant exchanges leads us to the problem of risk (*ġarar*). Unlike *ribā*, *ġarar* cannot be found in the Quran, but it is quoted in the Prophet's *sunna*. *Ġarar* describes things with unknown fate (*mağhūl al-'āqiba*); famous is the definition given by Mālik in *al-Muwaṭṭa'*: "it is included in *ġarar* and risky transactions the case of a man whose camel or slave, whose price is fifty dinar, is lost or escaped, and who is told by another man: 'I will buy it for twenty dinars'. Thus, if the buyer finds it, the seller loses thirty dinars; if not, the buyer loses twenty dinars."[21] Besides, Mālik underlines that if what has been lost is found and it is not known whether its value has increased or decreased or if it has some defect, this makes the contract even more aleatory. On this basis, jurists see *ġarar* whenever it is uncertain whether one of the parties will receive the equivalent of what it has given or what it wanted to achieve by concluding the contract. In these cases, there is an enrichment that, without a reason that justifies and makes legitimate the profit of one party at the expense of the other, must be considered unjust and therefore illegitimate. The general rule is that what belongs to a Muslim is not licit for another unless the owner gives his consent and there is no consent where profit or loss depends on blind fate; this is why buying an unborn (*emptio spei*), or buying future or still green harvest (*emptio aleae*) is not allowed.[22]

At the very beginning of Islamic history, the economy was dominated by self-financing and direct financing, this last one based on the direct relationship between the owner of the capital and the entrepreneur using it. The limit of these systems was represented, in the case of self-financing by the possibility that the entrepreneur did not have profits to reinvest; and in the case of direct financing by its being territorially limited to the lender's proximity (in order to allow him to easily be informed about the financed activity) and subject also to the further limit of confidence in the project's chances of success. Quite soon, business practice produced the figure of

---

[20] PICCINELLI, G.M., s.v. "ribā", *Digesto*, IV ed., XVII civile, 1998, 494–497; PAPA, M., *La definizione di contratto e l'autonomia contrattuale in diritto musulmano: dai principi della shari'a alle legislazioni contemporanee*, in Roma e America. Diritto romano comune, 7, 1999, 277–297.

[21] *al-Muwaṭṭa'*, XVII, 34, 1942; MĀLIK IBN ANAS, *al-Muwaṭṭa', Manuale di legge islamica*, TOTTOLI, R. (ed.), Einaudi, Torino, 2011, 498.

[22] SANTILLANA, D., *Istituzioni di diritto musulmano malichita con riguardo anche al sistema sciafiita*, Istituto per l'Oriente, Roma, Vol. II, 1938, 118–121.

the financial intermediary as the one who could collect money from savers and provide it to entrepreneurs (indirect financing, *muḍārib yuḍārib*); as a consequence, we have the progressive replacement of interest on money with alternative forms of profit, developing a system of risk participation on a corporate basis through which profits and losses are shared pro quota.

It is therefore not surprising that the expression "Islamic banking" today identifies interest-free banking activity, which is based on the sharing of profits and losses (PLS, profit and loss sharing) by all parties involved. What comes to the fore is the use of contractual instruments that allow the bank to become a real entrepreneur and, by participating in the business risk, to justify its earnings. The financing of commercial activities through PLS is primarily done through types of contractual partnership: *mušāraka*, a contractual company in which both the bank and the entrepreneur contribute capital and in which both have the right to manage the business; and *muḍāraba*, in which the bank provides the capital, the entrepreneur provides the work and the right of management belongs only to the latter. Both cases are examples of PLS partnership in which the bank is allowed to receive a predetermined percentage of the profit since it bears the risk of the failure of the company and, therefore, also of the non-recovery of the invested funds.

Alongside the partnership scheme, the Islamic bank can use instruments that allow it to directly manage the business activity; in these hypotheses, the remuneration of the banking activity is given by the sale price or the rent or commissions for the services provided. The following contracts can be used for these purposes: *murābaha* (mark-up sale), *bay ʿ mu ʾaǧǧal* (sale on credit), contracts where immediate payment is made for the future delivery of a product such as *istiṣnāʿ* (order to manufacture and supply a commodity for the purchaser) or *salam* (sale *anticipato praetio*), *iǧāra wa iqtinā ʾ* (leasing).

The Islamic bank, as an expression of respect for ethical-religious principles and values, suffers from a number of conditioning factors: in investments, the bank is required to verify, in addition to the credibility of the project and the entrepreneurial skills of the client, also the 'ethicality' of the financed operation, since an Islamic instrument could never be used to pursue purposes against *šarīʿa*.[23] The collection of savings must also comply

[23] It is intuitive that investment in businesses dealing with pork, alcohol, gambling or pornography are contrary to Islamic principles; less obvious is the prohibition of financing business dealing with the production of tobacco as well as armaments and destructive weapons; a negative evaluation can also exclude companies based in countries in which fundamental human rights are not guaranteed. ELMELKI, A. & MOUNIRA, B., *Eth-*

with ethical criteria: the objective is to attract the saver, presenting him/her with deposit instruments that are remunerative while not providing for the payment of interest.

Islamic economic finds its roots in theology and in Islamic jurisprudence and law. The Muslim believer is urged to enjoy the good things (*al-ṭayyibāt*) bestowed by God with measure and obeying the precepts (*aḥkām*) of Islam: therefore, the emphasis is on just exchange, just price, fairness, productive labour, prohibition of exploitation of the weaker party in an exchange, having in mind the satisfaction of human needs while enabling the believer to serve higher ideal.

References

ABU SAHLIEH, S.A.A., *Il diritto islamico. Fondamenti, fonti, istituzioni*, Roma: Carocci, 2008.

D'EMILIA, A., *Scritti di diritto islamico*, raccolti a cura di F. Castro, Roma: Istituto per l'Oriente, 1976.

ELMELKI, A. & MOUNIRA, B., *Ethical investment and the social responsibilities of the Islamic banks*, in International Business Research, 2, 2, 2009, 123–130.

FAROOQ, M.O., *Self-interest, homo islamicus and some behavioural assumptions in Islamic economics and finance*, International Journal of Excellence in Islamic Banking and Finance, 1, 1, 2011, 52–79.

GLEAVE, R.M., *s.v.* "maḳāṣid al-sharīʿa", in *Encyclopédie de l'Islam*, Vol. XII, 2007, 580–581.

HALLAQ, W.B., *Sharīʿa. Theory, practice, transformations*, Cambridge: Cambridge University Press, 2010.

KHADDURI, M., *s.v.* "maṣlaḥa", in *Encyclopédie de l'Islam*, Vol. VI, 1991, 727–729.

KHALILEH, H., *Merchant, Muslim*, in *Medieval Islamic Civilization. An Encyclopaedia*, New York: Routledge, 2006, 498–499.

MĀLIK IBN ANAS, *al-Muwaṭṭa', Manuale di legge islamica*, TOTTOLI, R. (ed.), Torino: Einaudi, 2011.

PAPA, M., *La definizione di contratto e l'autonomia contrattuale in diritto musulmano: dai principi della shari'a alle legislazioni contemporanee*, in Roma e America. Diritto romano comune, 7, 1999, 277–297.

PICCINELLI, G.M., s.v. "ribā", *Digesto*, IV ed., XVII civile, 1998, 494–497.

---

ical Investment and the Social Responsibilities of the Islamic Banks, in International Business Research, 2, 2, 2009, 123–130.

SANTILLANA, D., *Istituzioni di diritto musulmano malichita con riguardo anche al sistema sciafiita*, Roma: Istituto per l'Oriente, Vol. II, 1938.
SCHACHT, J., *An Introduction to Islamic Law*, Oxford: Clarendon Press, 1964.
WARDE, I., *Islamic Finance in the Global Economy*, Edinburgh: Edinburgh University Press, 2010 (second edition).
ZILIO-GRANDI, I., *Le virtù del buon musulmano*, Torino: Einaudi, 2020.

Chapter 3

PRECONDITIONS AND SUGGESTIONS FOR ISLAMIC FINANCE TO GENERATE SUSTAINED ECONOMIC GROWTH

Murat Çizakça

SUMMARY: 1. Introduction. – 2. Pre-conditions. – 3. Modest Contribution of Islamic Banking Towards to Economic Development. – 4. The Real Potential. – 5. Waqfs, Universities and Venture Capital. – 6. *Esham* and Public Debt. – 7. Conclusion. – References.

1. Introduction

Nowadays it is often argued that Islam is in crisis. I beg to differ! Since the Qur'an is immutable and has been so ever since the seventh century, the crisis cannot pertain to this religion. A crisis certainly exists but the culprit is not Islam; it is, instead, the massive and wide-spread poverty of Muslims.[1]

Much of this poverty is caused by the dissolution, dismemberment and the subsequent colonisation of the once powerful and rich Islamic empires by Western imperialism. So, when after the Second World War a multitude of newly independent countries emerged from the old empires, pockets of extreme wealth generated by oil have now been locked in some countries and emirates with tiny populations while other Islamic countries with large populations and potential are starving for capital. The result is a hugely unequal distribution of wealth across the Islamic world.

Today, Islamic countries are lagging not only behind the West but also the rest of the world, according to almost any economic criteria.[2] So the main question this paper deals with is whether Islamic finance can make

[1] While the Qur'an has indeed been fixed, I acknowledge that statements of Prophet Muhammad, the so-called *ahadith,* have not. Much of the Islamic radicalism is based upon fabricated *ahadith*. Thanks to the digitalisation of Qur'an, such *ahadith* can now be filtered out with relative ease. For, no authentic *hadith* can ever contradict Qur'an. So, if notwithstanding this, many Muslims are still influenced by such fabricated *ahadith,* this is due to their lack of reasoning and education. Inadequate education, on the other hand, is an economic problem.

[2] AHMET KURU, *Islam Authoritarianism and Under-development*, 66, fns. 1–5.

any difference. I have a straightforward answer to this question. Providing certain preconditions are met, yes, Islamic finance can make a difference and in doing so, it can create major profit potential not only for Muslims but for non-Muslims as well. Put differently, widespread poverty in the Islamic world is a problem that needs to be tackled through co-operation between Muslims and non-Muslims. The latter should not hesitate to co-operate, because we are living in a small and highly integrated world. Continuous poverty in any one region ends up affecting the developed world in the form of massive illegal economic migration and/or poverty-stricken, frustrated and angry young men easily influenced by radical preaching.

Viewed from this perspective, Islamic finance appears to be promising. For here is a financial system that operates within Islamic jurisprudence. It has the potential, therefore, to be embraced by the masses. This is important as mass-embracement avoids the so-called transplant effect, which reduces the chances of successfully borrowing an institution from another culture.[3] An indigenously developed system therefore has obvious advantages when compared with another one borrowed from elsewhere. This way of thinking has led to an over-optimistic obsession of Islamic economists with Islamic finance and banking. But these academicians are missing the point that unless certain pre-conditions are met, Islamic finance, on its own, notwithstanding its authenticity, cannot facilitate sustained economic growth in the Islamic world.

2. Pre-conditions

What then are these pre-conditions? I would argue that the first one should be to get rid of all the dictators Islamic world is infested with. This is indeed the first pre-condition. For rule of law cannot exist under dictatorships and without the rule of law, property rights also cannot exist. Without solid property rights, economic development cannot be achieved. It should also be recognised that most of the dictators in the Islamic world have been supported by Western powers. The crisis Mr. Macron has referred to, therefore, should actually pertain to this corrupt Western double standard which, while upholding democracy in the West, does not hesitate to undermine it in the Islamic world. Herein lies the potential Western contribution: the West must stop supporting the dictators. Indeed, just putting an end to supporting the dictators would be a major contribution.

Once dictators are swept out, those who replace them and have the

[3] BERKOWITZ, D. et al. (2003).

power to take economic decisions, must be sensitive to the wishes and demands of the population. This is possible only in democracies.

Democracy, however, is not an isolated system. It comes as a complex package of institutions that include a parliament and an independent judiciary that checks the executive, as well as a set of freedoms comprising, particularly, freedoms of expression, worship and entrepreneurship.

These principles and institutions are all specific to the West. So, we must ask the inevitable question: How applicable would they be in the Islamic world? The good news is that all of them have been found to be in perfect harmony with the basic teachings of Islam.[4] While borrowing them from the West, a significant transplant effect should therefore not be expected.

3. Modest Contribution of Islamic Banking to Economic Development

Now, let us make a heroic assumption here that these pre-conditions have somehow been fulfilled. What then would be the contribution of Islamic finance towards economic development in Islamic countries? Islamic banking, the most visible component of Islamic finance, does not have a great potential. This is because Islamic banking today has diverged from the original project of its founder, Dr. Ahmad al-Naggar, who established the very first Islamic bank in 1963 in Mit Ghamr, Egypt. Al-Naggar had envisaged Islamic banks as risk-sharing financial institutions, friendly to capital hungry entrepreneurs, which also contained important characteristics of micro-finance.[5] Combining entrepreneurial aspects as well as micro-finance and doing so within an authentic Islamic framework, it was highly original and had great potential. But after impressive operations of merely four years, the whimsical dictator Gamal Abdul Nasser decided to close it down. The prevailing Islamic banking today has abandoned these ideas and focused on imitating conventional Western finance.

There are three basic reasons for this: first, Islamic bankers have received their initial training primarily in the conventional system and second, they are under the pressure of their clients who expect to be rewarded for depositing their cash in ways similar to the conventional system. This leads to the third reason, the so-called mismatch of funds problem: while depositors deposit their funds with the banks for the short run, financing

[4] Çizakça, (2020; 2014). See also Kamali (1998).

[5] On Naggar type Islamic micro-finance see Çizakça (2020). On the successful application of micro-finance, see, e.g., Yunus (2003).

entrepreneurs yields returns in the long run. To deal with these problems, Islamic banks, not only shun entrepreneurial finance, they also imitate conventional instruments and make them appear compliant to Islamic jurisprudence. Often, they do this by deliberately complicating their transactions so as to disguise the interest element embodied in them. But every additional step they take for this purpose increases their costs. As a result, Islamic banking generates modest profits despite the fact that there is great demand among Muslims for banking services. It is this almost insatiable demand, but not the cost efficiency of their transactions, which enables Islamic banks to expand their activities globally.

One major achievement of Islamic banking must be mentioned here. Notwithstanding the drawbacks mentioned above, they have, by and large, facilitated the transformation of non-banking Islamic societies into banking societies. The huge importance of this for channelling the savings of the masses into major investment projects is obvious.

Despite their success and the important role they play in Islamic economies, Islamic banking constitutes but a small part, just the tip of the iceberg, of Islamic finance. The real potential lies elsewhere. In the rest of this chapter I intend to explain this.

4. The Real Potential

Islamic economic and financial history informs us that the following institutions have been successfully employed by Muslims. I have deliberately used the term "successfully" here. For it indicates that these are highly sophisticated institutions that have been time-tested. The first ones that come to mind are the partnership techniques. As far as these partnerships are concerned, time-testedness is an understatement. For some of these partnerships have been deciphered by historians in the cuneiform tablets of ancient Babylonia dated around 2000 B.C. Known as Harranu partnerships, they were diversified further in new Babylonia around 600 B.C.[6] Carefully studying the details of these partnerships provided by Lanz, I reached the conclusion that they constituted the origins of the Islamic partnerships that emerged centuries later.

Subjected to an Islamic filter, these partnerships constituted the backbone of Islamic finance, from the seventh century onwards. They were so perfected by the classical Muslim jurists that they were borrowed by medieval Europeans.[7] The Islamic *Mudaraba* partnership which medieval Euro-

---

[6] LANZ (1976).

[7] UDOVITCH (1969).

peans called *Commenda*, dominated and financed the European commercial revolution during the thirteenth century and afterwards. *Commenda* was apparently so important that Acemoğlu and Robinson trace the beginning of the decline of Venice to the exclusion of the rising bourgeoisie from *commenda* transactions.[8]

Remarkably, we observe all the basic characteristics of *Mudaraba/Commenda* in rude health even today. Indeed, the dynamic Californian venture capital is basically a modernised *Mudaraba*! Since I have already provided substantial evidence for this statement, I will not go into details here.[9] In sum, venture capital is true Islamic finance and once the pre-conditions are fulfilled, it would be in perfect harmony with the traditions and jurisprudence of the Islamic world. Since it is also known perfectly well in the West, herein lies a great potential of co-operation across cultures.

Another huge potential exists in non-governmental organisations, or NGOs. A specific NGO format known in the West as charitable trusts or foundations also has its distant origins in ancient Mesopotamia and Egypt.[10] Similar to the business partnerships mentioned above, they were also subjected to an Islamic filter during the seventh and eighth centuries and incorporated into Islamic jurisprudence, where they are known as waqfs.[11]

A waqf was established by the well-to-do, who donated a part of his/her wealth for a specific charitable purpose, usually for education or health. Once donated and registered by the local judge, *kadi*, the capital of the waqf, was considered to have become the property of God. It therefore immediately began to enjoy strong property rights. Thus protected, it became very difficult for unscrupulous rulers to confiscate such donated assets. This meant that they enjoyed longevity. There are, indeed, many waqfs all over the Islamic world that have survived for centuries.

Once incorporated into the Islamic jurisprudence during the seventh-eighth centuries, waqfs were then borrowed, again, by the medieval West. The best-known example of this process is Merton College of Oxford. A careful analysis of the endowment deed of Merton College convinced Professor Gaudiosi that the legal format of this deed was identical to an Islamic waqf. Since Walter De Merton, the founder of the Merton College, had close contact and even deposited his wealth with the Knights Templars, he was perfectly well informed about Islamic waqfs. So it is by no means surprising that he should establish his college in that format.

---

[8] ACEMOĞLU and ROBINSON (2012).

[9] ÇIZAKÇA (2011, Ch. 15).

[10] BORGOLTE, (2017).

[11] Since waqfs have become part of the English vocabulary, they are not italicised here.

Since waqfs usually financed, organised and maintained schools and colleges as well as hospitals, they were the primary providers of human capital. Human capital, on the other hand, is considered by Gary Becker, a Nobel laurate in economics, as the most important and effective component of economic growth. [12]

Nowadays, probably the most powerful waqf in the world, with its capital of more than 50 billion USD, is the *Bill and Melinda Gates Foundation.* Thus, once again we observe an Islamic institution *par excellence,* functioning with great success in the West.

From medieval Islamic waqfs to the Gates Foundation, with some 15 centuries in between, this institution obviously evolved. A major turning point, well-conceived but not applied, was the very first attempt to combine waqf with *Mudaraba.* This happened back in the eighth century when Imam Zufer was asked whether a waqf could be established not only with real estate but also with cash. Zufer not only replied affirmatively but also explained the *modus operandi* of such a waqf. "Yes," he said, the founder can establish his waqf with cash and invest this capital with *Mudaraba* and then channel the profits generated to the charitable purpose of the waqf. Had this model been applied it would have constituted a perfect merger between waqf and *Mudaraba.* But it was not meant to be. Founders were too risk averse to subject their waqf*s'* capital to *Mudaraba,* a risky partnership. So, they preferred to invest the cash capital of their waqfs with *istiglal,* a legal trick that disguised the interest embodied.

Reluctance of cash waqf founders to invest their waqf*s'* capital with *Mudaraba* had unfortunate consequences for Muslim entrepreneurs. This is because *Mudaraba* is an entrepreneur friendly partnership for the following reasons:

1. It is a capital-labour (entrepreneurship) partnership. The entire capital is provided by the capitalist. This enables young and penniless entrepreneurs to obtain capital purely on the strength of their projects.
2. Since the focus is on the feasibility and profit potential of the project, the entrepreneur does not have to provide collateral, a condition normally very difficult, if not impossible, for young entrepreneurs to fulfil.
3. In case of loss, the entrepreneur does not lose his/her meagre capital. All pecuniary loss accrues to the capitalist partner.

The road to waqf-*Mudaraba* combination remained closed for centuries. The first turning point had to wait until the early twentieth century when three *fatwas* were obtained, two in Egypt and one in Iraq, which permitted

[12] See BECKER, (1995) and PIKETTY (2017).

the establishment of waqfs not only with cash but also with shares and PFPD instruments.[13] This was the birth of, at least at theoretical level, waqfs of stocks. Actual application came later when Vehbi Koç, a well-known secular Turkish businessman supported by certain members of the parliament, succeeded to push through a new waqf law in 1967 which allowed the establishment of cash waqfs with shares of joint-stock companies.

A comparative analysis of this evolution has already been made, where I have explained that for all practical purposes a waqf of stocks is actually akin to a combination of waqf and *Mudaraba.*[14] This is because purchasing shares of a company leads to a risk sharing partnership between the purchaser and the entrepreneur, which is the essence of *Mudaraba.* In short, the combination originally envisaged back in the eighth century finally came to be applied in the twentieth. That the combination has finally found wide-spread application is important for a number of reasons. First, from the perspective of Islamic jurisprudence, the dubious *istiglal* has been replaced by waqf of stocks, a perfectly legitimate instrument. Second, the information asymmetry problems associated with the old cash waqfs have also been solved. Indeed, while in old cash waqfs all management strategy and decisions were firmly stated in the endowment deeds by the long-deceased founders, the trustees who were facing contemporary problems had no power to make the necessary changes in response to the ravages of time. With waqf of stocks, by contrast, all management decisions are taken by professional managers of companies, whose share the waqf holds. Third, establishing a waqf with company shares, opens up the possibility of combining waqf with venture capital. A crucial step in this direction was taken by the Turkish General Directorate of Waqfs on 6 August 1999 when waqfs were permitted to buy shares of start-ups not even listed in the stock-exchange.[15]

If we take a step further, there is no reason why a waqf, specifically with the purpose of financing young entrepreneurs, should not be established. Such a waqf, which focuses on start-ups, would combine the best features of waqf and *Mudaraba*/venture capital. It can function in a variety of ways.

First of all, it can obtain its initial capital through personal donations from well-to-do persons. Second, people with modest means can also contribute capital, their savings, through crowd-funding. Third, share-holders

---

[13] Permanently Funded Public Debt. This will be explained below. On the *fatwa*s issued see ÇIZAKÇA (2000).

[14] ÇIZAKÇA (2000).

[15] ÇIZAKÇA (2000).

of various companies can donate their shares and thus create a waqf of stocks. In this case, annual dividends are made available for *Mudaraba* investments. All of these methods would be entirely compatible with Islamic jurisprudence.

If established by a risk averse founder, the waqf of stocks could purchase shares of various well-established companies so as to form a portfolio. It would then spend the annual dividends on financing start-ups of young entrepreneurs. Alternatively, if it is established by a more ambitious founder keen on financing as many promising start-ups as possible, the waqf then would spend its entire capital on start-up financing. When it makes profits, it simply adds them on to its original capital, *corpus,* and if it makes losses, its capital would be depleted. What matters here is that whether expanded or depleted, the capital of this waqf has originally been donated. Therefore, unlike the manager of a venture capital (VC) company, who is under pressure to perform to satisfy its share-holders in the shortest possible time, the trustee of the waqf/VC manages donated money. The latter is clearly more patient capital. Although obviously both standard venture capital and waqf/VC need to be managed with utmost care, having more patient funds, waqf/VC can afford to invest in even longer term and high-risk high-gain projects. Put differently, waqf/VC can invest in high technology start-up projects with the greatest potential for long term profits thanks to its more patient capital.

5. Waqfs, Universities and Venture Capital

Universities and their labs can also be viewed in this context. As mentioned above, there have always been close links between waqfs and universities throughout history. Such links continue today as well. Presently in Turkey, there are more than 70 modern waqf universities. Many of these waqfs are founded with shares from holding companies, which channel a part of their profits annually to these universities. This structure carries with it an important potential. The research needed by these companies to survive in the harshly competitive business world can be outsourced to the associated universities within a venture capital framework. In this framework, capital would be provided by the company that requests the research and a professor with his graduate research team would be the entrepreneurs. The academic team would establish their own start-up and the company that needed the research would buy their shares with the understanding that the capital thus provided will be spent to set up the lab needed. The research then commences in the specialised lab situated in the university but jointly owned by the university, outsourcing company and the academicians.

When the research is successfully completed a number of options would emerge. Either the outsourcing company can buy more of the shares of the academic start-up and become the owner of the patent, or it would let the academic team to develop their start up to a full-fledged company and benefit from the rising value of its shares it holds. Put differently, the outsourcing company would simply sell the shares of the academic company it holds with profit and exits the project. Whatever the case, this would be a win, win, win situation with the outsourcing firm getting the technology it needed, the graduate students getting their Ph.D.s as well as money and the university getting a state of the art lab.

Finally, a new waqf law that incorporates many of the points mentioned above has been prepared by IRTI (the research arm of the Islamic Development Bank) and the Kuwait Public Foundation and will be proposed to all Islamic governments. [16] It goes without saying that assuming this proposed draft law is accepted by most Islamic countries, a significant potential forEast–West and North-South financial/technological co-operation would arise.

6. *Esham* and Public Debt

Another potential for long term technology investment exists in Islamic public finance. Nowadays all Islamic states borrow from global money markets. This is so even for Saudi Arabia. This proud custodian of the two holiest cities of Islam borrowed 17.5 billion USD in 2016 from the global money market. This was naturally a usurious transaction and pays even 2.1% more interest than the US treasuries. Had Saudi monetary authorities been better informed about Islamic economic/financial history, they could have avoided this, which must have been an embarrassing transaction, and borrowed money without interest. Economic/financial history does, indeed, inform us as to how this could have been done.

Both medieval Europe and the Islamic world have developed financial instruments enabling governments to borrow from the public without recourse to interest. Known in Europe with the general name, *Permanently Funded Public Debt* (PFPD) and in the Ottoman Empire as *esham,* these instruments securitised a fraction of the annual returns of a tax-source. Persons who bought a share, *sehm,* obtained the right to receive the annuities that pertained to that share for the rest of their life. There were also more expensive perpetual shares as well. The unique feature of these doc-

[16] ÇIZAKÇA (2014).

uments was the fact that redemption of the shares bought was always at the discretion of the borrower. Put differently, as long as the borrower (state) paid the annuities on time, it was under no obligation to pay back the principal. It is precisely this feature which makes it an interest free instrument. For, in a usurious transaction the borrower has to return the principal borrowed at a certain pre-determined date together with the interest. Since in this case it is the borrower who decides when to redeem his debt, *esham* is not usurious. Moreover, from Islamic perspective, *esham* directly follows the Qur'an, which advises that when writing a contract, the weak partner (the borrower) should dictate the terms. [17]

I argue here that a modernised version of *esham* can save all Islamic governments from the embarrassment of borrowing with interest. Moreover, this can be important for financial inclusion. As Piketty has argued, selling PFPD instruments in Europe used to be a far better method for people. After all, the PFPDs were replaced by heavy taxation. So, while for centuries PFPD holders earned substantial returns for generations, between the two world wars when the PFPDs were replaced by higher taxation, investors still had to hand out their savings in the form of taxes but ended up getting nothing in return. [18] This European argument is just as valid for Ottoman investors who had benefited ever since 1774 from *esham* annuities.

The characteristics of *esham* summarised above, render it perfectly suitable for financing venture capital activity in the Islamic world. Since redemption date and conditions are decided by the borrower (state), capital raised by the state by securitizing fractional revenue sources becomes patient capital. It can even be argued that together with waqfs, *esham* can provide the most patient capital for *Mudaraba*/venture capital investments. Thus, it would be perfectly logical for the state to set up *esham* funds and then to channel these to venture capital companies. This process should be done by equity finance; that is, the state should purchase minority shares of venture capital companies. The word minority must be emphasised here. The selection of an entrepreneur to be financed is a highly skilled and difficult job. It should never be entrusted to government bureaucrats. Put differently, *esham* funds should be channelled to venture capital companies through equity finance, but selecting the entrepreneurs to be financed should be within the purview of the venture capitalists.

One successful example of channelling state funds to entrepreneurs can

[17] II:282. The exact words are: "Let him who incurs liability to dictate" (Cairo: Dar al-Kitab al-Mısri, Yusuf Ali translation, n.d.).

[18] PIKETTY (2017).

be observed in Israel. The so-called YOZMA programme of Israel provides state funds on condition that the entrepreneur first obtains funding from an American venture capital company. If that is the case, then the government of Israel matches these funds at the rate of two-thirds. This programme not only allows the selection of the entrepreneur to professional venture capital companies, it also enables the Israeli government to channel its funds to the desired target without any bureaucratic corruption.

Moreover, the patient capital that *esham* and waqfs provide solves the mismatch of funds problems faced by Islamic banks. Therefore. not Islamic banks but these two institutions are far more potent to finance entrepreneurship.

With respect to Islamic public finance, *esham* shares can also be used for open market operations of Islamic central banks. Indeed, when these banks wish to inject money into the economy, they can redeem the *esham* shares held by the public. Conversely, when they want to withdraw cash, they issue new *esham* shares. Obviously, when the public begin to buy these shares, money will be withdrawn from the economy and be channelled to the central banks.

7. Conclusion

The relevance of all this for Muslim countries is the fact that they combine waqf, *Mudaraba* and *esham*, all time-tested authentic Islamic instruments of finance and also wide-spread and well-known in the West. Herein is the great potential forEast–West co-operation. There is no reason whatsoever why Western companies should not participate in *Mudaraba*/venture capital transactions in the Islamic world as such transactions are not only legitimate but also well-known in both civilisations. But the *conditio sine qua non* is that the preconditions stated at the beginning of this paper are fulfilled and the selection of the entrepreneur must be within the purview of the professional venture capitalists with the state confining itself to fund-matching only.

Islamic banking constitutes only a small component of Islamic finance. Naggar-Yunus type micro-finance and Tabung Haji type pilgrimage financing have already proven themselves in contemporary Egypt, Bangladesh and Malaysia, while waqfs of stocks and *esham* have been time-tested in Turkey.

Islamic venture capital/*mudaraba* can obtain funds from both waqfs of stocks and from a modernised *esham* system. *Esham* can also revolutionise and rescue government borrowing from *sukuk* dominated quasi usurious instruments and transform public finance into genuine Islamic norms.

Moreover, while doing so, it can also allow Western capital to participate in potentially high profit projects in the Islamic world. Open market operations of Islamic central banks can also be truly Islamised utilizing *esham*.

In this paper I have focused on those truly Islamic and time-tested instruments that are well-known in the West as well and are therefore open to East–West co-operation. The gist of this chapter is that providing the pre-conditions are fulfilled, potential for Islamic finance and East–West co-operation in the future is substantial.

References

ACEMOĞLU, DARON, & ROBINSON, J.A., *Why Nations Fail*, New York: Crown Business, 2012.

BECKER, G.S. (1995). *Human capital and poverty alleviation*. World Bank, Human Resources Development and Operations Policy.

BERKOWITZ, D., *The transplant effect*, in The American Journal of Comparative Law, 51, 2003, 163–200.

BERKOWITZ, D., PISTOR, K. & RICHARD, J-F., *Economic development, legality and transplant effect*, in European Economic Review, 47(1), 2003, 165–195.

BORGOLTE, MICHAEL, *Weltgeschichte als Stiftungsgeschichte*, Darmstadt: Wissenschaftliche Buchgesellschaft, 2017.

ÇIZAKÇA, MURAT, *Have Muslims been actually ordained to opt for liberal democracy?* www.academia.edu/38243524

ÇIZAKÇA, MURAT, *A History of Philanthropic Foundations: Islamic World from the Seventh Century to the Present*, İstanbul: Bogazici University Press, 2000.

ÇIZAKÇA, MURAT, *Islamic Capitalism and Finance: Origins, Evolution and the Future*, Cheltenham: E. Elgar, 2011.

ÇIZAKÇA, MURAT, *Democracy, economic development and Maqasid al-Shariah*, in ÇIZAKÇA, M.(ed.), *Islam and the Challenges of Western Capitalism*, Cheltenham: Edward Elgar, 2014, 178–201.

ÇIZAKÇA, MURAT, *A critical assessment of the* Waqf *Law being prepared by IDB/IRTI and Kuwait Foundation*, in MEHMET KURTOĞLU (ed.), *Dünya Vakıflar Konferansı* (World Waqfs Conference), Ankara: VGM Yayınları No. 113, 2014, 427–438.

ÇIZAKÇA, MURAT, *Why Islamic Institutions function best in the West*, in Turkish Journal of Islamic Economics, 7(2), 2020.

ÇIZAKÇA, MURAT, *A broad look into Islamic finance*, April 2020. www.academia.edu/41882805

GAUDIOSI, MONICA, *The influence of the Islamic Law of* waqf *on the development of the trust in England: The case of Merton College*, University of Pennsylvania Law Review, 136(4), 1988.

KAMALI, MOHAMMAD HASHIM, *Freedom of Expression in Islam*, Kuala Lumpur: Ilmiah Publishers, 1998.

KURU, T. AHMET, *Islam, Authoritarianism and Underdevelopment: A Global and Historical Comparison*, Cambridge: Cambridge University Press, 2019.

LANZ, HUGO, *Die neubabylonischen harranu Geschaeftsunternehmen,* Berlin: J. Schweitzer Verlag, 1976.

PIKETTY, THOMAS, *Capital in the Twenty-first Century*, Cambridge, Mass.: Harvard University Press, 2017.

UDOVITCH, A., *At the origins of the Western Commenda: Islam, Israel, Byzantium*, in Princeton Near East Papers, No. 9, Princeton: Princeton University Press, 1969.

YUNUS, MUHAMMAD, *Banker to the Poor*, New York: Public Affairs, 2003.

Part 2

FUNDAMENTALS OF MEDITERRANEAN ECONOMICS AND FINANCE

Chapter 4
THE ECONOMICS AND FINANCE OF THE MIDDLE EAST AND NORTH AFRICA

Jamus Jerome Lim

1. Introduction

The Middle East and North Africa (MENA) region has often been, as an economic entity, neglected relative to other regions. Not generally as wealthy as Western Europe or North America, nor as vibrant or rapidly-developing as East Asia, nor possessing the industrial core and geographical endowments of Latin America, the MENA region has, as its defining characteristic, one key endowment necessary for life in the modern global economy: energy resources.

This has meant that much of the modern understanding of the economics and finance of the region has largely been framed in a fairly unidimensional manner, and typically in reference to the economies of the West (the primary export market for Middle Eastern energy). Indeed, the very name by which the region is defined – the Middle East – stands in contrast to the geographical position of the region as it sits on the Asian continent (West Asia).

Such a perspective has, undoubtedly, shaped the manner in which modern analysts view the region. While the influence of energy exports is undeniably a distinguishing feature – some would argue, *the* key distinguishing feature – of the economic fortunes of the region (especially in terms of its relations with the rest of the world), it nevertheless underplays the contribution that the region has had in terms of its contribution to contemporary political-economic organisation and knowledge.

The objective of this chapter is to provide an overview of the economics and finance of the Middle East and North Africa, informed by this rich political-economic heritage. Our coverage extends from the Eastern limits of the region, including Egypt, Iraq, Iran, and the Gulf Arab states – sometimes collectively known as the *Mashreq* (the "place of sunrise") – to the Western bounds of the Northern African states, often collectively referred to as the *Maghreb* (the "place of sunset"). We also emphasize the region's linkages to the rest of the world, but not just to the occident, but also the orient.

In the first half of this chapter, we examine the economic history of the region, along with its modern economic organisation and structure. We then consider the MENA region in comparative perspective, paying attention to both the real and financial dimensions. In the second half, we turn to a discussion of one key financial aspect that is of particular relevance to the MENA region: sovereign wealth funds (SWFs). We contrast the region's SWFs with those elsewhere, and discuss in detail asset allocation for a modern, sophisticated SWF that is based in the region.

2. A Brief Economic History of the Region

The Middle East and North Africa is the cradle of at least two of the six so-called "pristine civilisations" in history: Mesopotamia (modern-day Iraq and Syria), and Egypt.[1] These were also the two oldest civilisations, and accordingly, set the stage for many of the modern political-economic institutions that persist till today.

These civilisations were part of the Fertile Crescent, which around circa 3,500 BCE saw the beginning of sedentary agriculture, along with the domestication of animals. Mesopotamia – literally, the "land between two rivers" (the two being the Tigris and Euphrates) – saw the transition away from gathering toward the farming of cereal (mainly emmer and einkorn wheat, and barley), pulses (lentils, chickpeas), and flax. Animal husbandry (mainly sheep and goats) was also more efficient than hunting. Similar developments were occurring along the Nile River. The food surpluses generated enabled the emergence of specialized professions, which are the origins of non-agricultural labour in the economy.

These settlements eventually began to coalesce into city-states in Meso-

[1] The other four comprise two in the Americas (Mesoamerican, in modern-day Mexico and Central America; and Andean, in modern-day Peru, but including parts of southern Colombia, Argentina, and Chile), and two more in Asia (Indus, in modern-day Afghanistan, Pakistan, and northern India; and Yellow River, in modern-day China).

potamia and a more coherent civilisation in ancient Egypt. Although sometimes forgotten, many elements of modern economic organisation can be traced back to these civilisations: principles such as property rights (to demarcate fields for agriculture), wage payment (for work in the fields), taxation (payments to temples, made possible with surpluses), banking and credit (necessary to meet temporary imbalances between when workers were paid and when their payments were due), and proto-government (led by the priests that served as intercessors to the gods to guarantee a good harvest).

Although the region sustained stable growth from these ancient times, it was subsequently overtaken by other civilisations, before coming back into pre-eminence during the Caliphate period, marked by the rise of Islam and the expansion of this empire from the Arabian peninsula first to the Levant (the countries of the Eastern Mediterranean), then on across North Africa and Southern Spain to the west, and Persia and central Asia to the east. This was the so-called Golden Age of Islam, where militaristic expansion led to vast wealth, and Baghdad – the capital of the Abbasid Empire – attained the enviable status of becoming the richest city in the world. Such wealth was followed by significant advances in learning and knowledge. Islamic scholars seized on texts from Greek and Roman culture, and cities such as Córdoba, Seville, and Shiraz expanded scientific inquiry along several different fields. Indeed, the significance of the region for Europe was that, after this Golden Age receded, many of the Arabic texts were subsequently translated (and in some cases, re-translated) back into European languages, preserving the continuity of hard-won knowledge. Consistent with theories of endogenous growth, knowledge and innovation were a major drive of economic advancement in the region.

By the beginning of the 14th century the Ottoman Empire was starting its expansion across much of the MENA region, even threatening, at the height of its expansion, the city of Vienna. Of course, the empire was successful – and endured for as long as it did – in no small part because of its ability to absorb human capital from across a multi-ethnic and multicultural region. Still, after several centuries, internal divisions led to a drawn-out decline, before it was overtaken by European powers in the 18th century. Still, the Ottomans persisted at least till the First World War, when its alliance with the Germans eventually led to its partition after its loss to the Triple Entente (of Russia, France, and Great Britain).

Unfortunately, the legacy of European presence in the region was, on net, somewhat negative. The starkest example of this was how the different partitions were often drawn without respecting ethnic, or institutional divisions. These would come back to haunt the region, where neat modern borders resulted in cleavages that upset longstanding historical relationships. European influence also led to a gradual hollowing out of what was proto-industrialisation. For instance, the late Ottoman empire was essentially self-sufficient in cotton and woollen textiles, but cheap European goods – chiefly from Britain – allowed the much more productive Midland factories to flood (and eventually crowd out) local industry. This deindustrialisation was further exacerbated by a focus of the European powers on extractive colonisation. Of course, European-led development was not an unalloyed bad; certain parts of the interior did benefit from the extension of a railroad network, even if its purpose was to support continued exploitation of resources and to expand potential markets.

3. The Emergence of the Modern Middle East

The weakness of the late Ottoman Empire set the stage for the MENA region, as we know it today. As the observant reader will have undoubtedly concluded from the historical overview, the beating heart of the region has always been centred around the Levant: after its founding by the Prophet Muhammad in the Arabian peninsula, the first Islamic caliphate (the Umayyads) had its capital in Damascus, the Abbasids founded their capital in Baghdad, and the Ottomans in Istanbul. Even secondary dynasties, such as the Ayyubids, Fatimids, or Mamluks, ruled from Cairo, relatively close to the original Mesopotamian/Egyptian civilisations.

There was one major instigator for shifting the centre of economic power away from this traditional core. In May 1908, the British-run Anglo-Persian Oil Company (which eventually became BP) struck oil in the area of Masjed Soleyman, in Southwestern Iran. This was followed by the discovery of large, productive wells in Saudi Arabia around 30 years later by the Standard Oil company (today, ExxonMobil).

By the middle of the 20th century, oil had become a mainstay in the region's economies, and this led to an irresistible shift of economic power and influence away from the traditional Levantine core toward what had, up till then, been the periphery. Indeed, the importance of oil (and energy more generally) is now so entrenched that observers of the region began to be categorized in terms of their relative endowments. Following one such taxonomy (Cammett, Diwan, Richards & Waterbury 2015) pairs relative energy abundance with population sizes, such that the economies of the region fall into four major types: the resource-rich, labour-poor (comprising the six Gulf Coooperation Council economies, along with Libya); the resource-rich, labor-abundant (economies such as Algeria, Iran, Iraq, Syria, and Yemen); the resource-poor, labour-abundant (e.g., Lebanon, Jordan, Egypt, Morocco, Tunisia); and the diversified and industrialized (principally Israel and Turkey).

Importantly, the region's oil-rich and oil-poor economies alike experience energy price-related economic fluctuations. For the former, this is mainly due to the enormous volatility that accompanies the nature of oil prices, which translates into dramatic shifts in these economies' terms of trade. For the latter, oil-poor economies are tightly linked to the cross-border capital, foreign aid, remittance, and external demand shocks that emanate from the oil exporters. Even a casual examination of the growth fluctuations of MENA economies reveals that business cycle shocks are first experienced by the resource-rich economies – such as the 1973 and 1979 shocks due to the Yom Kippur War and Iranian Revolution, and the 1990 invasion of Kuwait – before transmitting on to the resource-poor economies, with a lag.

Inflation patterns in MENA, likewise, echo this energy price cycle, as opposed to the manufacturing/electronics cycle in East Asia, or the somewhat more volatile commodity price cycle, which is more typical in South Asia (Figure 4.1). Since the region is not as integrated in terms of production value chains, the transmission mechanism for the energy price cycle mainly occurs on the nominal side, through price (and attendant terms of trade) changes.

Figure 4.1 Consumer price inflation, Asian regions, 1965–2016

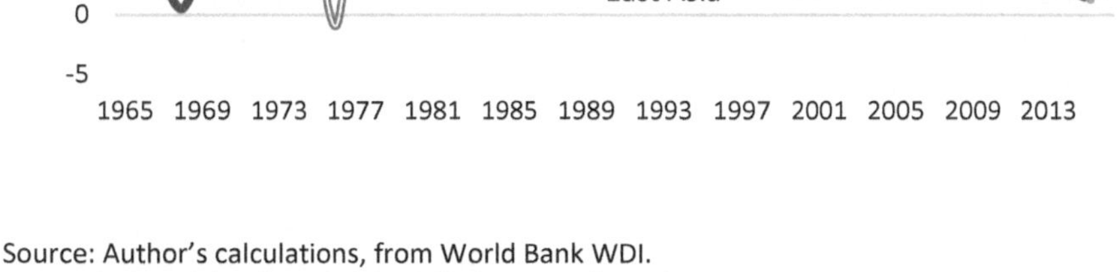

Source: Author's calculations, from World Bank WDI.
Notes: GDP-weighted annual CPI inflation rates for Asian regions.

4. The Structure of MENA Economies Today

Beyond the importance of the energy price cycle, the region's economies have gradually experienced changes in their economic structure since the 1960s. While the rapid industrialisation period of the 1970s and 1980s was characterized by high levels of public investment, these were typically inefficient (as revealed by high incremental capital-output ratios). By the 2000s, however, many had begun to experience a shift toward more efficient private investment. Although investment rates in the region lags those of high-investment East Asian economies, capital accumulation has steadily improved over time, averaging between 20 and 25% of GDP since 2000.

This accumulation of physical capital has also been accompanied by improvements in human capital accumulation. Many of the region's labour-abundant economies did, in fact, undergo a demographic transition around the 1970s and 80s, and fertility rates have declined to lows that are more characteristic of upper-middle income countries (of between two to three births per woman). The resource-rich economies, owning to fairly generous subsidies to support family formation, have lagged in this regard. Even so, fertility rates have likewise declined from highs of seven to something closer to three in most of these countries.

The decline in fertility has occurred in tandem with improvements in female labour force participation. Although rates remain somewhat low by OECD standards – owing to longstanding cultural reasons that discourage female labour – participation began to pick up substantially starting in the 1970s. In some countries, such as Kuwait and Qatar, rates are now even comparable to those of Southern European countries.

Unfortunately, the combination of high factor accumulation on these two fronts have not been accompanied by productivity improvements; in a number of resource-reliant economies – such as Saudi Arabia – total factor productivity (TFP) has even averaged a negative rate since the 1990s. Perhaps more worrisome, there are few signs that TFP is set to improve in the future.

One important factor that could inhibit a larger TFP growth contribution in the future is the fact that the economy remains reliant on services-led growth. Part of this likely stems from the deindustrialisation that occurred in the late Ottoman period, which has persisted till today. Even after many MENA economies pursued a path of liberalisation around the 1980s – belatedly embracing export-oriented industrialisation, instead of import substitution – manufacturing activity remained limited to light manufacturing, and even so, to only a number of economies, such as Lebanon and the United Arab Emirates (UAE). While it is not inconceivable that a services-led exporters could elevate TFP – this is, essentially, India's big bet – it should be kept in mind that, hitherto, manufacturing productivity has typically significantly outstripped that of the services sector as a whole, to the order of around 2 percentage points.

Perhaps even more corrosive for raising TFP is the fact the institutional quality remains challenged across the region. One measure of voice and accountability, the Polity IV score, reveals that most MENA economies remain heavily authoritarian. The score – which ranges from –10 (full autocracy) to +10 (full democracy) – is in negative territory for the typical MENA country, with only Tunisia (+7) registering as a solid democracy. Most Gulf Cooperation Council (GCC) nations,[2] such as Oman (–8), Qatar (–10), and Saudi Arabia (–10), are strongly autocratic.

For the region's economies to succeed in raising TFP, then, they will have to manage a transition where historically large public sectors will need to retreat and handoff economic activity to the private sector. In all fairness, this process has already begun. State expenditures, which peaked at around half of GDP for many of the region's economies in the 1970s and 80s, has since fallen, and currently stand at around between 30 and 40% of GDP for most countries. There is still room for continued shrinkage, of course. In Egypt, for example, the military remains involved in many sectors of the economy. And the employment of the native-born in the GCC economies is still largely channelled toward the (inefficient) public sector. But the significant decline thus far bodes well for aspirations for a growth engine that is more reliant on the private sector.

5. Financial Development in MENA

By and large, the region remains behind in terms of financial development. Even for the economies with the most sophisticated financial systems, measures of financial development lag those of comparable peer economies. For example, domestic credit to the financial sector for the UAE in 2019 amounted to around 78% of GDP; in contrast, equivalent metrics for two East Asian economies, Malaysia and Thailand, were 121 and 143%, respectively (and they are, moreover, only upper-middle income countries). Until the listing of Aramco, Saudi Arabia's stock market capitalisation only amounted to 63% of GDP (again, about half that of comparable East Asian economies), and two of the oldest stock exchanges in the region –

---

[2] The GCC nations are energy-abundant economies of Bahrain, Kuwait, Oman, Qatar, Saudi Arabia, and the UAE, and are also sometimes collectively referred to as the *Khaleej* (literally, "gulf").

Beirut and Cairo – can only claim capitalisation of around 14% of their respective economies.

Despite the relative unsophistication of MENA financial systems, the region has seen its fair share crises. In 2001, Turkey built up large twin (fiscal and current account) deficits, sustained by foreign financial inflows pursuing high-yielding bonds, which rapidly reversed when political instability led to a loss of confidence. The emirate of Dubai in the UAE was also a casualty of the global financial crisis, when liquidity shortages plagued the mass of pre-crisis debt used to financed rapid real estate construction; the emirate was eventually bailed out by neighbouring Abu Dhabi, and the debt restructured. Most recently, Lebanon underwent a financial crisis when deteriorating public finances called into question confidence in the country's banking sector (the largest holder of local-currency government debt, which had been financially-engineered to appeal to Lebanese diaspora seeking high returns), and an ill-considered proposal to tax WhatsApp messages catalysed a crisis that led to a collapse in the nation's twin deficits.

6. The MENA Region in Comparative Perspective

In many ways, the region is *sui generis*. As mentioned in the previous section, many states remain heavily authoritarian. This state of affairs persists, in part, because of the continued reliance of the region's governments on energy rents as a source of revenue. Data from circa 2000 reveal that the share of government revenue attributable to energy amounted to between 70% (Algeria) to as high as 85% (Kuwait) (Noland & Pack 2007). This share, even in other resource-rich comparators, is typically much lower; Botswana only derives 66% of government revenues from diamond sales, and even the Venezuelan public sector's reliance on oil amounts to around a third of income. Without a direct channel that demands greater democratic accountability in exchange for fiscal contributions – the flow of tax receipts – it is easier for MENA governments to ignore pressures for greater voice.

In mitigation, it does not seem like MENA governments run deficits that have been blatantly profligate. While it is true that most (non-resource-abundant economies) run deficits, these have not generally been much larger than that prevailing in Latin America or South Asia (albeit generally larger than East Asia).

Private saving is, likewise, comparably middling: saving and investment range between 20 to 25% of GDP, lower than East Asia, but generally higher than most other developing regions. The *efficacy* of investment, however, is generally wanting; the "bang for the buck" in terms of such high investment rates has lagged behind those of many other economies worldwide, insofar as translating investment into output growth is concerned.

As discussed previously, human capital growth has been steady expanding since the 1970s. Some MENA regions have been more successful on this front, relatively speaking, than others; the average years of education in Jordan, for instance, has mostly kept pace with that of Taiwan; among resource-rich nations, Algeria's has largely matched that of Indonesia. Even so, educational attainment in the region – especially for the high-income GCC – lags behind OECD nations, and there is no Arab university that feature in global rankings.

From a monetary perspective, MENA central banks have generally chosen to pursue a fixed peg, especially to the dollar (the main currency by which the region's central commodity – oil and gas – is priced). This is the case not just for the energy exporters – such as those in the GCC, Iraq, or Syria – but also non-energy exporters such as Algeria, Lebanon, and Morocco (although the Algerian dinar and Moroccan dirham are pegged to baskets of each country's major trading partners, which afford somewhat greater currency risk diversification). Indeed, only the region's most diversified and industrialized economies (principally Israel and Turkey) maintain floating exchange rate regimes.

7. The Sovereign Wealth Funds of the MENA Region

This relative stability in the exchange rate is supported, in part, by the presence of a large number of sovereign wealth funds (SWFs) across MENA. The majority of MENA SWFs fall in the commodity-energy category (Table 4.1), although the specific type of energy source may differ. The Qatar Investment Authority (QIA) and State General Reserve Fund of Oman, for instance, derive significantly more of their financing from natural gas revenue, as opposed to the Abu Dhabi Investment Authority (ADIA) or the Saudi Arabian Monetary Authority (SAMA), which are centred on oil. There are no known SWFs from the region that have been funded via surpluses – whether in terms of fiscal or foreign exchange reserves – although SAMA is the central authority for managing the state's forex surpluses, and entities such as ADIA do receive, for the purposes of management, excess fiscal surpluses from any given year.

Table 4.1 Sovereign wealth funds by earnings source and subtype

Earnings source	*Subtype*	
Commodities	Energy	Other resources
Surpluses	Fiscal	Forex reserves

Source: Adaptation by author from Reisen (2008).

The dissimilarities, however, stem not so much from their funding source but their respective objective. SAMA, like many central banks, operates as a reserve investment vehicle, and generally allocates to short-term, liquid instruments. In contrast, entities such as ADIA and the QIA operate more as savings vehicles, with mandates to invest oil surpluses for the benefit of future generations. A number of these operate as hybrids; the Kuwait Investment Authority, for instance, provides stabilisation functions – to insulate the fiscal budget and/or the economy from large commodity price shocks – in addition to its savings investment function; for major shocks, ADIA has been tapped for stabilisation purposes as well. One final fund objective has to do with development. These tend to allocate funding toward government policy priority areas, and operate alongside more traditional development institutions, such as development banks.

Certain states operate multiple SWFs. The best example of this is the UAE, which not only maintains separate funds for each emirate, but also purpose-specific funds. The investment portfolio of Mubadalah, for example, is focused heavily on supporting specific economic sectors in Abu Dhabi, such as tourism, logistics, and aluminium,[3] while the Abu Dhabi Investment Council (ADIC) takes on higher-risk exposures, and the International Petroleum Investment Company (IPIC) to invest in global hydrocarbon assets[4] (ADIA is a more traditional diversified global portfolio manager, and generally eschews investment in regional assets). On one hand, there are benefits from ensuring that the different investment objectives do not clash – for instance, stabilisation funds may need to sell assets to support an economy in recession, which may run counter to maximizing long-run returns – but this approach does introduce additional complexity and could constrain scale economies.[5] Other states

[3] Via its investment in DUBAL, a Dubai-based aluminium producer. The justification for this is that it is a complementary industrial activity that can take advantage of the Emirate's abundant energy resources.

[4] The three entities have since been merged, ostensibly to reduce costs, streamline operations, and – in IPIC's case, because of the 1MDB scandal.

[5] It is worth noting, however, that economies of scale in the operation of financial investments are not immediately obvious. Indeed, many funds struggle with securing

appear to have followed this lead. Saudi Arabia, for example, repurposed the Public Investment Fund away from mainly development objectives toward a more diversified savings function, while retaining SAMA's liquidity/reserves management role.

8. Investment Strategies of MENA SWFs

These varied objectives notwithstanding, SWFs – and those based in MENA are no exception – tend to allocate assets in a manner consistent with their mandates. For instance, saving funds generally hold long-term, illiquid assets such as equities and other alternatives (principally real estate), while stabilisation funds are biased toward liquid assets, such as fixed income and cash (Kunzel, Lu, Petrova & Pihlman 2011). That said, given the maturity of a number of regional SWFs – in particular, a number of those based in the GCC – asset allocation tends to be extremely diversified, and portfolios are relatively complex, with allocations to all major asset classes, as well as investment alternatives typically held by only the more sophisticated institutional investors, such as infrastructure and private equity (Gelg, Tordom Halland, Arfaa & Smith 2014). Even so, the majority of GCC SWF holdings remain basic bond-equity mixes, heavily based on the U.S. dollar (Setser & Ziemba 2009).

Beyond these basic mandates, the investment decisions by SWFs generally follow the basic tenets of standard portfolio theory. Of course, the fact that ownership vests to governments means that they may potentially be subject to political influences, and there is some evidence that funds subject where political involvement is more prevalent tend to compromise portfolio optimisation strategies (Bernstein, Lerner & Schoar 2013). Nevertheless, it is reasonable to treat such additional political constraints as part of the broader effort to construct a portfolio via constrained mean-variance optimisation. Indeed, it is not unusual for large institutional portfolios to incorporate explicit liquidity buffer or minimum asset class exposure constraints, and to simply add politically-directed constraints to the mix.

At risk of pedantry, the main principles underlying optimal portfolio allocation are as follows.[6] The objective is to maximize total return by choos-

---

excess returns when their assets under management swell, since their larger size also rules them out from investing in non-scalable opportunities, and their investments themselves could move markets.

[6] Many reviews of the principles of portfolio optimisation exist, both in articles and textbooks. PEROLD (2004) is an accessible introduction that also stresses the relevant developments in theory, along with the main principles involved.

ing different assets, with uncertain rates of return. By diversifying across assets – so long as risks are not perfectly correlated – a portfolio is able to achieve a reduction in the amount of risk, without any attendant decrease in expected return (equivalently, one is able to achieve a higher expected return for the same amount of risk). Portfolios may be constructed from combinations – including negative and, with leverage, greater-than-unity allocations – of risky assets to derive a so-called efficient frontier. In the presence of a riskless asset,[7] it is also possible to construct a linear combination of this asset with a portfolio that offers the higher risk-return combination (known as the portfolio with the highest Sharpe ratio). Various constraints – such as those associated with liquidity – can be included, as required, which will alter the choice of optimal portfolio.

Of course, expected returns and the nature of relationships between difference asset classes do not fall out of the sky. Real-world portfolio allocation requires estimates of expected returns, along with a parameterisation of the full variance-covariance matrix for all assets held in the portfolio. Institutional investors worldwide, including sophisticated SWFs in MENA, undertake this exercise daily.

9. Real-World Portfolio Allocation in a Typical MENA SWF

Given the importance of professional portfolio allocation practices in securing the financial future of the region's SWFs, it is worth examining this issue in greater detail. This section provides a case study based on the actual processes in place in one such MENA SWF.

The first step in the portfolio allocation exercise is to establish a benchmark "policy" or "reference" portfolio. This is usually a combination of publicly-traded equities and bonds, in very broad benchmarks. The global equity benchmark, for example, would be an index such as the MSCI ACWI Investable Market Index (IMI) or the FTSE All-World Index (an alternative, of course, is to construct one's own GDP – or capitalisation-weighted index of country-specific indexes). The global bond benchmark generally applies to sovereigns – as the lower-risk asset class – and could either be a similar BofA Merrill Lynch Global Government Bond Index, or more narrowly just sovereigns from developed markets. One even simpler possibility is to utilize a U.S. Treasury bond index, given that returns across most developed country bonds are highly correlated in any case.

---

[7] In reality no asset is truly riskless, although for all intents and purposes, short-term U.S. Treasury bills are generally viewed as the benchmark "riskless" asset.

The second step is to ascertain the principal's investment objectives and risk tolerance. This is a function of the SWF's mandate; typically, a mandate to maximize long-run expected returns will suggest a more aggressive allocation toward risky assets, since the investment horizon – of ten years or longer – allows the SWF to ride out the sort of deep drawdowns associated with typical market/business cycle frequencies. There is also the need to elicit the overall risk appetite of the principal, although it is probably fair, subject to discussions with the principal, to model preferences as risk-neutral.

The next step is to formulate a common set of economic premises (on nominal GDP growth – which by extension implies projections for real growth and inflation, along with any attendant exchange rate conversions), in what is sometimes known as "capital market assumptions." Generally, these are best understood as projections that follow a building-block approach: incrementally projecting of various contributions to growth, to obtain a final number (Figure 4.2).

Figure 4.2 Projections of growth contributions, Saudi Arabia, 2020–2030

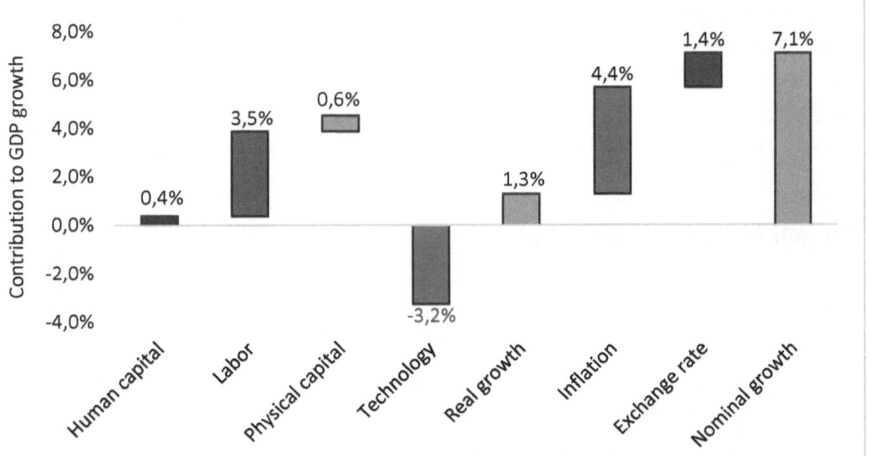

Source: Author's calculations, from Barro & Lee (2015, 16), Consensus Economics (2017), ILO (2014), UN (2013, 15), World Bank (2019).

This country-specific exercise would essentially be repeated for all economic regions for which asset exposures exist. The assumptions are then used to derive expected returns for various asset classes. Of course, each of these could apply capital market assumptions in a slightly different fashion. For instance, fixed-income projects generally take nominal growth as the starting point, before layering on term and credit premia, while real estate could utilize real growth projections instead, and subsequently add on forecasts of rental income yield along with capital appreciation. In other cases, the capital market assumptions could be applied to various different models, and expected returns are an average across models. For example, equities would draw on nominal growth (adjusted by foreign sales exposures) to obtain market-specific earnings growth, and the asset class specialist could then choose to apply initial valuation adjustments using various alternative models, before tacking on buybacks/dilutions and/or expected dividend income.

The variance-covariance matrix is often inferred from history, although the lookback period with which to build this matrix falls within the domain of the analyst. Moreover, this matrix need not be static; the historical distribution can always be used to obtain simulated bounds using Markov Chain Monte Carlo methods.

The mean-variance optimisation process yields what would be a strategic asset allocation (SAA), which is evaluated vis-à-vis the reference portfolio (excess returns in this case are sometimes referred to as "enhanced" beta). The SAA need not be the only source of active management relative to the benchmark, of course. Sophisticated SWFs may also adopt short-run – in this case, usually within the six-month to two-year window – deviations from the SAA, which constitute active bets to garner above-market returns (or alpha) via tactical asset allocation (TAA). Finally, within each investment department, the chief investment officer may decide to exercise asset selection choices, which in turn layer on yet another source of alpha.

10. MENA's Economic Future

The region finds itself at crossroads in its economic future. Following the events of the Arab Spring – where vast swathes of the population across the Middle East and North Africa put paid to the notion that cultural norms of the region precluded a greater interest in voice and accountability – it has become clear that there is a need for a new growth model in MENA that extends beyond oil.

Such an endeavour is easier said than done, of course. Only two MENA economies – Israel and Turkey – have successfully transitioned their economies to high-income, industrialized ones, built on a diversified economic base. A number of other economies – notably Iran, Lebanon, Tunisia, and the UAE – have made marked progress on that front, but most remain stuck in the (upper) middle income trap, while the last has yet to demonstrate that the Dubai model can be replicated across the entire nation (which would lend credibility to the country's high-income status).

Other economies that have tried to diversify their economies and reduce industrial concentration have run into various political economy problems. Syria, for example, made substantial progress in export diversification (Lim & Saborowski 2012), but struggled with overcoming entrenched oligopolistic business interests, which inhibited further reform. This is, to a lesser extent, also the case in Egypt, where the military holds sway over significant parts of the economy.

Worse, the inability to consolidate economic diversification has also meant that factor allocation inefficiencies remain, which inhibit a more efficient deployment of accumulated human capital. This is the case especially within countries, where underemployment of professionals is countries like Egypt, Jordan, and Morocco has resulted in brain drains as their native talent seek opportunity elsewhere (usually in the higher-paying Gulf states).

In a sense, the prospective challenges that economies in MENA face come down to a choice between two models, which are well-captured by projections of potential economic growth for Saudi Arabia versus Egypt (Figure 4.3a and 4.3b). A decomposition of the contributors to economic growth [8] reveals that the historical economic performance of the former has heavily relied on physical capital accumulation, with little long-run reliance on technology, as revealed by a negative TFP contribution, on average. In contrast, the latter has seen solid accumulation of not just physical capital, but also positive contributions from human capital – both historically, as well as in the impending future due to demographic tailwinds – as well as a modest (but still positive) contribution from productivity.

Importantly, while we often use the "technology" shorthand to refer to TFP, it is also the case that TFP could embody other unobserved elements, such as management acumen, intangible assets, or institutional resilience. It is this last aspect – developing credible, participatory, and high-quality institutions – that the region faces the greatest uphill challenges, both over the past century, as well as into the next.

---

[8] These are obtained via standard growth accounting methods, using historical data to infer parameters, and obtaining projections from various sources, along with assumptions about trend evolution.

Figure 4.3a Decomposition of output growth, baseline projection for Saudi Arabia

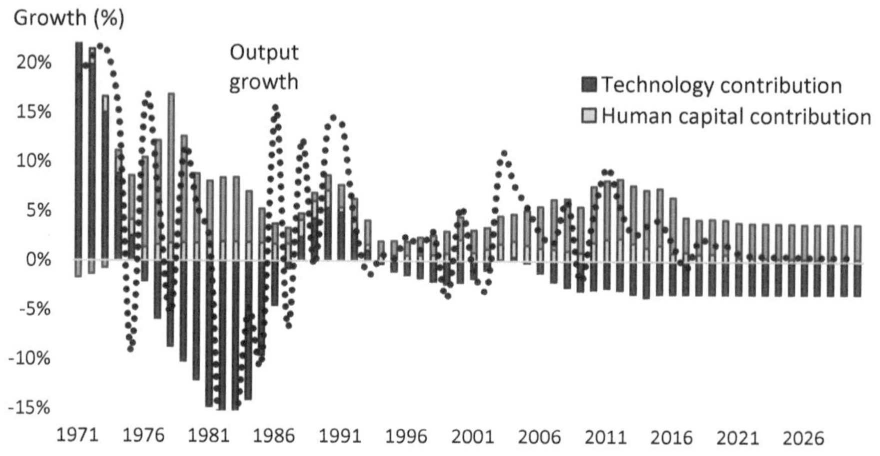

Source: Authors' calculations, from Barro & Lee (2015, 2016), IIASA (2010), ILO (2014), UN (2013, 2015), World Bank (2017)

Figure 4.3b Decomposition of output growth, baseline projection for Egypt

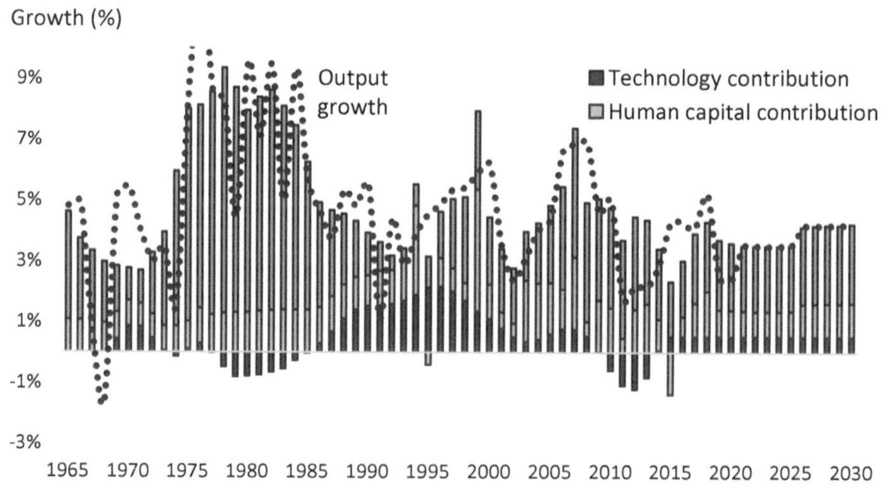

Source: Authors' calculations, from Barro & Lee (2015, 2016), IIASA (2010), ILO (2014), UN (2013, 2015), World Bank (2017)

References

ABDELAL, RAWI, *Sovereign Wealth in Abu Dhabi*, in Geopolitics 14(2), 2009, 317–327.

CAMMETT, MELANI, ISHAC, DIWAN, ALAN, RICHARDS, & WATERBURY, JOHN, *A Political Economy of the Middle East*, 4th ed., Abington, England: Routledge, 2015.

GELB, ALAN, TORDO, SILVANA, HALLAND, HÅRVARD, ARFAA, NOORA, & SMITH, GREGORY, *Sovereign Wealth Funds and Long-Term Development Finance*, in Policy Research Working Paper 6776, Washington, DC: The World Bank, 2014.

KUNZEL, PETER, LU, YINQIU, PETROVA, IVA, & PIHLMAN, JUKKA, *Investment Objectives of Sovereign Wealth Funds*, in IMF Working Paper, WP/11/19, Washington, DC: International Monetary Fund, 2011.

LIM, JAMUS JEROME, & SABOROWSKI, CHRISTIAN, *Export Diversification in a Transitioning Economy: The Case of Syria*, in Economics of Transition 20(2), 2012, 339–367.

NOLAND, MARCUS, & PACK, HOWARD, *The Arab Economies in a Changing World*, Washington, DC: Peterson Institute for International Economics, 2007.

PEROLD, ANDRÉ, *The Capital Asset Pricing Model*, in Journal of Economic Perspectives, 18(3), 2004, 3–24.

REISEN, HELMUT, *Commodity and Non-Commodity Sovereign Wealth Funds*, in Deutsche Bank Research Notes, 28, Frankfurt am Main, Germany: Deutsche Bank Research, 2008.

SETSER, BRAD, & ZIEMBA, RACHEL, *GCC Sovereign Funds: Reversal of Fortune*, Center for Geoeconomic Studies Working Paper, New York, NY: Council on Foreign Relations, 2009.

Chapter 5

THE EU COOPERATION POLICY WITH THE NORTHERN AFRICAN MEDITERRANEAN COUNTRIES AND THE MIDDLE EAST

Giuseppe Colangelo

SUMMARY: 1. Introduction. – 2. From the Early Cooperative Instruments to the Barcelona Process. – 3. Two New Instruments in the 2000s: The European Neighbourhood Policy and the Union for the Mediterranean. – 4. The Recent Changes in the European Neighbourhood Policy. – 5. An Overview of the Trade Flows across the Mediterranean Sea. – 6. Conclusions. – References.

1. Introduction

The shores of the Mediterranean sea have been the place where several ancient populations developed and met each other, giving rise to profitable trade but also to long and cruel wars. One single population has never been able to prevail definitively over the others. Even now, the north (and the west) of the Mediterranean belongs to the South of Europe where the respect for human rights, democracy, the rule of the law and the market economy are pillars of their own economic and social development model. The diffusion of Christianity (and of Catholicism after) has played a crucial role in this area over centuries in modelling the mentality of people and their way of doing things. The clear separation between political authority and religious authority, reached after a secular process, is another important feature in this area. In the South (and in the East) of the Mediterranean sea instead, both in Maghreb and in Mashreq, this historical process has not occurred; still another process, a very different one, has occurred: the Muslim religion has largely prevailed in this region causing large social and economic inequalities in the population, in part due to its autocratic and despotic governments.

Furthermore political authority is often, even nowadays, largely intertwined with religious authority. Building an Islamic state is often a target in this part of the Mediterranean. But another important part of the puzzle is given by the long and important history of the Jews, God's elected people, with their own religion and traditions, of which they are very proud. They have always been a very closed large social group separated from any other population. They have been the object of several persecutions in history;

among them, Hitler's Nazi persecution has been the most terrible. This situation of difficult relationships with different populations and their different cultures has been exacerbated by the issue of the foundation of the Israeli State after the end of the Second World War and the Nazi persecution of the Jews. This State was formed in the Palestinian territory in 1948, largely inhabited by Arab-Palestinians and not only by Jews. As a consequence, a violent conflict between the Jewish and the Arab exploded in the Middle East in 1948 and even now, although there is no formal war, it is far from being solved once and for all. [1] This long and deep enmity is a strong handicap for the development of close and friendly relationships among the Mediterranean people. For the European countries and the EU, it is very difficult to be friend of both the Arabs and the Jews, who hate each other.

Different countries with very heterogeneous cultures live, then, close to each other on the shores of the Mediterranean sea. The potential for all sorts of conflicts, both explicit and more hidden, is still large. They need to know each other better, to talk to each other, to try to solve common problems together, in the perspective of a better mutual understanding and a peaceful coexistence. If this does not occur, one part could try to solve its own problems on the shoulders of the other; nationalism could develop again, causing new wars.

In 2011 the extraordinary events of the so-called Arab Spring, a wave of social protests asking for democracy that took place in all the North-African and Middle-East Mediterranean countries, changed the political situation dramatically. The EU tried to intervene, fostering the democratic transition, at least in some of these countries. While a slow democratic process started in some countries (e.g., Tunisia, Morocco and Jordan) in a relatively peaceful context, in other countries like Syria and Libya, devastating civil war took place with military intervention of foreign armies and soldiers. The Assad government survived in Syria only because of the intervention of Russia and Iran. The country, however, has been destroyed and millions of refugees have had to escape to close countries like Lebanon and Jordan, but also to the EU; moreover, the north-east part of the country was lost temporarily because of the formation of the Islamic State promoted by Isis terrorists under the leadership of al-Baghdadi. It took time and effort to reconquer it. In Libya, the Arab Spring revolution caused the end of the Gaddafi regime and his murder; the country is split in two parts with two different governments in struggle with each other: Tripolitania vs Cyrenaica. This explosive situation paved the way for the formation of two new

---

[1] For more details on the Middle-East conflict between Israel and the Arab countries see FRASER (2009).

very harmful threats to Europe from South Mediterranean: Islamic terrorism and illegal migration. The European Union cannot hide from these serious problems and must intervene with external action and its own diplomatic structure without leaving it all in the hands of the national member states. It is very important to assess its political relevance, to see whether the EU is able to solve common problems like those coming from the relationships between the geographically close countries.

The EU has created different instruments to get peaceful relationships and common development across the Mediterranean, such as: the EuroMed partnership, which emerged in Barcelona in 1995; the European Neighbourhood Policy, set up in 2004 and renewed in 2014–2015 as a reaction to the Arab Spring; and the Union for the Mediterranean, created in 2008.

In this chapter we analyse the road of cooperation walked by the EEC first and by the EU after, in their relationships with countries in the south-east of the Mediterranean sea from the 60s to the present. We want to identify and describe the best common projects pursued, the successes but also the failures observed in the process, in order to be able to give some policy suggestions.

With these purposes in mind, in Section 2 we illustrate the cooperation policy pursued by the EEC in the 60s with the first association agreements signed in a logic of bilateral agreements, the first idea of a global common policy for the Mediterranean in 1972 and the interesting establishment of the EuroMed partnership in 1995 in the so-called Barcelona process. In Section 3 we describe and assess two new instruments of cooperation across the Mediterranean: the European Neighbourhood Policy that is also (but not only) addressed to the Mediterranean region at the EU's south-east border, and the Union for the Mediterranean set up in the 2008 Paris summit and strongly supported by the French former President Sarkozy. In Section 4 we focus on the recent revision of the European Neighbourhood Policy that took place in 2014–2015, specifically to meet the new challenges posed by the Arab Spring in 2011 in the south-east of the Mediterranean region. We assess its common projects, its action plans and give suggestions on its future possible evolution. In Section 5 we look at macroeconomic data on trade flows across the Mediterranean countries, that are helpful to form a more detailed analysis. We notice that, even today, too many partner countries still have a too limited trade with the EU. Concluding comments in Section 6 end the chapter.

2. From the Early Cooperative Instruments to the Barcelona Process

The European Economic Community (EEC) started very early in the 60s, just a few years after its institution through the Rome Treaty, establishing formal cooperative and commercial relationships with Arab Mediterranean countries. In part, this was due to the nature of former colonies of some of these countries: for example Northern African countries like Morocco, Tunisia and Algeria were all French colonies that obtained political independence few years before; Egypt was a colony of the British Empire; Libya was a colony of the Italian fascist government for a decade. But, also, the Mediterranean countries without a colonial history had an important interest in getting preferential commercial agreements with the EEC, to receive financial cooperation and direct investment. They were searching for significant help in their efforts for development. All the cooperative agreements in the 60s were formally approved according to a bilateral approach. In 1963, an association agreement was signed between the EEC and Turkey; in 1964, a non-preferential commercial agreement was signed with Israel;[2] in 1965, with Lebanon; in 1969, an association agreement was signed with both Morocco and Tunisia; in 1972, a non-preferential commercial agreement was signed with Egypt. As Barizza (1984) reports, between 1976 and 1977 new cooperation agreements were signed by the EEC with most of the above-mentioned countries and others, one after the other: Morocco, Tunisia, Algeria, Israel, Egypt, Syria, and Jordan. Lebanon was excluded because of its civil war that went on from mid-70s to early 90s. Two of the most important aspects of these cooperation agreements were financial cooperation and trade cooperation: according to the former, Mediterranean countries could have access to loans issued by the European Investment Bank, to special loans and also, although in a more limited amount, to non-refundable funds from the EEC, especially to build basic infrastructures like highways, routes, ports, airports; according to the latter, EEC gave to these countries the advantage to enter the EEC market with their own products with a tariff discount, in some cases with a tariff exemption, even if almost always for a predetermined amount of quantity. In general, tariffs were lower for manufactured goods and higher for agricultural products. Even if Mediterranean partners would have preferred more help from the EEC on their agricultural products, the EEC had to limit its internal mar-

[2] It is well known that Israel is geographically belonging to the Mediterranean Middle East but it is definitely not an Arab country; rather, it is the strongest enemy of the Middle-East Arab countries. The EEC has found it very difficult to be friend and partner with two subsets of countries, so enemies between themselves. Another peculiarity regards Libya: after Gaddafi *coup d'etat* in 1969 and his anti-western policy pursued for decades with support to terrorism and terrorist attacks to western aircrafts (the most important attack was the PanAm air destruction in Lockerbie in December 1988 with hundreds of deaths), no significant cooperation has been pursued under his government by the EEC and then by the EU.

ket to these products, to avoid a clash with its Common Agricultural Policy (CAP) and a conflict of interest with southern EEC members, due to tough competition on some agricultural markets between EEC members and Mediterranean partners. The chance of having these types of conflict has increased with the south enlargement of the Community that took place in the 80s when first Greece (1981) and then Spain and Portugal (1986) became EEC members. Although the bilateral approach has largely dominated during the early years of cooperation, in 1972 at the Paris summit, nevertheless, for the first time, a Global Mediterranean Policy by the EEC was mentioned. It had never happened before: a multilateral approach was suggested as a helpful instrument to improve the relationships among EEC and Mediterranean partners. Sixteen diverse countries were involved in this global policy, with a very different degree of friendship with the EEC (e.g., Albania, Algeria, Libya, Greece, Spain, Israel, Portugal, Turkey, Yugoslavia among others): for this reason it was not possible to pursue a common, multilateral, global policy and this attempt did not produce significant results and consequences. The successful approach remained the bilateral one. The multilateral approach was revisited many years later in 1990 with the so-called New Mediterranean Policy, but developed more extensively only with the so-called Barcelona process, some years later. It was indeed only in 1995 with the Barcelona declaration and with the rising EuroMed partnership that a multilateral approach had a first relevant development in relationships across the Mediterranean sea. The Barcelona declaration was signed by all the 15 EEC members and by 12 non-EEC Mediterranean countries: Algeria, Egypt, Israel, Jordan, Lebanon, Morocco, Syria, Tunisia, Turkey, the Palestinian Authority, Malta and Cyprus. It is well-known that the last two mentioned countries became EU members in 2004. The multilateral approach was meant to complement, not substitute, the bilateral approach.

The early 90s represented an optimistic period in the relationships between Israel and its Arab neighbours; in 1993 the Oslo agreement was signed and it seemed that a stable peace could be reached in the Middle East in the near future. As Panebianco (2012) remarks, the Barcelona process was conceived and launched in this atmosphere of optimism about global political relationships in the Mediterranean region and that could well have led to a better and more fruitful cooperation between the different countries on the shores of the Mediterranean sea. Unfortunately, it was soon clear that this optimism was unfounded. Rabin, the Jewish Prime Minister who signed the Oslo Agreements, was killed in November 1995, just a few weeks before the Barcelona Conference, and nationalistic leaders emerged as political winners in the countries involved and the achievement of a stable peace in the Middle East was still critical. Another reason that could possibly have a significant effect on the start of the Barcelona process was the willingness of the EU southern countries to balance the high attention to the east border given by the EU after the collapse of the Soviet Union with equal attention to the south border, as Attinà (2004) pointed out.

The main goal declared at the Barcelona Conference was to increase social welfare in the Mediterranean region by improving cooperation in three large fields: politics, economics, and culture. As per the political cooperation (or partnership) they intended to pass the main political values shared by EU countries on to the Mediterranean partners for their use: the EU hoped that values – like respect for human rights, for the rule of the law, for democratic principles, for peaceful conflict resolution and for international law – could be followed by its Mediterranean partners, at least in the long term. Reaching this very ambitious target could well mean getting much more political stability and security in the region.[3] Economic cooperation aimed at setting up a Mediterranean Free Trade Area (MEFTA) by 2010,[4] on the one hand, launching several specific relevant projects in the fields of energy, water, building infrastructures and regional development to struggle against unemployment, underdevelopment and poverty and thus reducing the immigration flows to Europe; on the other hand, increasing the amount of EU investment and financial cooperation in the region. The third large field of cooperation was the cultural one: partners need to know each other better in terms of culture, language, education, research and religion, to improve dialogue and mutual understanding. Since the Barcelona Conference, several forums of multilateral cooperation have been set up: Ministerial Meetings at least once a year, the EuroMed Committee formed by senior officials to prepare the ministerial meetings, the European Mediterranean Parliamentary Assembly (since 1998) with both plenary sessions and committee sessions. The European Commission, too, was involved in managing the Barcelona process.

Regarding economic cooperation, the main tool for getting the Free Trade Area within 2010 remained a bilateral one; new association agreements between the EU and each Mediterranean partner were signed be-

---

[3] This goal is in a sense closer after the Arab Spring in 2011 in some countries where some democratic elements have been nested, but at the same time it is much more distant where it caused a civil war like in Syria and in Libya.

[4] As a first step, this led to a South-South Free Trade Area with the Agadir Agreement signed in 2004 among Morocco, Tunisia, Egypt and Jordan that became operative in 2006. In 2016, Palestine and Lebanon joined the agreement. These South-South trade flows however remain nowadays much smaller than those between the EU and its Mediterranean partners in a North-South relationship, as HEDOUI *et al.* (2019) report.

tween 1995 and 2002: Tunisia, Morocco and Israel in 1995; the Palestinian Authority in 1996; Jordan in 1997; Egypt in 1998; Algeria and Lebanon in 2002.

Some interesting results, even if not exceptional, have been reached by the EuroMed partnership: the Anna Lindh Foundation for the cultural exchange and the intercultural dialogue was financed for the first time by all the partner countries and it has been very active since that moment; the university cooperation network and the foreign policy institutes network (Euromesco) were built up; there was a significant improvement in diplomatic cooperation; a pivotal Programme for the Mitigation, Prevention and Management of Natural Disasters was launched by Italy and Egypt in 1996 (later, France and Algeria joined the programme); the Euromediterranean Fund for Investment and Partnership operated by the European Investment Bank was set up with an ability to lend up to two billion euros per year.

An accurate estimate of European Funds invested in the Mediterranean region in the first ten years of the EuroMed partnership is about 25 billion euros. Roughly, 3.5 billion were made available by the EU for the partnership in the period 1995–1999; 4.5 billion euros in the period 2000–2006; 10 billion euros came from the MEDA fund managed by the European Commission; 7 billion euros were lent by the European Investment Bank to Mediterranean partners. On top of this, other money was given to partners through the bilateral agreements. It was not an enormous amount of money invested in those countries but neither a negligible one.

3. Two New Instruments in the 2000s: The European Neighbourhood Policy and the Union for the Mediterranean

In 2004 the European Union created a new external policy, the European Neighbourhood Policy (ENP), with the aim, stated in Article 8 of the Treaty on the European Union (TEU), of setting up a space of prosperity with the geographically close countries. It is based on the EU's intangible values, to be followed by their Mediterranean partners as well, and on tighter and better forms of cooperation. There are two identified sets of neighbour countries to whom ENP is to be applied: the eastern border set, including former Soviet Union members, now independent from Russia (Armenia, Azerbaijan, Belarus, Georgia, Moldova, and Ukraine), and the southern border set, hence the Mediterranean countries, both of North Africa and Middle East.

For both sets of neighbour countries, a multilateral institutional framework was set up in 2008–2009: the Eastern Partnership, including the former set of countries, and the Union for the Mediterranean, including the latter. Besides this multilateral instrument, the ENP works through bilateral agreements and action plans between the EU and each partner country. Among the most used bilateral agreements, there are the association agreements, the partnership and cooperation agreements, and more recently also the deep and comprehensive free trade agreements. In this framework, action plans are decided over the short and medium run with each partner country. A mix of multilateral and bilateral institutional instruments is therefore the way in which a Mediterranean policy is actually implemented by the European Union.

The Union for the Mediterranean (UfM) was instituted in 2008 at the Paris summit on the proposal by the then French President Sarkozy;[5] all the 27 EU member countries are now UfM members and 15 non-EU partner countries are also UfM members: Albania, Algeria, Bosnia-Herzegovina, Egypt, Israel, Jordan, Lebanon, Mauritania, Montenegro, Monaco, Morocco, Palestine, Syria (whose participation has been suspended because of its civil war), Tunisia and Turkey. Libya has got the status of observer and the Arab League can participate to all the meetings. We can well claim that UfM is now seen as the natural continuation framework of the former EuroMed Partnership set up in Barcelona in 1995 that remained active up to 2005. Its aims are the same stated in the Barcelona declaration. In 2010, the UfM Secretariat, the first permanent structure of the Union, was established in Barcelona. The actual General Secretariat of the UfM is the Egyptian Nasser Kamel. The UfM is chaired by a co-presidency: one for the North and one for the South Mediterranean, to have more symmetric relationships between the EU and its Mediterranean partners. Since 2012, the EU has assumed the North Presidency and Jordan the South Presidency. The UfM's deliberative organ is the SOM (Senior officials' Meeting) from the Ministries of Foreign Affairs: they approve the budget and the Secretariat agenda, prepare the meetings of the Ministers of Foreign Affairs and other Ministers, and appoint the General Secretariat and six general vice secretaries. A Euro Mediterranean Parliamentary Assembly is also active and gathers at least once a year for a plenary session. Two hundred and eighty members constitute this Assembly: 132 from the EU

---

[5] The initial UfM project by Sarkozy, that gave a strong leadership to France in the Union and that did not establish the UfM membership for all the EU members, was stopped by Germany who asked for a significant reform toward Europeanization of UfM and more symmetry among the involved EU members. Germany's request was accepted and led to an important change in the initial project. For more details see GILLESPIE (2011) and CARDWELL (2011).

(representatives of both the national parliaments and the European Parliament); 8 from the European participating countries (Albania, Bosnia-Herzegovina, Monaco and Montenegro); 130 from the partner countries of the South and East shore of the Mediterranean sea and 10 from Mauritania. The parliamentary assembly adopts decisions and recommendations that the Senior Officials Committee must translate in operative projects and programmes that will form the agenda of the General Secretariat after formal approval by the Committee.

More than 30 fields of cooperative intervention have been identified and listed. Many of these fields had already been identified in the Barcelona EuroMed Partnership: among others, energy, water, employment, women's empowerment, youth, education, transport and urban development, infrastructures, environment and climate change. A couple of recently financed investment projects are very noticeable: SESAME (Synchrotron-Light for Experimental Science and Applications in the Middle East), set up in Jordan with the EU financial support as the first international research centre opened in the Middle East; and PRIMA, a partnership on water management and food production in the Mediterranean region.

Looking at every country in a more detailed way, we notice that almost all the Mediterranean partners have signed an association agreement with the EU recently. The following list considers the operative agreements: the Palestinian Authority in 1997, Tunisia in 1998, Israel and Morocco in 2000, Jordan in 2002, Egypt in 2004, Algeria in 2005, Lebanon in 2006. Only Syria and Libya are missing because they are both are involved in civil wars and do not have the right conditions to pursue development projects.

In 2011, the Arab Spring occurred with protests and social riots asking for more democracy in all the countries of North Africa and the Middle East. Some governments fell and new governments, able to introduce more democratic rules, were formed in a relatively peaceful and non-violent environment, like in Tunisia and Algeria; in Syria, this was not possible and a violent and long civil war between the Assad government and Syrian people – especially in the north of the country – started. The army intervention of both Iran and Russia allowed Assad's Syrian government to survive, but the effects of this long civil war were harmful: several cities and important infrastructures were destroyed, millions of Syrian refugees escaped to close countries like Jordan and Lebanon but also to the EU, and a vast territory in the north-east of the country was temporarily lost and controlled by the Islamic State, set up by the terrorist groups of Isis. In Libya, the Arab Spring led to the murder of President Gaddafi and the country split in two parts: Tripolitania and Cyrenaica, which were controlled by two different governments in war between them. In July 2013, General Al Sisi led the intervention of military forces against President Mohamed Morsi, the leader of the so-called Islamic Brotherhood, an Islam fundamentalist large political group, that lost the power. The year after, Al Sisi became President of Egypt, after having resigned from the Army.

In the same period, and correlated somehow to these radical changes and civil wars, Islamic terrorism increased the number of terrorist attacks in some EU countries and illegal migration to southern Europe became much bigger than in the past. This new and detrimental situation dramatically hit the EU countries, especially those at the south border, who tried to organize a united answer at the level of the European Union. In order to have safer stabilization of the southern border, the EU decided to make a deep revision of the European Neighbourhood Policy, that we are going to examine in the next section.

4. The Recent Changes in the European Neighbourhood Policy

The EU revised the ENP after the Arab Spring of 2011, giving more importance to the implementation of democratic principles in the Mediterranean partner countries and the occurrence of a more inclusive economic development. The democratic progress in those countries includes targets like free elections, the implementation of human rights, the struggle against corruption, the independence of the judicial system from political power, and the democratic control of the army. The ENP has been organized according to the principle of "more for more": more economic aid and investment to countries that make more progress in the democratic transition. These rules were written in a specific EU regulation (n. 232/2014). In November 2015, a joint communication of the European Commission and the High Representative of the Union for the Foreign Affairs and Security Policy started the institutional process for a new revision of ENP, to make it more strategic, flexible, and consistent, in accordance with a precise request made by the European Parliament. In May 2017, the European Commission and the High Representative of the Union for Foreign Affairs published a joint report on the implementation of the revision of the ENP. In April 2018, the European Parliament approved a report on the instruments for the external financing of the EU included the ENP, calling for a new reform of the instruments; the European Commission answered this question by issuing a rule proposal two months after, proposing a unitary and more simplified architecture of instruments in the fields – the Neighbourhood Policy, Development Cooperation and International Cooperation, together with a significant budget increase. The European Parliament approved this proposal on March 2019 and it will become operative in the next EU financial multiperiod plan 2021–2027. The Neighbourhood policy budget will become about 22 billion euros, with a large increase of more than 40% relative to the budget established in the previous multiperiod plan. In March 2019, the European Parliament also approved a resolution on the political situation in the Mediterranean region after the Arab Spring, asking for more democratic reforms in those countries; it also requested that the EU put more effort and work in reaching better and more effective results in the Mediterranean non-EU countries as they move towards a more democratic political life and more inclusive economic development.

The ENP action plans, with projects and priorities, are still made country by country, according to a bilateral approach. The EU budgeted an endowment of 15.4 billion euros for ENP in the period 2014–2020. On top of this, financial help is provided to each country at a bilateral level and there is the intervention of both the European Investment Bank (EIB) and the European Bank for Reconstruction and Development (EBRD) with loans. A new instrument that aims at improving the management of the difficult issue of migrations across the Mediterranean is called the Mobility Partnership and was set up in 2016. [6] Another new instrument to be used to promote free trade at a bilateral level is the Deep and Comprehensive Free Trade Agreement that has been signed with Morocco and Tunisia. Morocco, furthermore, has been given advanced status in its relationships with the EU, while Tunisia has a privileged partnership; they have received more EU financial help, together with Jordan, according with the principle of "more for more," given that they have done more progresses in the field of political reforms. A special strategic partnership on energy has been recently signed with Algeria, the most important gas producer of the region and among the top producers in the world.

In 2013, moreover, the EU offered Israel and the Palestinian Authority a special privileged partnership but this has been made conditional on them making progress in the peace process. The EU has invested a considerable amount of money in improving living conditions in the Gaza strip and to training the security forces of the Palestinian Authority.

More progress was made in antiterrorism cooperation: European antiterrorism experts are now working in partner countries like Tunisia, Lebanon, Jordan, Israel, and Egypt, together with the local police forces. Preventing money laundering and other illegal ways of financing terrorism are other significant fields of action.

Two new financial instruments for ENP have been set up to solve spe-

---

[6] Through the Mobility Partnership the EU tries to reduce illegal migration, promoting legal migration and making visa issues for Mediterranean partners' citizens easier, helping in training local police for the shores' detection. Countries involved in this Partnership are Libya, Morocco, Egypt, Tunisia, Jordan and Algeria.

cific emergency situations: the Trust Fund for Syria in 2017 with a financial endowment of 1.3 billion euros[7] and the Emergency Trust Fund for Africa. Besides this, there is the new European Fund for the Sustainable Development with 3.5 billion euros invested by the EU up to 2020. This Fund, if supported by the Mediterranean partners as well, could become an important instrument in financing development projects in the region.

The impression of having the general conditions to see the start of a new and more powerful regional policy by the EU in this area is real, pushed by the need of mitigating Islamic terrorism and mass migration.

5. An Overview of the Trade Flows across the Mediterranean Sea

Let us now focus on the most recent annual data on trade flows between the EU and its Mediterranean partners. Data are changing slowly from one year to the other, so it is sufficient to present data only for the most recent year available. In Table 5.1 we report the data collected by Eurostat on this subject for 2019.

Table 5.1 Trade flows between the EU and its Mediterranean partners, 2019, billion euros

Partner country	*Total trade*	*EU imports*	*EU exports*	*Trade balance*
Turkey	138.1	69.8	68.3	–1.5
Algeria	33.2	16.3	16.9	0.6
Morocco	39.7	16.3	23.4	7.1
Israel	33.1	13	20.1	7.1
Egypt	27.4	8.3	19.1	10.8
Tunisia	21	10	10.9	0.9
Libya	20.4	15.9	4.5	–11.4
Lebanon	6.2	0.4	5.8	5.4
Jordan	3.7	0.3	3.4	3.1
Mauritania	1.5	0.7	0.8	0.1
Syria	0.7	0.06	0.6	0.54

Source: Eurostat.

[7] The EU and its member countries however have given a great amount of money to Syrian population (not to the Syrian government, whose relationships with the EU were stopped in 2011) for humanitarian assistance to the refugees, more than 17 billion euros from 2011.

We can see that the value of the interchange in some cases is very small, almost negligible. It is true that civil war and a difficult political situation do not help to establish good and large economic trade but for Syria, Mauritania, Jordan and Lebanon, the EU trade is really too small. If we consider the dimension of its economy, Egypt also has an exiguous EU trade, only 27.4 billion euros; Morocco and Algeria, which are smaller economies than Egypt, have a less limited EU trade. So there is a lot of room to increase the trade across the Mediterranean and to expand the markets. Even the trade with Israel, given the high development of the Israeli economy and its capacity to produce important goods, seems too low: only 33.1 billion euros. Paradoxically, the country with by far the largest total trade with EU is Turkey, which is not developing particularly active neighbour relationships with EU at the moment; rather, Turkey is now involved in potentially troublesome relationships with Greece and then with the EU on the question of the right to inspect the sea depth in searching for raw materials like oil and gas in Greek waters, even if close to the Turkish shore. The EU has got a trade surplus with all its partners except for Libya (–11.4) and Turkey (–1.5). The highest EU surplus is with Egypt (10.8), then Israel (7.1), Morocco (7.1), and Lebanon (5.4).

6. Conclusions

The EEC started to develop cooperative relationships with Mediterranean countries, using a bilateral approach, very early in the 60s. Later, new multilateral instruments were built up and used together with the old bilateral tools. On the one hand, the availability of multiple tools (e.g., the association agreements, the EuroMed partnership, the European Neighbourhood Policy, the Union for the Mediterranean) allows the EU to diversify the treatment country by country according to the degree of respondence and adherence to the European values while having at least a minimum standard of cooperation reached by all. On the other hand, however, the risk of inefficiencies could increase with the number of tools used and a lack of coordination among them. Failure in coordination increases with the number of tools used and some inefficiencies arise. The EU itself has recently realized that the cooperation tools available are too many and an integration and a simplification of them is urgently needed. Further reform in this direction is ongoing and will become operative next year.

The chaotic situation that emerged in countries like Libya and Syria due to the civil war started after the Arab Spring in 2011 and the economic crisis of the last years has determined a worsening in the effects on the EU, coming from the threats of Islamic terrorism and illegal migration starting from the Mediterranean region. The instruments created by the EU in the last decades, with the purpose of developing good neighbouring relationships with its Mediterranean partners, can now be used to achieve these defensive targets. For this reason, instruments like ENP and the Union for the Mediterranean have become more important. However, they should be reformed and made more powerful, from the perspectives of greater visibility and defensive use. More money should be invested by the EU in the Mediterranean region, to allow a more significant development there and to reduce economic migration and Islamic radicalization. Nevertheless, it is a tough challenge at the moment: the EU, in fact, needs to provide massive financial investment in its own member countries to recover from the Covid pandemic that has led to a long and deep recession in all the EU territories. Will the EU be able to lead different but equally important policies internally and externally at the same time? It is very challenging and the outcome is highly uncertain.

References

ATTINÀ, F., *The Barcelona Process, the Role of the European Union and the Lesson of the Western Mediterranean*, in The Journal of North African Studies, 9, 2, 2004, 140–152.

BARIZZA, F., *Il Commercio della Comunità Economica Europea con il Resto del Mondo*, Il Mulino, Bologna, 1984.

CARDWELL, P.J., *EuroMed, European Neighbourhood Policy and the Union for the Mediterranean: Overlapping Policy Frames in the EU's Governance of the Mediterranean*, in Journal of Common Market Studies, 49, 2, 2011, 219–241.

EUROPEAN COMMISSION, *Joint Communication to the European Parliament, the Council, The European Economic and Social Committee and the Committee of the Regions, Review of the European Neighborhood Policy*, 18th November, 2015.

EUROPEAN COMMISSION, *Relazione Congiunta al Parlamento Europeo, al Consiglio, al Comitato Economico e Sociale Europeo e al Comitato delle Regioni, Relazione sull'Attuazione del Riesame della Politica Europea di Vicinato*, 18th May, 2017.

EUROPEAN PARLIAMENT, *Dopo la Primavera Araba: Prospettive Future per il Medio Oriente e il Nord Africa*, Resolution, 27th March, 2019.

FRASER, T.G., *Il Conflitto Arabo-Israeliano*, Bologna, Il Mulino, 2009.

GILLESPIE, R., *The Union for the Mediterranean: An Intergovernmentalist Challenge for the European Union?* in Journal of Common Market Studies, 49, 6, 2011, 1205–1225.

HEDOUI, M.A., NATOS, D., & MATTAS, K., *EU Agricultural Integrated Policies: The Case of EU and Mediterranean Countries*, in *New Medit*, 3, 2019, 17–29.

PANEBIANCO, S., *L'Unione Europea "Potenza Divisa" nel Mediterraneo*, Milano, Egea, 2012.

Part 3

BANKING, FINANCE AND BUSINESS OPPORTUNITIES

Chapter 6

GLOBAL ISLAMIC FINANCE:

PRINCIPLES AND PRODUCTS

Flavia Cortelezzi

SUMMARY: 1. Introduction. – 2. The Geography of Islamic Finance. – 3. Reasons for Growth. – 4. The Principles and Pillars of the Islamic Economic Model. – 5. From Principles to Product. – 5.1. Profit and Loss Financing Products. – 5.2. Non-Profit and Loss Financing Products. – 5.3. Sukuk. – 5.4. Takaful. – 6. Problems and Perspectives. – References.

1. Introduction

The Islamic financial system (IFS) is part of the modern economy and it is established on the religious beliefs that emerged in some Muslim countries. What is distinguishing about the Islamic financial system is that it is based on a variety of "sharia-compliant" products, services and financial practices, that are in accordance with the Koran (al Qur'àn).

In the last years, numerous studies have noted the expansion[1] and growing importance of Islamic Finance[2] (IF) across many parts of the

---

[1] See HANIEH, ADAM, *New geographies of financial power: global Islamic finance and the Gulf*, in Third World Quarterly, 41:3, 2020, 525–546.

[2] Islamic Finance is the subject of growing interest as it provides an alternative banking system to the world economy. An Islamic financial system is a segment of the overall Islamic economy that would underpin an Islamic social order that could be an alternative to capitalist liberalism and socialist planning. It would offer the faithful the opportunity to reconcile their economic activity with their religious beliefs. According to LONE, F.A., *Islamic Finance: An Introduction*, in Islamic Banks and Financial Institutions, Palgrave MacMillan Studies in Banking and Financial Institutions, Palgrave MacMillan, London, 2016, the notion of investing finance in an ethical way is essential. On the one hand, interest is forbidden in Islam; on the other hand, the management of investment is a must, so Islam has developed an alternative financial system which encourages the promotion of trade without interest. In this system, therefore, risk is shared rather than being transferred while taking the business transactions into consideration. The literature on the subject is very wide. See among the many, without pretension of completeness EL-DIWANY, T., & AHMAD, T., *Islamic Banking and Finance: What It Is and What It Could Be. Bolton: 1st Ethical Charitable Trust*, 2010; ZAMIR, IQBAL, & ABBAS, MIRAKHOR, *An Introduction to Islamic Finance: Theory and Practice,* 2nd edition, Wiley.

world. Although small compared to conventional finance, the value of assets held by IF industry was estimated at around 2.4 trillion globally at the end of 2019, and it has been seeing an increase of more than 40% since 2013.[3] This growth encompasses a diverse range of countries and economic sectors, and has been strongly welcomed by international organizations such as the World Bank, the International Monetary Fund (IMF) and the United Nations Development Programme (UNDP). According to these institutions, IF is an important instrument to improving global inequality, tackling poverty and widening financial inclusion, since it is based on principles of a just, fair, and equitable distribution of income and wealth during the production cycle, and is thus 'highly aligned with the spirit of the Sustainable Development Goals'. For these reasons, IF is seen as an alternative means of development financing that allow to meet the funding shortfall for infrastructure and other projects.[4]

Islamic finance has developed over a long period of a profound rethinking of the cultural, religious and social identity of Muslims and with the affirmation of its distinctive characteristics.[5] The first theoretical models, concentrated on the banking sector, were formulated in the 1950s, when many Muslim-majority countries achieved political independence from western colonial powers. The first Islamic banks were formed in the following decade, operating mainly in the retail sector, which aimed at satisfying the demand for sharī'ah-compliant products from the most observant Muslims. These were often attempts to rediscover their Islamic identity after decades of foreign domination, carried out mainly in some North African countries. The process accelerated sharply in the 1970s, in conjunction with the oil crisis and the surge in the price of crude oil. The consequent huge inflow of liquidity into the countries of the Gulf Cooperation Council (GCC) supported the establishment of several institutions offering Islamic financial services, which multiplied mainly in the countries of the Middle East and the Persian Gulf. In 1975, the establishment of the Islamic Development Bank (IDB) in Saudi Arabia represented the first involvement of institutions and governments in the development of Islamic finance. Numerous initiatives, both entrepreneurial and academic, continued to flour-

---

[3] Islamic Finance grew at double digit rates during the past decade, from about USD$ 200 billion in 2013 to USD$1,8 trillion at the end of 2013. For a detailed analysis, see IMF, Islamic Finance and the Role of IMF, 2017.

[4] *Ibidem*.

[5] For a retrospective on this point see FILIPPO DI MAURO, PIERLUIGI CARISTI, STÉPHANE COUDERC, ANGELA DI MARIA, LAUREN HO, BALJEET KAUR GREWAL, SERGIO MASCIANTONIO, STEVEN ONGENA & SAJJAD ZAHER, *Islamic Finance in Europe*, ECB Occasional Paper Seriesno 146, June 2013.

ish in the 1980s, i.e., Iran, Pakistan and Sudan started the process of Islamization of their financial system (in the case of Pakistan without ever completing it). In the Nineties, interest in Islamic finance also involved institutions and markets of western countries: some conventional banks inaugurated Islamic branches within their subsidiaries operating in the area, or set up entirely sharī'ah-compliant branches. In 1995 the first two stock market indices relating to sharī'ah-compliant financial instruments (the Dow Jones Islamic Index and the Financial Times Islamic Index) were launched. In those years, the market began to feel the need for greater regulation of Islamic financial institutions, especially in accounting; this is due to the differences in opinion between the various Islamic legal schools and the contrasts between the theoretical model of Islamic banking and the concrete operation of these institutions which risked weakening the sector's development prospects. An initial response to this need was the Accounting and Auditing Organization for Islamic Institutions (AAOIFI), created in Bahrain in 1991, with the aim of developing accounting and governance rules compatible with Islamic finance. In the last decade, in correspondence with the acceleration of the sector's growth, numerous supranational institutions have been created. A leading role among these is played by the Islamic Financial Services Board (IFSB), established in 2002 in Malaysia: it represents the main coordination, regulation and standard setting body, with functions similar to those of the Basel Committee for the conventional banking system.[6]

Since then, the Islamic financial activity has grown significantly, both in terms of volume and scope. The Islamic financial system and the way most players perceive it have changed profoundly: there has been a diversification of products and players and an intensification of the cross-border dimension.

Nowadays, Islamic finance is no longer seen as opposed to a "secular," global financial system, but as an integral part of it. Today, an Islamic financial system exists to provide a variety of religiously acceptable financial services to Muslim communities and also as an alternative for non-Muslim clients seeking ethical investments and greater risk diversification.

The paper is organized as follows. In Section 2, we examine the geography of Islamic Finance and the main drivers of its expansion. We then discuss the main principles and pillars of the Islamic Economic Model (Section 3) and its main instrument (Section 4). In Section 5 we highlight the main problems and perspectives and conclude.

---

[6] See IFSB, *Core Principles for Islamic finance regulation (banking segment)*, Islamic Financial Services Board (2015).

2. The Geography of Islamic Finance

The role of Islamic finance is increasing every year and it is now diffused in more than 70 countries worldwide,[7] including countries of Europe, CIS, USA, Australia, etc., where more than 300 Islamic financial institutions operate nowadays (see Figure 6.1). It is recognized as "systematically important in Asia and the Middle East," by a recent IMF study.[8]

Figure 6.1 Diffusion of Islamic finance in 2019

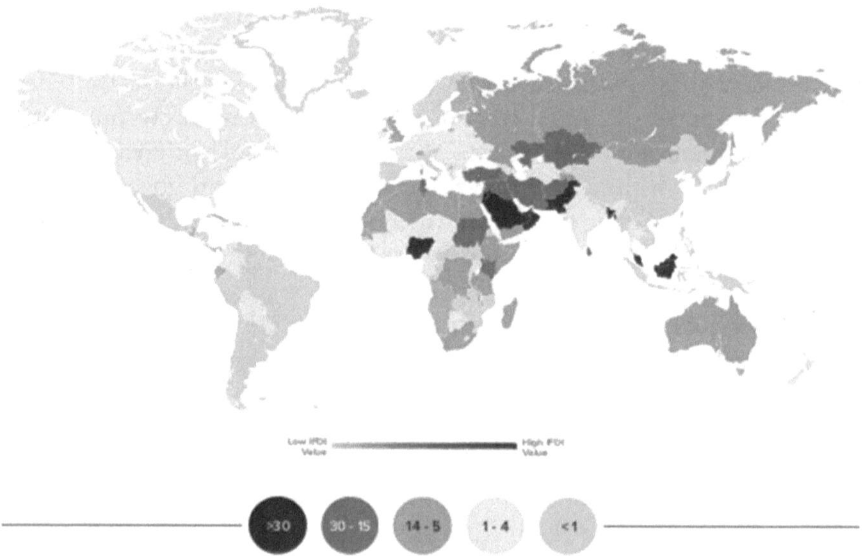

Source: Islamic Finance Development Report (2020).

In terms of value, Islamic financial assets increased worldwide from USD 150 billion in the mid-1990s to about USD 1.6 trillion by end-2012.[9]

---

[7] See G. SHABSIGH, A. HARON, M.A. NORAT, I.W. SONG, M.E.H. KHATAT, D. MURPHY *et al.*, *Ensuring financial stability in countries with Islamic banking*, United State of America, New York (2017) www.imf.org/en/Publications/Policy-Papers/Issues/2017/02/21/PP-Ensuring-Financial-Stability-in-Countries-with-Islamic-Banking.

[8] IMF, *Islamic Finance and the Role of IMF*, 2017.

[9] Islamic finance has developed significantly over the years to become a noticeable part of the international financial system. The value of Islamic financial assets worldwide increased from USD 150 billion in the mid-1990s to about USD 1.6 trillion by end-2012, led by the Islamic banking sector and the global sukuk market. On this point see FILIPPO DI MAURO, PIERLUIGI CARISTI, STÉPHANE COUDERC, ANGELA DI MARIA,

As it is possible to note from Figure 6.2, MENA and GCC Countries are the main drivers of this phenomena.

Figure 6.2 Breakdown of global IFSI by sector and by region

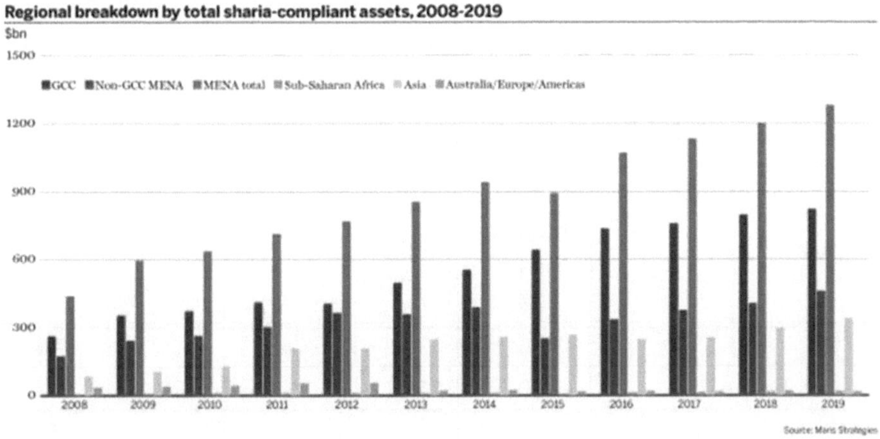

Source: The banker, 2019.

The estimated value of the three main sectors of the industry (banking, capital markets and takaful) amounts to approximately USD 2.4 trillion in 2020.[10] The robust growth was led actively by the Islamic banking sector and the global sukuk market (see Table 6.1).

Table 6.1 Sectoral composition of the global IFSI

Sector	December 2019 (%)
Islamic Banking	72.4
Sukuk	22.3
Takaful	4.2
Islamic Funds	1.1
Total (3)	**100**

Source: Author's elaboration on IFSB 2020.

LAUREN HO, BALJEET KAUR GREWAL, SERGIO MASCIANTONIO, STEVEN ONGENA & SAJJAD ZAHER, *Islamic Finance In Europe*, ECB Occasional Paper Seriesno 146, June 2013.

[10] IFSB (2020).

Despite the formidable growth over the last few years, Islamic finance still accounts for a relatively small share of global finance, and remains mostly localized in selected areas of the world, particularly in the Middle East and Far Eastern Asia (see Figure 6.2 and Table 6.2). To get a general idea, Table 6.2 provides an overview of the geographic distribution of the globalized IF sector, in terms of Sharia complaint assets – both globally and within the Gulf Cooperation Council (GCC) states.

Table 6.2 Breakdown of global IFSI by sector and by region

Region	Sector				
	Banking asset (%)	Sukuk (%)	Islamic funds (%)	Takaful (%)	Total share (%)
GCC	48.36	37.66	35.58	43.22	45.4
South East Asia	13.60	55.81	26.1	11.16	23.5
Middle East and South Asia	33.09	3.51	16.13	41.96	25.9
Africa	1.93	0.32	1.56	2.03	1.6
Others	3.02	2.70	20.63	1.63	3.7
Total	**100**	**100**	**100**	**100**	

Source: Author's elaboration on IFSB 2020.

It is possible to note that the biggest share (ca 45.4%) of the world Shari'a-compliant assets is located in the GCC states, followed by South-East Asia (23.5%), the non-GCC MENA (Middle East North Africa) region, which hosts another 25.9%.

If we analyse the domestic market share for Islamic banking services in relation to the total banking sector, it has continued to increase, breaking deeply into the sector. Among the GCC states, Saudi Arabia is the undisputed leader with 70% of the GCC states' share. Improvements in market share were also made across other systemically important jurisdictions, including Kuwait, which is now at 40.6%, the UAE 20.6%, and Bahrain 14.2%. The importance of the GCC states is far from surprising, since the initial rise of the IFS sector was closely linked to the presence of petrodollars, which abounded (and still abound) in the Gulf.

Among the non-GCC states, Iran[11] and Sudan have intended to fully Is-

---

[11] In Iran the Islamization of the entire banking system was closely related to the Islamic revolution in 1979. The process has proved to be successful since Sharia com-

lamize their economies, making all assets theoretically Shari'a-compliant, from the 1980s onwards. Compared to the previous years, a substantial improvement in market share was also observed in Kuwait, now at 48%, Malaysia 28%, Bangladesh 25.1%, and Jordan 16.2%. In addition, several countries have recently been introduced in the monitoring list of Islamic banking market-share (see Figure 6.3): Palestine, which boasts a 10% market share for Islamic banking, Djibouti (15%), Senegal (5%), Bosnia and Herzegovina (3.6%), Sri Lanka (1%), Kyrgyz Republic (1.5%) and Tanzania (0.7%).

Figure 6.3 Islamic banking share in total banking assets by jurisdiction

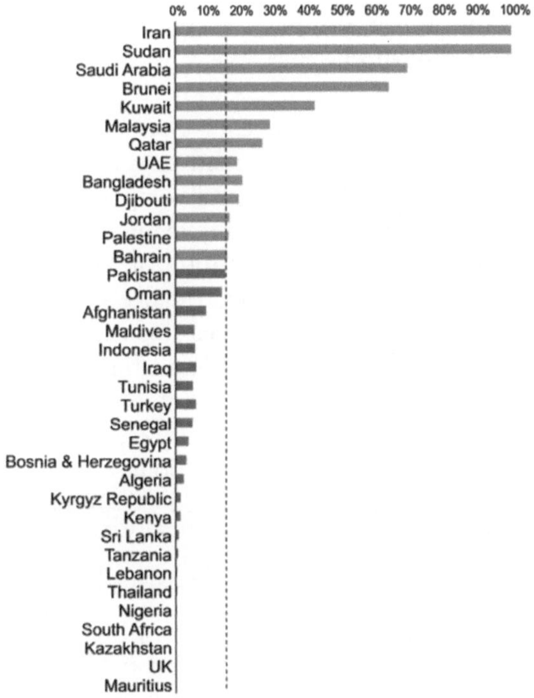

Source: IFSB 2020.

There is therefore a strong expectation of increase in some emerging countries of the Middle East, in Asia and in Africa where Islamic finance supports economic development and where 175% increases have been recorded in the last five years.

---

plaints assets represent 100% of all Iranian assets. For a retrospective on Islamic Banking see KULSHRESTHA, P., & ALI, M., *An Overview of the Islamic Banking Development in the United Kingdom, Malaysia, Saudi Arabia, Iran, Nigeria, Kenya and Uganda*, in Political Science, 2019.

To refine our level of analysis, we focus on the geographical location of the major players in the IFS sector. The IF sector is dominated by firms from the Middle East, mainly located in the GCC states and Iran. Focusing on the top firms in terms of headquarters location, [12] it appears that a relatively small number of cities plays a crucial role within these most important Shari'a-compliant regions. Tehran has the largest headquarter presence with twelve top 100 firms, but the lion's share of these firms are non-listed government-owned institutions. Within the GCC states, top cities such as Manama and Kuwait City are leading the way, followed by other regional centres such as Dubai, Doha, and Abu Dhabi. [13]

Therefore, Islamic finance has established itself mainly in the Arab countries of the Gulf, but it also has a strong presence in some non-Arab countries. [14] Outside the Middle East, the most important player is Malaysia (10.8%).

The Malaysian Islamic financial system is both robust and fast growing. [15] The Malaysian market has highly diversified players, with a strong presence of Islamic banks, investment banks, takaful companies, development financial institutions, savings institutions, fund management companies, stock brokers, and unit trusts in its economy. With the rapidly changing international Islamic financial landscape, Islamic finance in Malaysia is becoming increasingly integrated into the international financial system. This development has occurred in all segments of the Islamic financial system in Malaysia – including the Islamic banking and the takaful industry – and in the Islamic money and capital markets (Bank Negara Malaysia, 2016).

Malaysia currently pursues a pro-active policy towards the IFS sector. For instance, the Ninth Malaysia Plan (2006–2010) aims at strengthening

---

[12] For a detailed description of Islamic banking geography see BASSENS, D., DERUDDER, B., & WITLOX, F., *Searching for the Mecca of finance: Islamic financial services and the world city network*, in Area 42 (1), 2010, 35–46.; and, more recently, NIKONOVA, TATIANA, V., YUSUPOVA, LILIYA, M., & NUGAEV, FATICH, SH., *Islamic financial institutions in the european economy*, in Journal of Economics and Economic Education Research, 2016, 17:144; and LAI, KAREN, PY, *Financial geography in International Encyclopedia of Geography: People, the Earth, Environment and Technology: People, the Earth*, in Environment and Technology, 2016, 1–8.

[13] BASSENS, D., DERUDDER, B., & WITLOX, F., *Searching for the Mecca of finance: Islamic financial services and the world city network*, in Area 42 (1), 2010, 35–46.

[14] ADAM HANIEH, *New geographies of financial power: global Islamic finance and the Gulf*, in Third World Quarterly, 41:3, 2020, 525–546.

[15] The growth rate of Islamic finance in Malaysia is impressive. Malaysia has the power to retain its leadership in global Islamic finance, despite the emergence of competition from other centres such as Hong Kong and Dubai. The Malaysian competition was way ahead of other countries, in terms of product offerings and sophistication, as they have been developing the market for 40 years.

Malaysia's position as a global IFS hub, as a centre for origination, distribution, trading, fund, and wealth management.[16] By making the country a global Islamic brand, Malaysia is also trying to tap liquidity from the Gulf States. Much of this Islamic "buzz" is located in Kuala Lumpur, which is home to the Islamic Financial Services Board. Simultaneously, the Malaysian offshore centre Labuan is developing IFS as a niche market to avoid competitive outbidding from other offshore financial centres.[17]

In 2013, the government of Malaysia has played a crucial role in the development of this sector by drafting legal reforms, creating a suitable business environment and providing qualified human resources. According to the International Monetary Fund, Malaysia also hosts the largest sukūk market,[18] which

Table 6.3 *Sukuk* market

Regions		Composition December 2019 (%)
Malaysia		32.82
Saudi Arabia	31.94	
Indonesia		13.38
Turkey		7.45
UAE		5.31
Oman	4.38	
Bahrain		3.36
Nigeria	0.51	
Quatar		0.38
Brunei		0.26
Morocco		0.15
Bangladesh		0.03
Gambia		0.03

Source: Author's elaborations on IFSB 2019.

[16] IMF (International Monetary Fund), 2007, *Malaysia: An Islamic capital market hub*, Retrieved October 15, 2008.

[17] ABBOTT, J.P., *Labuan: Treasure island, pet project or ghost town?* in *Offshore financial centers and tax havens: The rise of global capital*, 1999 Edited by: Hampton, M.P. & Abbott, P.A. 192–211, New York: Palgrave MacMillan.

[18] It is followed by Saudi Arabia (31.94%), by Indonesia (13.38%) and Turkey (7,45%). IFSB, 2020.

accounts for about 32.8% of the global Islamic bonds and represents the largest market in terms of outstanding size and number of issues.[19]

The other countries targeted in the internationalization process include Turkey, Sudan, Bangladesh, Pakistan and Indonesia, as well as countries that have introduced legislation around Islamic banking very recently (Bosnia, Nigeria, Senegal and Kenya). There are also exceptions. In countries with very populous Muslim communities such as India, Islamic finance is almost absent.

But also in non-Muslim countries, the IFS sector is now gaining momentum. Islamic banks demonstrate a much greater propensity to internationalization and show a greater interest in geographical overseas expansion than their conventional counterparts. The majority (53%) of all GCC bank subsidiaries are located in North America/EU or in offshore financial centers. Europe clearly has the upper hand with London and with Paris, to a lesser extent, as IFS hubs are increasing.

However, Islamic banking in the European Union countries is still at an early stage of development. There is only a small number of banks, offering Islamic financial products and services in the EU. In 2004, Islamic Bank of Britain (IBB) became the first fully-fledged Islamic bank, not only in the UK, but in the whole European Union. There are several examples of IFS firms that are present either through branch offices (e.g., Faisal Private Bank in Geneva, a subsidiary of the Manama-based Ithmaar Bank) or newly established full-fledged Islamic financial institutions. Additionally, conventional financial institutions have opened Islamic 'windows' to cater to the local Muslim population (e.g., HSBC through its subsidiary HSBC Amanah). Both in Europe and in the USA, Shari'a compliant products are now available at the retail level.

3. Reasons for Growth

The demand for Sharia-compliant financing and banking products that have recently come to light in many Muslim and non-Muslim countries (Europe and USA) does not seem casual. Let us consider some of the reasons that are causing this phenomenon.[20]

---

[19] WORLD BANK, *Malaysia's Domestic Bond Market: A Success Story. World Bank*, Washington, DC. © World Bank, 2020, https://openknowledge.worldbank.org/handle/10986/34538 License: CC BY 3.0 IGO.

[20] NIKONOVA, TATIANA, KOKH, IGOR, & SAFINA, LILIYA, *Principles and Instruments of Islamic Financial Institutions*, in Procedia Economics and Finance, 24, 2015, 479–484.

First of all, the generally growing need among Muslims for a Shari'ah-compliant financial system seems to be driving the growth of Islamic finance.

Earlier Muslims were not familiar with banking operations, and the concept of a bank as a modern institution is new to Islamic societies. Initially, many Muslims did not even understand the extent and importance of banks in their everyday lives, even when living in non-Islamic countries. However, once they realized that interest payments from conventional banking are at odds with the prohibited *rhiba*, they naturally looked for alternative modes of financing. Early initiatives in the 1960s led to the establishment of Islamic financial institutions in Egypt, India, Malaysia, Pakistan, Saudi Arabia, and later in Iran and Sudan, where Islamic finance was adopted as the only financial system countrywide.

Thus, it is not surprising to see that Muslims continue to look for Shari'ah-compliant financial institutions around the world, as these become more mature and integrated into conventional financial systems. While offering a wider range of services, large segments of the Muslim population are still underserviced by conventional finance – only 24% of adults have a bank account and 7% have access to formal financing, compared with 44% and 9%, respectively, for non-Muslim populations.[21]

In Europe, Islamic finance is still at a fairly embryonic stage, but a number of factors would tend to support its further development, e.g., the growing Muslim population within European jurisdictions, government incentives and the measures introduced to create an environment conducive to a growing and thriving Islamic finance industry.[22] There is a wave of issuing licenses and permits, which allows the start-up of retail banking services (mortgages, insurance and loans) in accordance with the Shari'ah. European governments have changed their policies and they now encourage paying more attention to the needs of Muslim communities in Europe. The fear of alienating a significant part of European society and the threat of the destruction of stability have played a great role in the process of changing the official position. Islamic banking and finance are now being finally considered as promising business opportunities – and not a "handout" of ethnic minorities – by government officials and traditional banks. In addi-

[21] DEMIRG DEMIRGUC-KUNT, ASLI, KLAPPER, LEORA, & RANDALL, DOUGLAS, *Islamic Finance and Financial Inclusion: Measuring Use of and Demand for Formal Financial Services among Muslim Adults*, Policy Research Working Paper, No. 6642, World Bank, Washington, 2013.

[22] BIANCONE, PIETRO PAOLO, & RADWAN, MAHA, *Sharia Compliant "Possibility for Italian SMEs"*, in European Journal of Islamic Finance, (1), (2015).

tion, a large number of professional investors want to include Islamic financial products in their portfolio for diversification purposes.

Second, there is currently a growing interest in Halal (allowed) financial products among non-Muslims as well. The investments of European banks in sukuk (Islamic securities) have increased interest among those private investors who would like to take ethical and/or religious aspects into account in their investment decisions. Choosing Sharia-compliant products they can be sure they don't invest in unethical products.[23]

Third, part of the industry growth is driven by the economic growth of the MENA region. Over the past decade, the MENA region has witnessed a solid growth path, which in turn has helped the Islamic finance industry, particularly banking assets.[24] The average real GDP growth in the MENA region has been about 4%, with the highest growth rate of 11% in Qatar and 5.2% in Saudi Arabia. Moreover, in GGC the growth is driven by the abundant liquidity flows from the recycling of petrodollars generated by high oil prices over the years.

Finally, there is the perception that the Islamic financial sector can support efforts to promote global financial stability. Islamic banks are more resilient to shocks than conventional banks, because *gharar* considerations prohibit them from investing in excessively risky subprime and toxic assets, as well as zero-sum betting on derivatives. By promoting risk sharing (as opposed to risk transfer) and endorsing investment in wealth creating activities, the asset-based nature of Islamic financing naturally curbs excessive leverage. It also restricts banks from investing in highly leveraged assets and short selling, suggesting that they are likely to foster financial stability and render the global financial system less prone to financial distress. The direct link between the financial and the real or trade sectors may also prevent technical speculations and potential bubbles. Further, increased monitoring by investment account holders may help impose market discipline on banks and maintain financial stability. Last, but not least, is the fact that multilateral organisations (e.g., the IMF) as well as a number of central banks have embarked on extensive studies/research initiatives to examine the prospects for Islamic finance within their respective economic blocs/regions.

---

[23] AHMED, HABIB, *et al.*, *On the sustainable development goals and the role of Islamic finance*, The World Bank, 2015.

[24] MUMTAZ, HUSSAIN, ASGHAR, SHAHMORADI, & RIMA TURK, IMF Working Paper, 2015.

4. The Principles and Pillars of the Islamic Economic Model

Islamic economics and finance find its origin in principles rooted in the rulings of the Shari'ah legal code. [25]

The holy texts of Islam establish detailed requirements about the behaviour of *Homo Economicus*. Sobriety, austerity and respect for the other, and equality between men are important cornerstones, as well as helping those who who need help without expecting anything in exchange.

Islam encourages work, gains and investment. However, businessmen's expectations of profit must go alongside the desire to serve their communities. They are expected not to cheat, lie nor behave dishonestly. Their employees must be remunerated fairly, and education, brotherhood and friendship at work are considered important virtues. Women should not have an economic role: they cannot participate in productive life, they have no freedom of initiative or, in certain cases, of movement. [26]

Money is considered as a means and not an end, thus not allowing its social and productive use. It is, therefore, simply a measure which represents the relative value of a product or service and a vehicle used to facilitate transactions. Money held in a bank account does not produce interest, as it is subject to taxation.

To conclude, the Islamic economic model is primarily intended to optimize the operation of each party's financial processes and is governed by some essential principles. In what follows, we discuss each principle together with its implications.

The Principle of Equity

This principle is usually invoked as the rationale for the prohibition of predetermined payments (*rhiba*). The idea is to protect the weaker contracting party in a financial transaction. The term *rhiba*, which means "hump" or "elevation" in Arabic, refers to any increase in wealth not related to a productive activity. *Rhiba* (the surplus) is any unjustified additional amount of money of capital in the loan, i.e., the interest on the loan. Thus, *rhiba* covers not only usury, but any interest in the usual traditional sense. Islam encourages profits only as a result of activities, leading to the formation of any final product, condemning the use of percent in profit. [27]

---

[25] IMF (International Monetary Fund), *Islamic Finance and the Role of IMF*, 2017.

[26] MAURI, MARCO, & HAMAUI, RONY, *Economia e Finanza Islamica*, Bologna: Il Mulino, 2009.

[27] "*The main objective of an Islamic Bank is to prohibit Muslims from dealing with in-*

The principle of equity is also the basis for prohibiting excessive uncertainty, i.e., *gharar*, defined as "*Preventable* ambiguity or uncertainty." When entering into a contractual relationship, the parties must fully disclose their intentions and information to each other, because the transaction that contains "*gharar*" will be prohibited. In any transaction, the subject of a contract must exist and must be specifiable and measurable. If either the subject of a contract or the price or both are not defined and not fixed in advance, the transaction will be considered suspicious by the Shari'ah.

Strictly related to the prohibition of uncertainty, it is also the prohibition of speculative behaviour, i.e., Maysir. Operations based on the random event or speculation and not on the action of the parties aimed at generating income are considered to be invalid in Shariah. In this regard, in the Islamic financial system it is extremely complicated to use the derivative financial instruments which have significant risk level.

Finally, the principle of equity and wealth distribution is also the basis of a 2.5% levy on cash or in-kind wealth (zakat), imposed by Shari'ah on all Muslims who meet specific minimum levels of income and wealth to assist the less fortunate and foster social solidarity.

The Principle of Participation

According to Shari'ah, "reward (that is, profit) comes with risk taking", so that investment return has to be earned together with risk-taking and not with the mere passage of time, i.e., the interest rate or *rhiba*.

Thus, there should be a link between financing activities and real activities. The capital owner is not lender but investor. In this way, there is risk sharing between the owner of capital and the user of capital, as there is no guarantee of regular income. In case of success of the project, the investor participates in the direct distribution of profits. The principle of participation is a cornerstone at the heart of Islamic finance. It ensures that increases in wealth should be due to productive activities.

The Principle of Ownership

The rules of "do not sell what you do not own" (i.e. short-selling) and "you cannot be dispossessed of a property except on the basis of right" establish

---

terest or usury (Rhiba) which has been strictly prohibited by Allah, and to protect them from one of the biggest sins." Dubai Islamic Bank Statement.

asset ownership before transacting. Thus, Islamic finance determines a strong link between finance and the real economy. Moreover, the contract is the most important condition of the transaction, i.e., the contracts should be respected (the sanctity of contract).

Haram versus Halal

Money, as "potential capital", will become capital only if it is invested in Halal industries. Islam investments must comply with the principles of Shariah and operations associated with certain types of products are prohibited. In particular, it prohibits moral grounds activities related to tobacco and other drugs, alcohol, pork products and gambling, involving money and non-money assets (*maysir*), speculation and traditional fixed-income financial products, pornography, armaments and destructive weapons.

5. From Principles to Product

The current Islamic financial system comprises a wide variety of Islamic financial products that are based on pillars above described. Despite their similarities, their purposes are different. We divide them into four categories: i) Profit and loss sharing, i.e., PLS contracts (*musharakah*; *murabahah*); ii) Mark up principle, i.e., non-PLS contracts (*mudarabah*; *ijarah*);[28] iii) *Sukuk*; iv) *Takaful*.

5.1. Profit and Loss Financing Products

These kinds of products are based on principles of equity and participation; they help to promote a more equitable distribution of income, leading to a more efficient allocation of resources. There are two types of PLS financing we discuss: *musharakah* and *mudârabah*.

Musharakah is a joint enterprise or venture and it is the most authentic form of Islamic financing. Thus, this product requires the signing of the partnership agreement between an Islamic financial institution and a customer, according to which both parties are funding the project together.

There should be the Capability of Partners, i.e., must be sane and mature and be able to enter into a contract.[29] Partners have a right to take

[28] Other contracts, we do not discuss here, are *Salam* and *Istinaa*.

[29] The contract must take place with free consent of the parties without any fraud or misrepresentation.

part in management; they seem to bear the greatest risk among all Islamic financing modes with the potential for earning the highest reward. However, whereas profits are distributed according to pre-agreed ratios, losses are divided in proportion to the participation of parties in the financing. If one or more partners choose to become non-working or silent partners, the ratio of their profit cannot exceed the ratio which their capital investment bears so the total capital investment in *musharakah*.[30] This type of contracts is often used to finance long-term investment projects and profits shall be distributed in the proportion mutually agreed in the contract.

In *mudârabah* one party supplies funding (financier as principal) and the other provides effort and management expertise (entrepreneur as agent) with a view to generating a profit.

Mudârabah is sometimes referred to as a sleeping partnership because the *mudarib* runs the business and the financier cannot interfere in management, though conditions may be specified to ensure better management of capital. The financial institution solely bears losses in case they occur, and in that case the *mudarib* (the trustee) gets no reward for its efforts. Islamic banks mainly make use of *mudârabah* financing to raise funds; *mudârabah* contracts are also used for the management of mutual funds. *Mudarabah* is typically used to finance short – and medium – term investment projects (e.g., in retail trade).

Concluding, there are three main differences between *musharakah* and *mudarabah*. In *musharakah* all partners invest and participate in the management of the business and can work for it. In addition, all partners share the loss to the extent of the ratio of their investment. In *mudarabah*, only *rab-ul-Maal* invests and he has no right to participate in the management which is carried out by the *mudarib* only. In addition, only the financial institution suffers losses because the trustee does not invest anything. However, this is subject to a condition that the *mudarib* has worked with due diligence.

5.2. Non-Profit and Loss Financing Products

Non-PLS contracts are most common in practice. They are generally used to finance consumer and corporate credit, as well as asset rental and manu-

[30] ASMADI, M.N., *Purchase Undertaking Issues in Musharakah Mutanaqisah Home Financing*', in ISRA International Journal of Islamic Finance, 3(1), 2011. Kuala Lumpur: International Shariah Research Academy. NIKONOVA, TATIANA, KOKH, IGOR, & SAFINA, LILIYA, *Principles and Instruments of Islamic Financial Institutions*, in Procedia Economics and Finance, 24, 2015, 479–484.

facturing. Non-PLS financing instruments include *murâbaḥah*, *ijārah*, and *istisna'*.

Murâbaḥah is a popular Shari'ah-compliant sale transaction mostly used in trade and asset financing. The bank purchases the goods and delivers them to the customer, deferring payment to a date agreed by the two parties. The expected return on *murâbaḥah* is usually aligned with interest payments on conventional loans, creating a similarity between *murâbaḥah* sales and asset-backed loans. However, *murâbaḥah* is a deferred payment sale transaction where the intention is to facilitate the acquisition of goods and not to exchange money for more money (or monetary equivalents) over a period of time. *Murâbaḥah* transactions are widely used to finance international trade, as well as for interbank financing and liquidity management.

Ijārah is a sale contract regarding the right to use an asset for a period of time. In this type of financing arrangement, the lessor (who must own the property) leases the property to the lessee in exchange for a stream of rental and purchase payments, ending with the transfer of property ownership to the lessee.

It is essentially a lease contract, whereby the leaser must own the leased asset for the entire lease period. Since ownership remains with the leaser, the asset can be repossessed in case of nonpayment by the lessee. However, the leaser is also responsible for asset maintenance, unless damage to the leased asset results from lessee negligence. This element of risk is required for making *ijārah* payments permissible. A variety of *ijārah* takes a hire-purchase form, whereby there is a promise by the leaser to sell the asset to the lessee at the end of the lease agreement, with the price of the residual asset being predetermined. A second independent contract gives the lessee the option to buy the leased asset at the conclusion of the contract or simply return it to the owner.

Istisna' is a contract which a commodity can be transacted before it comes into existence. The unique feature of *istisna'* (or manufacturing) is that nothing is exchanged on the spot or at the time of contracting. It is perhaps the only forward contract where the obligations of both parties are in the future. In theory, the *istisna'* contract could be directly between the end user and the manufacturer, but it is typically a three-party contract, with the bank acting as intermediary.

5.3. *Sukuk*

Sukuk investments represent a distinct class of securities issued by sovereign and corporate entities. Like bonds, *sukuk* have a maturity date and holders are entitled to a stream of income over the life of the sukuk, along with a final payment at maturity. However, *sukuk* are asset-based rather than asset-backed securities, with the underlying asset being necessarily Shari'a-compliant in both nature and use. *Sukuk* holders might be responsible for asset-related expenses, and the sale of sukuk results in the sale of a share of an asset. Bonds, in contrast, are pure debt obligations issued to finance any activity and whose value rests on the creditworthiness of the issuer. *Sukuk* price can vary both with the creditworthiness of the issuer and the market value of the underlying asset. However, while *sukuk* and shares of stock are similar in the sense that they represent ownership claims and that the return on both investments is not guaranteed, *sukuk* must be related to as a specific asset, service or project for a period of time.

5.4. *Takaful*

For a long time the insurance contract represented a taboo in the Muslim world. According to Islam, Allah's affects every event in the life of human beings. Even the death of a beloved person, the loss of an asset or a damage suffered are the result of His will. In a conventional insurance, the insurer receives a sum of money (the premium) from the insured, in the hope of making a profit. The insurer expects that the amount of claims reimbursed is lower than the amount of premiums collected, thus configuring a speculation. In addition, as a rule, the insured party pays a certain premium for an uncertain benefit that may be null or far greater than the premium paid, thus leading to uncertainty. In Islamic insurance, insured parties cooperate to each other, contributing to the creation of a fund from which they draw for the payment of compensation. There is no insured-insurer relationship but but a joint participation in the fund and the guarantees are not traded. Conventional mutual insurance resembles *takaful* in many ways since the end is not speculative profit, but the element of uncertainty remains as a relevant difference.

6. Problems and Perspectives

Having considered the basic principles and tools of financing used by Islamic financial institutions and mechanisms for their implementation, we can mention the following possible benefits and challenges.

First, it is often argued that Islamic finance is inherently less prone to crisis and it is more stable than conventional finance because its risk-sharing feature reduces leverage and encourages better risk management on the part of both financial institutions and their customers. Moreover, financing is asset-based and thus fully collateralized and it involves prohibitions against speculation. Last, but not least, Islamic economic and financial principles are inherently socially oriented, entail moral development and a more stable business and, consequently, may have an impact on reducing the level of corruption and dishonesty in the economy. For all of these reasons, Islamic financial institutions are considered to be a good platform for increasing access to financial inclusion, including access to finance for SMEs, thereby supporting growth and economic development.

Nonetheless, Islamic finance faces a number of challenges. For example, up to now in many countries the industry is governed by a regulatory and supervisory framework developed for conventional finance. The industry is still largely a nascent one, lacking economies of scale, and operating in an environment where legal and tax rules, financial infrastructure, and access to financial safety nets and central bank liquidity are either absent or, if available, do not appropriately take into account the special characteristics of Islamic finance (Askari, Iqbal, and Mirakhor 2010; Ernst and Young 2014; IFSB, IsDB, and IRTI 2010).

References

AHMED, H., *et al.*, *On the Sustainable Development Goals and the Role of Islamic Finance*, The World Bank, 2015.

BASSENS, D., DERUDDER, B., & WITLOX, F., *Searching for the Mecca of Finance: Islamic Financial Services and the World City Network*, in Area 42, 1, 2010, 35–46.

BIANCONE, P.P. & RADWAN, M., *Sharia Compliant "Possibility for Italian SMEs"*, in European Journal of Islamic Finance (1), 2015.

DEMIRG DEMIRGUC-KUNT, A., KLAPPER, L., & RANDALL, D., *Islamic Finance and Financial Inclusion: Measuring Use of and Demand for Formal Financial Services among Muslim Adults*, in Policy Research Working Paper, No. 6642, Washington: World Bank, 2013.

Di Mauro, F., Caristi, P., Couderc, S., Di Maria, A. Ho, L., Grewal, B.K., Masciantonio, S., Ongena S., & Zaher, S., *Islamic Finance In Europe*, ECB Occasional Paper Seriesno, 2013, 146.

EL-DIWANY, T., & AHMAD, T., *Islamic Banking and Finance: What It Is And What It Could Be*, Bolton: 1st Ethical Charitable Trust, 2010.

HANIEH, A., *New Geographies of Financial Power: Global Islamic Finance and the Gulf,* Third World Quarterly, 41, 3, 2020, 525–546.

Hussain, M., Shahmoradia, & Turk, R., IMF Working Paper, 2015.

IMF (International Monetary Fund), *Islamic Finance and the Role of IMF*, 2017.

IMF (International Monetary Fund), *Malaysia: An Islamic Capital Market Hub*, 2007.

IFSB, *Core Principles for Islamic finance Regulation (banking segment)*, Islamic Financial Services Board, 2015.

IFSB, *World Bank. 2020. Malaysia's Domestic Bond Market: A Success Story*, World Bank, Washington, DC. © World Bank, 2020, https://openknowledge.worldbank.org/handle/10986/34538 License: CC BY 3.0 IGO.

KULSHRESTHA, P., ALI, A., *An Overview of the Islamic Banking Development in the United Kingdom, Malaysia, Saudi Arabia, Iran, Nigeria, Kenya and Uganda*, in Political Science, 2019.

LAI, KAREN PY., *Financial Geography*, in International Encyclopedia of Geography: People, the Earth, Environment and Technology, 2016, 1–8.

LONE, F.A., (2016) *Islamic Finance: An Introduction*, in Islamic Banks And Financial Institutions, Palgrave Macmillan Studies in Banking and Financial Institutions, London: Palgrave MacMillan.

MAURI, M., & HAMAUI, R., *Economia e Finanza Islamica*, Bologna: Il Mulino, 2009.

NIKONOVA, T.V., YUSUPOVA, L.M., & NUGAEV, F. SH., *Islamic Financial Institutions in the European Economy*, in Journal of Economics and Economic Education Research, 17, 2016, 144.

SHABSIGH, G., HARON, A., NORAT, M.A., SONG, I.W., KHATAT, M.E.H., & MURPHY, D., *et al.*, *Ensuring Financial Stability in Countries with Islamic Banking*, New York: United State of America, (2017) www.imf.org/en/Publications/Policy-Papers/Issues/2017/02/21/PP-Ensuring-Financial-Stability-in-Countries-with-Islamic-Banking.

ZAMIR, IQBAL & ABBAS, MIRAKHOR, *An Introduction to Islamic Finance: Theory and Practice*, 2nd Edition, Wiley, 2011.

Chapter 7
FRAMEWORK AND FUNCTIONING OF THE ISLAMIC BANK AND DIFFERENCES WITH CONVENTIONAL BANKS

Paolo Biancone and Silvana Secinaro

SUMMARY: 1. Islamic Banking Systems. – 2. Islamic Bank Regulation. – 3. Concepts and Principles underlying Islamic Banking Activity and the Supply of Financial Products. – 4. Islamic Banks versus Traditional Banks. – 5. Islamic Equity Crowdfunding. – References.

1. Islamic Banking Systems

The Islamic banking system is defined as a financial system in which the guiding principles of its operations and activities are based on Islamic or Sharia rules. All the operations must be based on the principles of the Shariah. The main factor that distinguishes the Islamic financial system is precisely the fact that all the transactions are developed without introducing the element of interest or *riba*. Additionally, another element consists in the aim of Islamic banks. Mainly, Islamic banks should provide for the financial needs of the Muslim population, as the management of the bank is based on the concept of justice and equity in the interest of society as a whole.[1] The history of Islamic financial operations can be traced back to the early days of Islam, when activities such as deposits, loans and exchange rates already existed. Even before the birth of Islam, Mecca was the centre of the Middle Eastern trade, but an organic system of financial institutions had never been created before.

Therefore, it is necessary to consider more recent times to see Islamic finance as a system characterised by moral principles, established itself in financial activities. The development of the modern Islamic financial system is generally traced back to the establishment of the Mit Ghamr Saving Bank in Egypt, in 1963.

There were some previous attempts to create institutions of this kind. Some scholars (Erol and El-Bolour, 1989) argue that the first attempt to

[1] Please see HARON, S., & AZMI, W., *Islamic Finance and Banking System*, Selangor (Malaysia): McGraw Hill, 2009.

establish a non-interest-bearing bank was made in Malaysia in the mid-1940s, while others recall the experiment in India in the 1930s.

The creation of the Mit Ghamr Saving Bank in one of the Muslim agricultural regions of the Nile Valley marked the real beginning of the modern phenomenon. It opened the way for the foundation of other Islamic banks. The local farming community appreciated the Sharia-compliant services a lot, and the number of clients rose rapidly from 17,560 in its first year of operation (1963/1964) to 258,151 at the end of the financial year 1966/1967, and so did the deposits from £40,944 (Egyptian pounds) to 1,828,375. Despite this success, its operations slowed down as a result of an unstable economic policy in Egypt and mid-1967 it was absorbed by the Egyptian National Bank (Egypt and Central Bank of Egypt). Because of this incorporation, the ban on interest payments was abandoned. However, it was restored in 1972 with the founding of a new financial institution, the Nasser Social Bank, whose success led Muslim operators to conduct studies on the guidelines for this new reality around the world.

The situation was difficult because the scarcity of literature on the subject was accompanied by the fact that many Muslim economists had trained in Western universities which did not have deep foundations in the Islamic economy.[2] The need to create institutions based on the principles of Shariah was very strong in those years.

However, the first steps in the foundation of Islamic banks came from private initiatives rather than governments, even if the full support of governments was always decisive for the success of the initiatives. Most of the established banks have been operating and generating profits for 30 years.

The development of the Islamic financial system has followed different lines across the various Islamic countries, different from each other in several aspects: historical, legislative, operational opportunities and government support. In some countries, such as Iran and Sudan, for example, the financial system is almost wholly Islamised; in others, such as Bahrain, Jordan, the United Arab Emirates and Yemen, there is a system of dualism where both Islamic and conventional banks operate in parallel but separately. In states such as Malaysia, the full support of the government has allowed the Islamic system to develop rapidly and the creation of infrastructure, such as the interbank capital market in 1994, has accelerated its development as well as ties with other countries. Finally, in countries such

[2] GLERATLIS, 1990, cites that when the Pakistani authorities wanted to introduce the Islamic financial system into the country, only one out of 19 economists called in to deal with the problem was an expert in Islamic economics, and eleven of these had attended universities run by Catholic or Protestant religious.

as Kuwait, Qatar and Turkey there is a mixed system where Islamic and conventional financial services are offered together and in agreement, with the existence of Islamic banks and Islamic branches in conventional banks.

2. Islamic Bank Regulations

Islamic banks, as organisations based on religion and profit, must comply with two types of regulations: the Islamic or Sharia law and the one issued by the various countries, which are favourable laws. As noted, however, Sharia law is the Islamic law that entirely regulates the life of Islamic organisations and society, concerning both faith and practice, personal behaviour and social/legal transactions.

In addition to Islamic law, Islamic financial institutions must observe human-made laws (positive law) in their activities. There is no uniform positive law for Islamic banks because while some countries have introduced specific Islamic financial laws for banks, others have issued regulations that must be followed by all the banks. Additionally, Islamic banks must observe other laws relating to the economic and financial activities of the country in which they operate. Finally, the Central Bank is usually responsible for the monetary and political control of Islamic Banks in the different countries.

Generally, both conventional and Islamic banks are governed by the same regulations as regards supervision and monitoring. However, it is not possible for Islamic banks to use those financial instruments that include interest rates. The existence of this double regulation to follow makes it essential for the Islamic bank to have a Sharia Supervisory Board, constituted from experts in the Islamic law, to ensure that the principles of the Sharia are not violated. From one bank to another, these bodies vary in the number of members, methods of evaluation and responsibility; this also explains why the annual balance sheets of the Islamic banks differ in content and methods of drafting.

The role and development of the leading organisations and associations concerning the Islamic banking system is valid worldwide, while sometimes limited to certain countries, providing general or specific services in aspects of Islamic financial institutions.

The function of these authorities is to identify and disseminate strict principles and uniform rules – such as legal, fiscal and accounting standards – and to promote agreements between countries and within the various financial institutions. Additionally, they create a system as harmonious and transparent as possible; their efficiency and validity are reflected in the stability and operational capacity of the financial system especially in periods, such as the current one, of rapid evolution and sudden change.

The Islamic Development Bank (IDB) represented one of the most important catalysts in the diffusion of Islamic banks in the world, both managing to mobilise the wealth of the Muslim countries through cooperation between them and promoting the economy and the growth of the less developed ones. The benefits of the projects and interventions are evident across the adhering countries and the whole Islamic community.

There have been four types of programmes carried out: project financing, technical assistance operations, financial activities in support of trade and specialised fund transfer operations between the affiliates. It was one of the founding members of the AAOIFI which, as will be seen, is now one of the most important bodies of the Islamic financial infrastructure.

Moreover, in those years, numerous organisations were founded by the banks with the objective of mutual protection and the development of activities with reciprocal benefits. The first organisation of this kind was the International Association of Islamic Banks, which, unfortunately, closed in 1997, after 30 years of profitable operations. In its place, the General Council for Islamic Banks was founded in Bahrain, which, however, did not have an incisive action on the sector, limiting itself, in fact, to the organisation of seminars and conferences.

Furthermore, many Central Banks, like those of Malaysia, created beneficial Associations in the development of banking activity and gave life to relevant bodies which today constitute the infrastructure of the Islamic banking activity.

The AAOIFI – Accounting and Auditing Organization for Islamic Financial Institution – based in Bahrain, was created in 1990 to develop issues related to accounting, auditing and ethical standards for Islamic financial institutions. Its structure consists of five divisions: The General Assembly, the Council of Trustees, the General Secretariat, the Accounting and Auditing Standards Committee and the Sharia Committee. The last two support the operating divisions for the development, respectively, of accounting standards and of ethical-moral standards. The primary purpose of the AAOIFI is to implement an efficient financial infrastructure that renders the system efficient. This role is essential as there are substantial differences in the interpretation of the Islamic law, both concerning the typology of products and the accounting representation of the operations: the absence of adequate standards of harmonisation creates confusion, uncertainty, contrasts and damages the transparency of the system.

The AAOIFI has no power of taxation, but the application of the accounting standards issued is expanding in different areas such as Bahrain, Dubai International Finance Centre, Qatar, Jordan, Lebanon, Sudan and Syria. In these countries, Islamic financial transactions and bank accounting strictly follow the AAOIFI standards. In others, such as Australia, Indonesia, Malaysia, Pakistan, Saudi Arabia and South Africa, regulations have been issued on standards and guidelines that reflect their accounting standards and pronouncements.

3. Concepts and Principles Underlying Islamic Banking Activity and the Supply of Financial Products

Islamic banks follow the precepts of the Shariah, offering financial products and services inspired by religious principles (Sharia-compliant), where the prohibition of the payment of pecuniary interest leads to an operating system based on profits and risks sharing.

The Islamic banking system, however, is not only based on the prohibition of interest (interest-free); besides the *riba* (interest, usury), there are other principles of the Shariah, affecting the banking system, to be respected: the prohibition of the exercise of speculative activities (*gharar* and *maysir*), the sharing of risks and profits (PLS), the compulsory payment of a religious obligation (*zakat*), and the ban on investing in prohibited activities (*haram*).[3]

In Islamic law, the *riba* interest-usury is considered a deadly sin, to such an extent of being compared to murder, fornication and idolatry by the literature.

In general, the *riba* is linked to the prohibition of interest, but in reality, it is a much broader notion connected to a literal meaning of "growth, increase". It is not limited to borrowing with interest, but to all payments of sums of money or fungible goods from one person to another, generating an uncompensated profit in either party. The pecuniary interest consists in fact in receiving compensation only for having made a certain amount of money available to a third party, i.e., it is remuneration in the absence of productive work.

Given the variety of situations, jurists distinguish different types of *riba* and, in the absence of a precise definition within Sharia, different schools of interpretation have been formed.[4] However, these reflections have not

[3] ISRA, *Islamic Financial System*, Kuala Lumpur: Principles & Operations, 2013.

[4] Since a more rigorous interpretation, according to one part of the doctrine, would not favour economic development, a concept of *riba* based more on "spirit" than on literal meaning has been proposed. According to this interpretation, the underlying reason for the prohibition lies in preventing injustice and protecting the weakest. Therefore, the payment of an interest rate would be objectionable if it affected a poor person. However, it would not be objectionable in the case of a rich person, and so it should be admitted to the extent that it maintained value despite inflation.

been taken into consideration until now: it is the literal meaning that constitutes the rule in the Islamic financial and commercial activity, where they tend to eliminate any evidence of pecuniary interest from operations. All the financial contracts must concern real tangible activities (asset-backed), and it is not admitted "making money out of money" (Kettel 2010): money only generates value and wealth if invested in a productive activity of goods and services. [5]

It is worth remembering that originally the European model of financial activity also considered the prohibition of interest, but the evolution has been different. [6]

In the worldwide diffusion of Islamic banks, two models of operation have been identified:

- pure Islamic bank: it is an autonomous bank whose activity is based on the principles of Islamic law with the exclusion of any other operation. This model of bank requires high technical and juridical skills to carry out valid and profitable investment activities. In recent years, there has been an increase in its numerical growth, but the average size is still limited compared to conventional banks. In the ranking of the first 100 world banks, there are no Islamic banks. Some studies have pointed out that more than half of the Islamic banks are, as far as assets are concerned, below the vital minimum identified in 500 million US dollars;
- Islamic windows in conventional banks: these are branches opened within conventional banks, exclusively dedicated to Islamic financial products. This system began in the early '80s and was established by Western banks to meet the needs of the Muslim clientele. In the management of the branches, the conventional banks acted only as intermediaries on behalf of Islamic banks. Subsequently, they began to offer Islamic products autonomously.

4. Islamic Banks versus Traditional Banks

Islamic banks are profit-making enterprises that develop the typical activities of funding and use of funds, together with other financial services. Their peculiarity consists in not paying/asking for interest and in leading

[5] HAMAURI, R., & MAURI, M., *Economia e finanza islamica*, Bologna: il Mulino, 2009.

[6] The Christian religion prohibited interest and usury in order to safeguard the poor, the weaker contracting party. However, this principle gradually faded over time in order to adhere to the needs of commercial activity. For Catholics, the prohibition of usury fell formally only in 1917, under Pope Benedict XV, with the publication of Codex Iuris Canonici.

financial activities according to the moral principle of risk/profit sharing with the clients. This definition sums up the main differences between the two banking systems very well.

First, Islamic financial institutions pursue objectives. They manage their activities based on the binding principles of the Koran. At the same time, Western banks operate without the obligation to follow precise religious dictates, even if, in the social and economic environment of reference, ethical principles of behaviour are increasingly referred to.

The fundamental aspect which differentiates the two systems lies in the payment of interest. As mentioned before, in the Islamic bank, this item, which constitutes the remunerative basis of the funding and use of the funds of conventional banks, is absent, because it is forbidden. The prohibition of interest has posed to the Islamic bank the question of how to replace the mechanism of the interest rate to make its operative structure profitable: the recourse to the principle of profit and loss sharing (PLS) has been the Islamic answer to this problem.

The Islamic bank does not profit from the difference between borrowing and lending rates, but participates in the profits deriving from the use of the funds. The depositors, in turn, participate in the distribution of the bank's profits based on a predetermined ratio. In this way, a sort of "society" is created between the Islamic bank and its depositors on the one hand, and the bank and its clients, users of the funds, on the other, who productively manage the depositors' funds.

This mechanism is profoundly different from the one used by conventional banks which, on the one hand, mainly carry out funding operations paying interest and, on the other, use the funds receiving interest.

From the Islamic logic of sharing the risk between the parties also derive the consequences that are reflected in the reliability of the clients: while conventional banks consider the creditworthiness and the eventual physical guarantees offered, Islamic banks appreciate, above all, elements such as the validity of the project and the managerial capacity.

The example shown in Table 1 is intended to clarify how the financial consequences for the bank, and the creditor client are dependent on the different approaches towards risk-sharing in the two banking systems.

In the case examined, the traditional bank requires an interest rate on the loan equal to 10%, while the Islamic bank applies a profit and loss sharing ratio of 50%.

The traditional bank makes a 10% profit on the loan regardless of the success of the project. The client only earns if the project pays more than 10%, i.e., the interest rate paid to the bank.

With the Islamic bank, instead, the bank and the client realise the same yield according to the profitability of the project: even if the return of the project results are low, the client will obtain a positive margin; in this case, with this mechanism, the client and the bank are both incentivised to achieve the success of the project because the more significant the yield of the project, the higher their rewards.

Additionally, Islamic banks include a body composed of members competent in finance and in Islamic moral rules which has the function of controlling and certifying, both preventively, the correct application of the Shariah in financial transactions. This is the Sharia Supervisory Board (SSB) whose judgements are binding and can limit the implementation and the use of new financial products and services.

The necessity of verifying the conformity of one's activity with the legislation in force also exists in Western banks. However, the duty to observe religious and moral principles creates greater complexity. Often, the Islamic banks must also turn to authoritative jurists and external committees to have a definitive opinion, with additional expense and waste of time. An interest is concentrated on the presence of the Sharia supervisory board. It is a body composed of few scholars of Islamic law, that certifies Sharia-compliant bank activities. It supports the shareholders' meeting, the board of directors and the top management and that, in some ways, appears very similar to the ethics committees which have spread in the Western economy following the boom of sustainable finance. The latter supervises regular banking activities so that they respect the rights of all stakeholders and minimises possible conflicts of interest. It often has consultative functions; it is mostly composed of internal members of the group but can make use of external professionals for the analysis of specific issues. The Sharia Board also has consultative functions, but above all, of audit and control. It has an independent nature. It can be considered, to all effects, the regent of the governance of the Islamic financial institution. It issues *fatwas* (sentences) on the launch of new products or operations and informs the public of what is to be considered *halal* or *haram*. All the financial institutions that offer Shariah-compliant products typically have a supervisory board called the Sharia board (or, as a minimum condition, a consultant) composed of experts in qualifications (these are the so-called religious experts). The Sharia board has the task of reviewing and approving the practices and activities of the bank to ensure they are permitted by Koranic law. Such skills, in the Islamic world, are a guarantee and increase the attractiveness on the part of the investors. The principles on which Islamic finance is based are subject to interpretation (there are four schools of thought in this regard). For instance, it often happens that the Sharia scholars, the *fiqh* experts, and Islamic jurisprudence, are not in tune, and what is lawful in one country may not be lawful in another. In this case, it is a question of interpreting not only the pillars of Islamic finance – such as the prohibition of interest, the prohibition of uncertainty, ethical investments, profit and loss sharing or asset backing – but also the way of considering the stakes which they believe to be an investment enterprise.

The IFSB (Islamic financial services board) has been instituted with the aim of standardisation, in support of the various Sharia boards. The IFSB issues regulations on the supervision, and the AAOIFI (accounting and auditing organisation for Islamic financial institutions) issues international standards on the accounting, auditing and corporate governance, and principles such as our IAS/IFRS accounting principles. Non-Islamic financial institutions can request a certification (a *fatwa*) to promote their products. It is an endorsement by an expert doctor of Islamic doctrine recognised within Islamic schools, as happened for the launch of the *Sukuk* by the company.

The "sharia scholars" who sit on the boards are not only guarantors of the correct functioning of the banking activity, but a point of reference and, therefore, an element of the defence of the reputation for the clientele. Around the world, various Sharia scholars often express strict judgments, the result of personal opinions and/or cultural influences. It is still being questioned whether these differences of interpretation are an obstacle or an asset to the Islamic economy. Surely the role of the board has acted as a protection against the crisis that in recent years has affected hundreds of financial institutions in the Western world.

The role of compliance insurers of every single financial choice made by the board can be well replicated in the Western economy by thinking of a body that ex-ante verifies that the service or product being launched is ethically oriented. Of course, the choices made by the board are not always well accepted by the management and often trigger internal clashes which, however, allow a vital barrier to be established against reputational downturns to which all institutional subjects are now subject.

5. Islamic Equity Crowdfunding

To comply with the Koran, Islamic finance requires socially responsible investments, with a real impact on the community; as has already been said, Sharia law prohibits interests on loans and speculation, but allows taxes applied to transfers and taxes in general, hence the inevitable similarity to crowdfunding and its participatory methods.

> Comparing traditional crowdfunding platforms to purely Islamic ones, it emerges that the difference is really minimal. In the first case, in fact, a

promoter presents a project, asking the community to support it in exchange for a reward, proportional to the financial subsidy. Participants are not investors, but rather contributors. The second makes use of the fatwā (a legal response issued by the Islamic authority) which imposes a ban on the application of interests, to which is added the concept of legality of the project: everything must be halal (i.e., allowed by the Sharia law). In other words, Islamic crowdfunding must avoid the promotion of prohibited substances and activities such as gambling, alcohol or the marketing of animal fat, but it is not just about wine, beer, ham or pork, as even make-up and clothing may contain haram (prohibited) components.

To be precise, there are four types of Sharia-compliant platforms:

1. Crowdfunding based on Islamic donation (donation-based crowdfunding): in the event of a donation, donors pay rather small amounts for a non-profit project or social development initiative, such as supporting a family with medical care or building a school in Africa or for a personal campaign, such as a person's treatment or medical bills.
2. Reward-based crowdfunding: donors contribute small amounts of money in exchange for a reward after the completion of the project. The reward is a product generated by the project itself.
3. Islamic equity-based crowdfunding: at this stage, investors provide large sums of money, so they become shareholders and share profits and losses.
4. The crowdfunding of Islamic debt (debt crowdfunding): the lenders grant a loan and expect the repayment of the capital and the distribution of the profit.

Islamic Finance is, ideally, an alternative way of financing based on ethical and socially responsible standards, which ensures fair distribution of benefits and obligations between all the parties in any financial transaction (Abdullah S., 1999). Crowdfunding carries these characteristics and provides the ground for new developments in the field, as it can use Islamic finance as an ethical and socially responsible tool to promote financing and development. Islamic finance and crowdfunding both conceptualise consumers as investors and can potentially provide investment opportunities with higher returns. Investors take an equity stake in the project and gain returns based on the principle of ensuring a fair distribution between shareholders and entrepreneurs. Sharī'a-compliant crowdfunding invests in *halal* socially responsible projects/products, shares the risks of the investment, and is characterised by the absence of an interest rate. The company takes equity stakes in the project, the model of product-based crowdfunding eliminates the issue of interest altogether (Ahlers, 2012). Regarding the certification of the Sharia-compliance of these platforms, the Religious Supervisory Board is the widely used component to ensure the Islamicity of Islamic banking at the private sector level.

Yomken is a product-based crowdfunding platform that opened in Egypt in October 2012. It is the first example of product-based crowdfunding and it defines itself as Sharia-friendly. Using the idea of crowdfunding, it wanted to develop a crowdfunding model suitable for Egypt and the Arab world. Wishing to have a social impact and promote solidarity in the context of Egypt after the Revolution, Yomken combined three different business models: crowdfunding, open innovation and Islamic finance. As new products are generally not financed by banks because their market demand is unknown, Yomken removes this risk by offering the new product through its platform in the pre-commercialisation phase. Yomken follows a two-fold process.

First, it links people who want technical solutions with people who have them, such as university students, researchers, specialists, or even companies, in order to make new products or improve the existing ones. Yomken partners with NGOs involve entrepreneurs, micro and SMEs, in order to locate small businesses facing technical challenges which require creativity and expertise, and link them with the wisdom of the crowd. Problem solvers are rewarded depending upon the case: they get a share of the benefits, a lump sum benefit, or an award from Yomken. On the site, users can post "challenges" and ideas for new innovations for free. The website creates a competitive environment amongst contributors in order to come up with the best solution.

Second, once the prototype is developed, a target number of buyers it set up according to its production costs, and the product is offered through Yomken's web-page on crowdfunding basis. If the target number of buyers is reached, the prototype is fundraised, produced, and delivered to them, showing that the market needs the product. In the event that the target funding amount is not collected, contributors retrieve their initial funding amount. That way Yomken removes the risk of innovations and assist new product ideas to become reality. To ensure that a product is delivered, Yomken finances the challenge temporarily until the crowdfunding phase is completed, "placing faith in these businesses before users do". This is a risk that the company is willing to take, as solutions might not reach the funding goal. The originality of product-based crowdfunding lies in the fact that in return, the investor does not receive interest but the product itself, which promotes the creation of new products and furthers innovation. Investors that pay for a product they wish to have can track the production process and see how their money is spent on the progress of the projects on a weekly basis. Transparency is a very important part of the project, and a direct link between the customer and the workshop owner is established from the beginning (Biancone, 2012). In order to understand their compatibility with Sharia, it is based on qualitative and quantitative criteria: the qualitative criteria relate to the type of industry in which companies cannot operate: this sector includes all activities not permitted (*haram*), namely: alcohol and pork products, pornography, tobacco, gambling, interest-bearing financial assets, weapons and defense, biology and animal genetics (cloning). The financial reports of companies are tested for amounts not exceeding certain thresholds and thresholds are different in the percentages and formulas among different global indices.

References

ABDULLAH, S., *Osmanlı medeniyeti tarihi*, Instanbul: 1999.

Ahlers, G.K., Cumming, D.J., Christina, G., & Denis, S., *Signalling in Equity Crowdfunding*, 2012.

BIANCONE, P.P., *Il bilancio della banca islamica e la rappresentazione dei principali contratti finanziari*, Milano: 2012, 1–184.

BIANCONE, P., *Islamic Finance Services and their Application to the Italian Financial System* in XVI Toulon-Verona Conference "Excellence in Services", Ljubljana (Slovenia): 2013, 85–98.

BIANCONE, P.P., *La banca islamica*, Vol. 2, Torino: 2017.

BIANCONE, P.P., & RADWAN, M., *Sharia Compliant "Possibility for Italian SMEs"*, in European Journal of Islamic Finance, 1, 2015.

BIANCONE, P.P., & RADWAN, M., *Sharia-Compliant Financing for Public Utility Infrastructure*, in Utilities Policy, 52, 2018, 88–94.

BIANCONE, P.P., & RADWAN, M., *Social Finance and Unconventional Financing Alternatives: An Overview*, in European Journal of Islamic Finance, 10, 2018.

BIANCONE, P.P., & RADWAN, M., *Social Finance and Financing Social Enterprises: An Islamic Finance Prospective*, in European Journal of Islamic Finance, 2019, 1–7.

BIANCONE, P., & MOHAMED RADWAN AHMED SALEM, M., *European Companies: Evaluation for Sharia Compliance "Opportunities and Challenges"*, in European Journal of Islamic Finance, 2016, 1–8.

BIANCONE, P., & MOHAMED RADWAN AHMED SALEM, M., *International Entrepreneurship from an Islamic (Sharia Compliant) Prospective "The Opportunities for Western Economies"*, in World Journal of Accounting, Finance and Engineering 1, 1, 2017.

BIANCONE, P., & SECINARO, S., *The Equity Crowdfunding Italy: A Model*

Sharia Compliant, in European Journal of Islamic Finance, 5, 2016, 1–10.

BIANCONE, P.P., & SHAKHATREH, M.Z., *Using Islamic Finance for Infrastructure projects in Non-Muslim Countries*, in European Journal of Islamic Finance, 2, 2015.

BIANCONE, P.P., & SHAKHATREH, M.Z., *Asset Life Sukuk to Fund Utility Companies*, in European Journal of Islamic Finance, 6, 2017.

BIANCONE, P., SECINARO, S., & BRESCIA, V., *Introduction of Islamic Finance in Brexit Time, Some Tips for the West*, in International Journal of Management Sciences And Business Research, 8, 2, 2019, 53–68.

Biancone, P., Shakatreh, M., & Mohamed Radwan Ahmed Salem, M., *Operational Risk Management Disclosure in Islamic Banks*, 2016.

EROL, C., & EL-BOLOUR, R., *Attitudes, Behaviour and Patronage Factors of Bank Customers towards Islamic Banks* in International Journal of Bank Marketing, 7, 6, 1989, 31–39.

HAMAURI, R., & MAURI, M., *Economia e finanza islamica*, Bologna: 2009.

HARON, S., & AZMI, N.W., *Islamic Finance Banking System*, Singapore: 2009.

ISRA, *Islamic Financial System, Principles & Operations*, Kuala Lumpur: 2013.

KETTELL, B., *Frequently asked Questions in Islamic Finance*, Chichester: 2010.

MOHAMED RADWAN AHMED SALEM, M., *Exploratory Step Towards Islamic Finance Adoption in Italy "An Empirical Analysis for Potential Users' Financial Behavior Towards Using Islamic Banking in Italy"*, 2017.

SADEGHI, V.J., & BIANCONE, P.P., *Shariah Compliant International Entrepreneurship: A Study of Islamic Finance in Europe*, in European Journal of Islamic Finance, 8, 2017.

SECINARO, S., *Equity Crowdfunding Sharia Compliant*, Vol. 1, Torino: 2017.

Chapter 8

MARKETING OF ISLAMIC BANKS

Cedomir Nestorovic

SUMMARY: 1. Introduction. – 2. The Marketing Environment for Islamic Banks. – 3. Marketing Concepts for Islamic Banks. – 3.1. STP for Islamic Banks. – 3.2. Ansoff's Matrix for Islamic Banks. – 3.3. Communication for Islamic Banks. – 3.4. Controversies. – 4. Conclusion. – References.

1. Introduction

In a free market with many competitors, marketing is a crucial function for companies that must differentiate their offer and serve their customers better than the competition. Islamic banks are no exception. They evolve in an environment where alternative offers exist in the form of conventional *and* Islamic products and services. Believing that Muslims will automatically prefer an Islamic offer, whatever the cost and characteristics of the product does not correspond to reality. Thus, Islamic banks, like any other company, must deploy all marketing efforts in order to win customers' trust and confidence. By Islamic banks we refer to "*pure players*", such as Dubai Islamic Bank, that function only according to Islamic principles, "*Islamic banking subsidiaries*", such as HSBC Amanah where the bank has parallel, segregated organisations for Islamic and conventional offers and "*Islamic windows*", where banks have a comprehensive set of products and services, including, but not only, Islamic products and services without separate organisations. Obeying to Islamic principles means that these banks will respect the following rules: no *riba* (interest rate), no speculation and gambling, no investment in *haram* (prohibited) activities, obligation of profit and loss sharing and obligation of tangible asset backing. Marketing definitions on their side have evolved over the time passing from focusing on one or several elements of the marketing mix (product, price, place, promotion) to customer-centric, value creation and social definitions of marketing. The latest definition from Kotler and Armstrong (2017) takes into account disruptions initiated by the digital age and customer engagement. The definition is as follows:

Marketing is the process by which companies engage customers, build strong customer relationship and create customer value in order to capture value from customers in return.[1]

How to engage customers will considerably depend on the environment in which Islamic banks operate. How they build customer relationship and create customer value will depend on strategies and tactics they will deploy. That is why we will divide the present paper in two parts: the first one dealing with the environment Islamic banks have to face, and the second one analysing concepts in marketing that can be useful for Islamic banks in engaging customers, especially through advertising.

2. The Marketing Environment for Islamic Banks

Islamic banks are part of the general market of Islamic products and services, where environment is the starting point for the assessment of the market potential (Nestorovic, 2016).[2] The *economic environment* gives the answer the question: do we have a market? This is a *sine qua non* question because without a market, there is no marketing. We will assume that there is a market expressed by increasing purchasing power and demography, in countries which are members of the Organization of Islamic Cooperation (57 members) but also in other countries where Muslims live in minority. The next environment is the *political legal environment* that answers the question: are there some political and legal barriers to the introduction of Islamic Banking? A political barrier can be boycotts that fall in two categories: official and non-official boycotts. Among the official boycotts, the boycott of Iran by the United States and some other countries does not permit Iranian Islamic banks to operate in these countries.[3] However, if Iranian banks cannot operate in Saudi Arabia, they can do it in nearby United Arab Emirates where Bank Melli Iran and Bank Sedarat Iran operate throughout the federation. When Saudi Arabia, Egypt, Bahrain and United Arab Emirates boycott Qatar, it means that the Qatar Islamic Bank cannot operate in these four countries. Boycotts can be unilateral when one

---

[1] PHILIP KOTLER, & GARY ARMSTRONG, *Principles of Marketing*, 17th edition, Pearson, 2017, 29.

[2] CEDOMIR NESTOROVIC, *Islamic Marketing: Understanding the Socio-Economic, Cultural, and Politico-Legal Environment*, Springer, 2016.

[3] For the US boycott of Iranian banks see the Press statement 'Sanctions on Iran's Financial Institutions' from October 8, 2020 on https://www.state.gov/sanctions-on-irans-financial-institutions while the EU and UN boycott on Iranian banks is tracked by the website Iran Watch on: www.iranwatch.org/sanctions.

country boycotts another one, for instance when India boycotts Pakistan and vice versa. The boycott between these two countries has been lifted in 2012 but the list of foreign banks in India does not show any Pakistani bank among the 45 foreign banks operating in that country and similarly, the list of foreign banks operating in Pakistan does not show any Indian bank.[4] A non-official boycott may come from NGOs, associations or individuals like George Clooney who launched a boycott of Brunei and its companies abroad because of the adoption of anti-LGBT laws.[5] This boycott had practically zero impact on Islamic finance from Brunei because the Bank Islam Brunei Darussalam does not have offices abroad except Singapore and Dubai. The legal environment is focusing on the status of Islamic finance in a given country. It can be compulsory, forbidden or authorised. Only Iran makes Islamic finance mandatory while Pakistan has introduced it as mandatory but does not observe it fully and Sudan has reversed its decision about mandatory Islamic finance in the country. The biggest Islamic countries such as Gulf countries, Egypt, Nigeria or Indonesia did not transform the entire financial system into an Islamic system. There is a coexistence between Islamic banks and conventional bank. As far as the prohibition of Islamic banking is concerned, it happened to be the case in series of Islamic countries such as Morocco, Tunisia, Algeria, Oman or Turkey but gradually all these countries have opened up even if for various reasons some of them do not accept the term Islamic banking. They prefer the term solidarity or participative banking instead. In other countries where there is a substantial Muslim population, such as the United States, the United Kingdom, Australia or Germany, Islamic banking is accepted. However, it is not the case in countries such as India or France, where for different reasons Islamic finance is still prohibited.

The third and most important environment for marketing is the *socio-cultural environment* because it answers a qualitative question: do potential customers want to buy Islamic banking products and services? The social environment puts the emphasis on society and the identification of the fundamental brick of the society. Is it the individual or the family? If the society is made of individuals, the bank has to target individuals in order to build awareness, explain why and how the Islamic offer is different from conventional finance and what is the advantage for the individual and the

---

[4] The list of licensed foreign banks is given by the State Bank of Pakistan on www.sbp.org.pk/ecib/members.htm and the Reserve Bank of India on https://m.rbi.org.in/scripts/bs_viewcontent.aspx?Id=3657.

[5] R. Sander, *George Clooney Will Continue Boycotting Brunei Hotels Over LGBTQ Death Penalty*, in Forbes (May 6, 2019).

society at large by adopting Islamic finance products and services. If the society is made of groups (ethnic groups, tribes, religious groups, political or philosophical groups), the bank will target groups of people instead of individuals. Sociologists and political leaders recognise that families are the building blocks of society.[6] Two types of family can exist: nuclear families and extended families. The nuclear family encompasses only two generations (parents and children) and only biological brothers and sisters form the same parents. Muslim countries can experience a high fertility rate (up to six or seven children per woman in some African countries) but in other countries like in the Middle East or Asia the total fertility rate tends to be close to two or three children per women.[7] The size of the family has implications on financial products because the savings that the family would like to put aside for the education of children, their marriage or inheritance will vary according to the number of people within the family. The extended family is composed of several generations and dozens or hundreds or relatives that believe they are part of the same family. The notion of extended family is widespread in some Muslim countries where the veneration of ancestors is still strong so people will refer to the same ancestor even if families have parted away. What is important from the family finance point of view is to assess the degree of solidarity between generations and siblings because the family can pool resources in order to compensate for a natural catastrophe or a wrong business decision. In that case having information about the purchasing power of the individual is not relevant. It is better to have information about the resources a family can put together for certain decisions such as opening a business or sending a member of the family to study abroad. Once the family has been defined, it is important to identify the most important member of the family, the person who takes decisions, especially financial decisions.[8] In the decision-making process, the most important person is the prescriber (the person who is taking the decision about the financial products), while the buyer is the person who

---

[6] The UN General Assembly's first formal recognition of the family unit's special status as the basic building block of civilised society came in 1989 when it passed resolution A/44/82 (1989) proclaiming 1994 as the first International Year of the Family. See www.nationsencyclopedia.com/United-Nations/Social-and-Humanitarian-Assistance-THE-FAMILY-SOCIETY-S-BUILDING-BLOCK.html#ixzz6djjcrFN0.

[7] For the size of Muslim families see Statista on www.statista.com/statistics/1090592/average-household-size-worldwide, and Pew Research Center: www.pewforum.org/2019/12/12/religion-and-living-arrangements-around-the-world.

[8] JIHNEE KIM, MICHAEL GUTTER, & TAYLOR SPRANGLER, *Review of Family Financial Decision Making: Suggestions for Future Research and Implications for Financial Education*, in Journal of Financial Counseling and Planning, 28, 2 (November 2017) 253–267.

actually puts money in a bank account, and the user is the end beneficiary of the whole process. In the case of a single-parent family, the parent is at the same time the prescriber, the buyer and the user. In the case of extended families and tribes the situation is more complex. The traditional Muslim family identifies the oldest couple as the decision maker. After them comes the son and the daughter-in law and after them comes the daughter of the oldest couple and the son-in law. It is clear that importance goes with age and male descendants. Family values are very much present in advertisements for Islamic banks. Kuwait Finance House for instance shows a father and a son together, while HSBC Amanah from Malaysia with a tagline *Islamic finance for life* talks about the investment for a newlywed couple. On the other side, Jordan Dubai Islamic Bank shows parents and children with the mother signing the acceptance to the bank account, pointing out a great involvement of women in modern Muslim families. Tradition is well present, but the situation can be more complex.[9] In an extended family, people do not necessarily live together, some members can be in Pakistan and others in the UK or in the United States. Let's imagine that the oldest couple lives in Pakistan and their sons live in the UK. The probability that the oldest couple in Pakistan is aware about all financial options that exist in the UK is very low. In that case, the children not only will decide about their own options, but they can in turn influence their parents into investing in some options they have identified as best, such as the cryptocurrency investments.

The next element is culture. There are hundreds of definitions of culture. We will use the definition coming from Geert Hofstede, one of the most influential authors in intercultural management and marketing. He used to say that culture is the software of mind[10] and the main question is how culture is established and transmitted from one generation to the other, especially when it comes to Islamic finance and what is the role of marketing in that. For the traditional channel of transmission of culture (family and religion), Islamic finance will have very few possibilities to intervene. Concepts of Islamic finance are not very well known by Muslims worldwide, the probability that people will discuss about them in family circles is rather low. As for religion, in mosques and in madrassahs they will not talk about Islamic finance either. The other two channels (education and mass

---

[9] MUSAWAH, *Who provides? Who cares? Changing Dynamics in Muslim Families*, *Musawah*, 2018, on www.musawah.org/wp-content/uploads/2018/11/WhoProvides Who Cares_En.pdf.

[10] GEERT HOFSTEDE, GERT VAN HOFSTEDE, & MICHAEL MINKOV, *Cultures and Organizations: Software of the Mind*, 3rd edition, Mc-Graw Hill Education, 2014.

media) are much more suitable for the marketing of Islamic banks. In education first, it is possible to organise workshops, demonstrations and discussions about how Islamic banks participate in social development and social justice. As for mass media, this is the main area where marketing can be developed fully with sponsorships and advertising. Since mass media are now mostly private, it is possible that Islamic banks own some of media outlets and in that case, there are many paths how to promote a certain brand. Social media open new venues for Islamic banks because it is possible to sponsor preachers, influencers, celebrities of any kind in order to make the brand visible. There are 57 Islamic countries in the world, on all continents, and the diversity among them is great. How to compare them and how to develop a unique offer for the Ummah (the whole Muslim community) is a serious challenge for Islamic banks. Cultural comparison among countries is also done by Geert Hofstede through his interactive website called *Hofstede Insights.*[11] Hofstede identified cultural dimensions like individualism vs collectivism, power distance, masculine vs feminine values, uncertainty avoidance, short vs long term orientation and indulgence and gives a possibility to look at the score and comparison between countries. For instance, the individualism vs collectivism dimension might refer to the reason why people chose an Islamic bank over a conventional one. Is the person looking for his/her direct benefit and profit, or is the person looking for social benefit by taking the services of an Islamic bank? In the case of power distance, it is interesting to find out if religious authorities have influence on banking decisions. In some countries there is still a monarchy where the King might have an influence on citizens. A highly regarded imam, preacher or rector of a famous university like Al-Azhar in Cairo can have influence on believers. The long-term approach is intimately linked to Islamic finance because of its emphasis on long-term benefits for the society rather than short-term profits. However, since many Islamic countries experience conflicts or tensions, it is very hard to think long-term, so the short-term can be sought by some customers. Finally, societies with a high indulgence index tend to profit from the accumulation of wealth which is in contrast with Islam that does not encourage accumulation of unproductive wealth and luxury items. On the contrary, what Islam looks for is distribution of wealth either through *zakat* or voluntary gifts like the *sadaqah* or food distribution during Ramadan. The above-mentioned website gives the possibility to compare up to four countries at the same time with about 20 Islamic countries covered. For some dimensions results are rather similar such as for Power Distance Index from a country to an-

[11] www.hofstede-insights.com

other, while for the others, differences are big between Islamic countries.

Islamic banks will look at these dimensions of culture especially when they want to export a concept from one country to the other. There are two problems for Islamic banks from the religious point of view. The first one is linked to the schools of *fiqh* or *madhabs* (schools of Islamic jurisprudence) that may have different approaches to Islamic finance. What can be used in Malaysia that practices the Shafii school of thought approves might not be accepted in Saudi Arabia that follows the Hanbali school. Islamic banks try to resolve this through the Shariah Supervisory Board where they appoint scholars who are experts in different schools of thought, who try to reach a consensus. The second problem is that in countries where Muslims live in a minority, there might be Muslims originating from different countries, with again different schools of thought. Here the situation is more complex because secular countries do not want to interfere in religious affairs and they will not try to harmonise the situation. It will be up to Muslims themselves to find out what kind of rules one Islamic bank follows and if they are willing to accept these rules.

3. Marketing Concepts for Islamic Banks

Islamic banks can use any of the marketing concepts, but two of them seem to be particularly interesting. The first one is the STP approach that refers to Segmentation, Targeting and Positioning and the second one is Ansoff's matrix.

3.1. STP for Islamic Banks

In STP, segmentation is very important, and the bank must identify the segmentation criteria first. [12] Criteria can be the usual criteria like age, gender, income, academic background, but also specific like religious consciousness and willingness to accept only Islamic finance and nothing else. There is a huge discussion among Islamic finance practitioners about the segment Islamic banking should serve. Is the Islamic bank for Muslims only or for everyone? Once the criteria for segmentation have been decided, the segments will be identified and assessed according to their economic potential, the financial literacy or location. If for instance in Indonesia, the

[12] See S.C. JAIN, *Marketing, Planning and Strategy*, South-Western Publishing Co, 1993 and PHILIP KOTLER, *Marketing Management Analysis, Planning, Implementation, and Control*, Prentice Hall International, 1997.

Muslim population does not have a high purchasing power compared to the Chinese Indonesian population and at the same time does not have the awareness and appetite for Islamic finance, it will be hard for Islamic banking to grow. And this is what is happening. In a country where Muslims represent more than 90% of total population, Islamic finance represents about 4–5% of total assets.[13] The second step in STP is to identify the bank's goal in targeting a specific segment. It can be the highest turnover possible. In that case the bank is not interested in profits. Only turnover and market shares are important. With that goal in mind, countries with big populations like Pakistan, Bangladesh or Indonesia might be the most suitable targets. If the goal on the contrary is to make profits, countries with the highest purchasing power could be the most interesting targets, namely Gulf countries but also the Muslim population living in Western countries. The Turkish-origin population that lives in Germany has a much higher purchasing power than the Turkish population in Turkey. That is why the joint venture Kuveyt Turk (Kuwait Finance House) operates five branches in Germany and no branch in Italy or Spain where people of Turkish origin are not numerous. The United Kingdom has the highest number of Islamic banks in Europe and these banks mainly target the population coming from the Indian subcontinent. Geographical criteria aside, the target can be early adopters first, people who are the first to adopt Islamic finance. This way, the bank does not look for turnover or profits, it will look for the evangelisation of the concept by focusing on awareness and acceptability. Traditionally, celebrity endorsements were used to target early adopters, but today with social media it can be through influencers and YouTubers. The choice is not necessarily a binary choice. Islamic banks can pursue different segments at the same time. It can have one offer for highest turnover and another offer for profits. That is what the biggest Islamic banks do: some products are for the masses while wealth management is reserved for the higher income bracket. Practically all Islamic banks have a wealth management or private banking division in order to cater to the upper market segment but very few have set up a proper division with a specific name like Dubai Islamic Bank with Aayan Exclusive Banking. The last step in STP is positioning. If the Islamic bank addresses only Muslims, in that case the Islamic bank will consider that its market universe and playground is composed of other Islamic banks only, even if the consumer has the possibility to see conventional banks too. If the Islamic bank con-

---

[13] BEELIN ANG, *Indonesia makes progress in Islamic finance*, in IPE Magazine (November 2020) available on www.ipe.com/indonesia-makes-progress-in-islamic-finance/10003500.article.

siders that it addresses everyone, in that case the perimeter will include all kinds of banks, not only Islamic banks. Some banks have stated clearly that they address only Muslims, while others on the contrary want to address everyone. Finally, the bank must decide if it will be positioned high, medium or low. This decision can be done on a relative base in comparison with competitors but it can also be done on an absolute basis, where the Islamic bank decides to go only for the upper market or for the low market; for instance, when the bank has been set up in order to deal with the saving accounts for the Hajj as it was the case with the Bank Islam, founded by Tabung Haji in Malaysia. The first Islamic financial institution was set up in Egypt under the name *Meet Ghamr Bank* in 1963 and it was a savings bank modelled after the German savings banks.[14] It is interesting to note the bank was looking for the lowest part of the population with three types of accounts: a deposit account with very small amounts and no maximum, another one with a maximum deposit cap and a third, *zakat* account with social services.

3.2. Ansoff's Matrix for Islamic Banks

The second concept largely used in marketing is the Ansoff's Matrix. H. Igor Ansoff (1918–2002) is most famous for his Product-Market Growth Matrix, a tool he created to plot generic strategies for growing a business.[15]

	Existing products	New products
Existing markets	Market penetration	Product development
New markets	Market development	Diversification

Market penetration is the name given to a growth strategy where the business focuses on selling existing products into existing markets. With this strategy, the Islamic bank wants to capitalise on the existing customer in the existing market. It does not look for new customers and does not want to launch new products. It only wants the existing customer to consume more of the existing product. For instance, if the customer usually pays for groceries in a supermarket with a debit card and in cash in a con-

[14] ZAYNEB HAFSA ORHAN, *Mit Ghamr Savings Bank: A Role Model or an Irreplicable Utopia?*, in The Journal of Humanity and Society, 8, 2 (June 2018), 85–102.

[15] IGOR H. ANSOFF, *A Model for Diversification*, in Management Science, 4, 4, July 1958, 392–414.

venience store, the Islamic bank would like the customer to use its debit card everywhere. Another option is when the customer uses the Islamic bank account in order to pay for *zakat* and social activities and a conventional bank account for savings. The Islamic bank would like that the customer uses the Islamic bank for both. There is much room for growth in Islamic countries because the highest Islamic banks' asset share is in Saudi Arabia (79%) while in many other countries it is under 50% like in Pakistan or in Oman where Islamic banks assets represent 15–16% while in Indonesia it is around 5%. The objective of Islamic banks will be to push existing customers to use more of their products in everyday life. That is why they put the emphasis on saving and deposit accounts and debit cards. The MCB Islamic Bank from Pakistan advertises the debit card with the following message: *Presenting MCG Islamic Bank UnionPay Gold Debit Card to cover all your needs, every time, everywhere* while the Faisal Bank, also from Pakistan, entices customers to use its debit card even for small amounts and partners with the fast-food chain KFC with special offers like free Pepsi when they use the Faysal Islamic UnionPay Debit Card.

As far as *market development* is concerned, it is used when the business seeks growth to sell its existing products into new markets. Market development is much riskier than market penetration since the firm expands into a new market. Many Islamic banks that started their own markets are now going to other Islamic countries with their expertise and reputation. When the Dubai Islamic Bank entered the Pakistani market, it insisted both that it is the first ever Islamic Bank in the world on one side and its expertise and excellence on the other side. Dubai Islamic Bank is now present in countries such as Bosnia, Indonesia and Sudan while Kuwait Finance House is present in Malaysia, Saudi Arabia, Bahrain, Turkey. Al Baraka Group from Bahrain has probably the largest footprint in Islamic countries since it is present in Jordan, Egypt, Tunisia, Sudan, Bahrain, Turkey, Algeria, Lebanon, Syria, Indonesia, Pakistan and Libya. The competition and the environment are not the same everywhere, so Islamic banks reconsider their marketing strategies and tactics, such as Kuwait Finance House targeting the Turkish population in Germany from their Turkic subsidiary or the Bank Chaabi, part of the Banque Populaire from Morocco that launched a specific product in France called Chaabi Harmonis, presenting itself as the only bank in France that follows ethical and Islamic principles. The demand coming from Western countries where Muslims represent a minority but where they hold an important purchasing power pushes Islamic Banks to develop their presence abroad, but it is much more difficult than in Maghrib countries which have recently opened their markets to Islamic finance and where the concept of Islamic finance will be easier to implement.

Product development in Ansoff's matrix is used when the firm aims to introduce new products into existing markets. The company wants to capitalise on existing customers and launch new products for them. It counts on the loyalty of existing customers who want to continue with the existing company. There are constant innovations in Islamic finance when Islamic banks want to mimic conventional banks and their products, so they do not hesitate to launch new products that can be borderline in Shariah acceptance. Many sophisticated, structured products are launched such as futures contracts or structured funds without tangible asset backing that can be dubious. On the other side, the success of *sukuks* is something that is completely legitimate as well as new options for the *waqf* and *zakat* payments. The financing of mosques in Singapore can be done through *waqf* vouchers for as little as SGD 100 participation, a practice that does not exist in many other countries. The concept of *waqf* is as old as Islam is. It consists in investments in tangible assets for the common good such as hospitals, mosques, schools etc. Cash *waqf*, which permit people to invest in commercial activities and returns, used for social purposes, were used mainly during the Ottoman Empire and then faded away. There is currently a revival of cash *waqf* in the Middle East and Malaysia and Singapore.[16] Islamic Real Estate Investment Trust schemes in Malaysia and Singapore such as Sabana REIT in Singapore or Al-Aqar Healthcare REIT in Malaysia are attracting attention of Islamic banks.[17] Pos Malaysia (Post Office) launched a pawn broking operation under the name Ar Rahnu in 2012 even though pawn shops have problematic status when it comes to Shariah screening because of the interest rate that is integral in the concept of pawn shops. In all these cases, innovation is on the way, either in terms of products or process with internet banking, mobile banking, voice and face recognition (as Al Baraka group does in Turkey with its smart banking).

Diversification is used when the business takes an initiative outside its core competencies with new products in a new market. This is the riskiest of the four strategies known as the "suicide cell". Well done, it can generate high returns. Islamic banks are not known for entering diversification. However, some cases exist. A few years back, Tabung Haji, the parent company of Bank Islam Malaysia, launched a *halal* beverage brand called TaHa. Tabung Haji had never been in the food and beverage business be-

---

[16] See the website IslamicMarkets and its section on cash *waqfs* on: https://islamicmarkets.com/education/cash-waqf and MOHAMMAD MAHBUBI ALI, *Unleashing the Potential of Cash Waqf*, in The New Straits Times (June 9, 2017).

[17] See MARSILA MHD RUSLAN, *The Financial Performance of Islamic Real Estate Investment Trusts (REITs) in Malaysia*, in Asian Academy of Management Journal of Accounting and Finance, 15, 1 (August 2019), 191–220.

fore, and it gave up after a few years. Purchases of football clubs can be seen as diversification, but only indirectly, since there are no Islamic banks owning them. Having companies, even sovereign ones, becoming sponsors of sports clubs is extremely common. Having individuals, private investment funds and companies buying out sports clubs is also common. What is not common is that sovereigns from another country buy out sports clubs, which is the case of PSG and Manchester United. Manchester United is owned by Abu Dhabi United Group for Development and Investment, a private equity company owned by Sheikh Mansour bin Zayed Al Nahyan, a member of the Abu Dhabi Royal Family. Sheikh Mansour does not manage any Islamic bank, but he sits as the Chairman of the Emirates Investment Authority and many other public and private institutions in Abu Dhabi, so Islamic finance is not far away. The other case is Paris Saint Germain, owned by the Qatar Investment Authority, the sovereign fund of Qatar. Among the different companies QIA is owner of, or has a significant stake in, are Qatar Islamic Bank and Al Rayan Bank established in the UK as the successor of Islamic Bank of Britain, the first UK Islamic bank.

3.3. Communication for Islamic Banks

Communication is always attentive to the target segment. Some Islamic banks want to address only Muslims because they believe that non-Muslims will not be interested in Islamic finance or because there are not many non-Muslims in their country. Looking at the experience in Malaysia, Kamarulzaman and Madun (2013) point out that Islamic organisations dealing with *zakat* and pilgrimage funds will automatically be clients of Islamic banks. They represent a captive market for Islamic banks, so the banks do not need to communicate very much to attract them.[18] The situation is completely different when it comes to individual customers, because they have a choice between Islamic and conventional products. The review by Alam and Seifzadeh (2020)[19] reveals that marketing topics for Islamic financial services found in literature mostly relate to consumer behaviour and new products or service adoption issues while communication is usually missed out except in the paper by Schottmann (2014) who analysed the print advertisements and customer websites of Islamic banks in Malaysia. Schott-

---

[18] YUSNIZA KAMARULZAMAN, & AZIAN MADUN, *Marketing Islamic Banking Products: Malaysian Perspective*, in Business Strategy Series, 14, 2-3 (March 2016), 60–66, 63.

[19] INTEKHAB ALAM, & POUYA SEIFZADEH, *Marketing Islamic Financial Services: A Review, Critique and Agenda for Further Research*, in Journal of Risk and Financial Management, 13, 12 (January 2020), 1–20.

mann noted an evolution of communication strategies of Islamic banks in Malaysia, passing from the emphasis on the religious obligations for Muslims to save and invest in shariah compliant products in the 1980s to the emphasis on economic benefit of investing in Islamic banks in the 1990s and onwards.[20] The religious duty according to his research is not a salient element for Islamic banks. One reason for that is that Malaysian Islamic banks also attract a significant number of non-Muslims, which is not necessarily the case in the Middle East/North Africa region where non-Muslims do not represent a considerable part of the population. Islamic banks will therefore use a combination of religious duties and economic benefit when they communicate, depending on the situation country per country. When it comes to religious duties, the communication will be based on enhancing Islamic values, family values and traditions. Their communication is mainly based on website communication and print advertisements.[21] Islamic banks seem to follow the hadith about the 'lenient businessman':

> May Allah have mercy on a man who is lenient when selling, buying, and seeking repayment.[22]

The term lenient can be replaced by tolerant, merciful, magnanimous. In all cases it would mean that the Islamic bank must have a comprehensive engagement with the client, beyond contractual obligations, and this engagement is based on ethics and Islamic values. Thus, the values and ethical statements will be prominently present in their advertisings as demonstrated in the following examples. NBF Islamic from Fujairah will insist on Islamic values under the motto *Modern banking inspired by traditional values.* In its mission statement the bank says:

> You lead a modern lifestyle, but you live by age-old traditions. At NBF Islamic, our clients trust us to bring them the benefits and convenience of modern banking practices that they know are grounded in time-honoured Islamic values. As a progressive bank, we're forward thinking, but our integrity comes first.

The term trust appears to be an important element in choosing the bank. Habib Metro from Pakistan presents the bank the following way:

---

[20] SVEN ALEXANDER SCHOTTMANN, *From Duty to Choice: Marketing Islamic Banking in Malaysia*, in South East Asia Research, 22, 1 (March 2014), 57–72.

[21] All the advertisements quoted can be found on www.islamicadsnetwork.net under the section Islamic finance, *waqf* and *zakat*.

[22] Hadith quoted by Al Bukhari, available on https://sunnah.com/bukhari:2076.

> The determination based on faith and trust, Habib Metro Islamic Banking offer Shariah compliant investments.

As for ADCB Islamic Banking from Abu Dhabi they also put the emphasis on Islamic values with a series of statements like the following ones: *You live with purpose. Why not bank with one?* or *Not all wealth can be measured in dirhams and fils.*

The institutional advertising in enhancing Islamic values will insist on the core elements of Islamic finance on one side and pillars of Islam on the other. As far the tenets of Islamic finance are concerned, the most important one is *riba* (interest rate). Banks will definitely say that their accounts are *riba* free as the National Bank of Pakistan says in its advertisements "you are invited to invest in your *Riba*-free Aitemaad Investment Account" and the Sindh Bank Islamic branches and windows list the different products they have in store: *Ijara*, *Murabaha* and Diminishing *Musharaka*. The Dubai Islamic Bank in its advertisement about *Halal returns* does not talk about *riba* but the term *halal* seems to replace it:

> Dubai Islamic Fixed Deposit Account offers the ideal mix of long and short term benefits to depositors seeking attractive and halal returns on their savings. With a history of high payoff, the Dubai Islamic Fixed Deposit Account is an excellent investment vehicle for depositors with excess funds.

The return on deposits is called *halal* because the bank cannot promise a fixed return on deposits. The return will depend on the performance of the bank. However, the bank promotes its track record and there is no reason to doubt a similar performance in the future. The pillars of Islam are very much used in the advertising of Islamic banks. The second pillar, which is *Salat* (prayer), is heavily present with pictures of the most beautiful mosques in advertising of the Dubai Islamic Bank that also runs a hashtag *Friday Blessing* with a verse from the Qur'an prominently displayed on the screen. The mosques are also present on advertisements from Habib Metro Bank while the Syria International Islamic Bank shows prayer beads. Zakat as the third pillar of Islam will be presented by Zakat Collection Organizations such as Zakat SG, part of Majlis Ugama Islam Singapura (MUIS) from Singapore or Beit al Khair Society in Dubai and many banks will propose a *zakat* calculator in order to help believers and clients to calculate the amount of *zakat* they have to pay. The fourth pillar (*Sawm*) will obviously be solicited during Ramadan when banks usually greet clients and believers with Eid Mubarak (or Hari Raya as the traditional greeting goes on in Malaysia) and propose them a specific donation (Qurban or Sadaqah) during that period. Ramadan is the ideal time for buying new household items, including cars. That is why all Islamic banks propose special offers for the financing of car purchase. Not only do they stress the fact that their loan has a 0% interest rate, but they also organise competitions or donations with different prizes such as the competition by Alizz Islamic Bank from Oman offering cash prizes and a special repayment scheme *Buy now, Pay later*. Finally, the last pillar of Islam is the Hajj package offered by the Dubai Islamic Bank (with Qurban or without Qurban), United Bank of Egypt or Emaan Islamic Banking, part of Silk Bank in Pakistan.

3.4. Controversies

Not everything is perfect in the advertising world. Controversies can also be raised and here are few of them. The Bank Muamalat Indonesia opened a branch in Malaysia in 2009 with the tagline on the advertisements: *First Purely Sharia*. This might be strange because it implies that other Islamic banks are not purely sharia. Can a bank be 60% sharia or 80% sharia and what does that mean? On the other side, the bank was founded by the Council of Ulema in Indonesia (MUI) back in 1991 but Islamic banks in the Middle East already existed at that time. Malaysian banks have been the first in the region to launch an Islamic offer with Bank Islam Malaysia Berhad (BIMB) founded in 1983 and in 2009 when Bank Muamalat Indonesia opened a branch in Malaysia, there were other Islamic banks in the country. It is difficult therefore to claim that Muamalat Indonesia is the *First Purely Shariah*.

Another controversy relates to the possibility or not that an Islamic bank can celebrate or send greetings for holidays that are not Islamic, for instance during Christmas.[23] Iranian banks do this. For instance, Ayandeh bank published, in 2019, a full-page ad with a decorated Christmas tree and the inscription *Merry Christmas*. The same year the Export Development Bank of Iran had a Christmas tree with the following mention: *Congratulation on the Birth Anniversary of Jesus Christ to Monotheists in the World*, while Bank Mellat was even more complete with this greeting: *Congratulations on the Birth Anniversary of Jesus Christ and New Christian year (2019) to all Christian Fellow Countrymen*. In some countries there is a controversy about knowing if Muslims can send greetings for non-Muslim holidays like Christmas, Diwali or Vesak, but it seems that this is not a problem in Iran or in Indonesia.

Other controversies can happen when sensitivities within the Islamic

---

[23] Muslims Forbidden from Extending Xmas Greetings, says PAS Youth, *The Malaysian Insight* (December 24, 2018).

world are not taken into account. This happened to Jordan Dubai Islamic Bank and Al-Madinah Advertising Agency (Publicis) when they launched an advertisement in Jordan in 2010. The ad was quickly removed, and statements released by the bank which blamed the agency Al-Madinah which in return admitted the mistake. The cause of this controversy was a single phrase on an ornament inside a mosque that was shown on the ad. The intention of the message, according to the statement, was to connect quality with Arabic calligraphy, but the sentence included the phrase (علي وي الله) which is related exclusively to the Shiite Muslims in a country where most of the population is Sunni, thus raising questions in the local media about the bank's relationships to Shiites.[24]

A final example of a controversy comes from the Dubai Islamic Bank which featured in one of its *Monday Motivation* series a quote from a famous Mufti, Ismail Menk. The problem is that the same Mufti Menk is banned in Denmark and Singapore because of his extremist views. This proves that when banks want to use Islamic values in their advertising campaigns, it must be done with extreme caution.

4. Conclusion

Islamic banks operate in a competitive landscape. Like any other company, they must use marketing strategies in order to attract customers. These strategies are the same for Islamic and conventional banks – there is no fifth P in the marketing-mix which will be specific for Islamic products and services. What will be different is the environment in which they operate and the range of communication messages they can use. The environment is challenging because of the economic, political, legal, social and cultural diversity of Islamic countries, members of the OIC and other countries where Muslims live in a minority. It is impossible to have the same offer from one country to the other because of this diversity. If the offer is different, so should the communication be. The communication will first identify the target (the person who decides about financial matters) and which cell of Ansoff's matrix the Islamic bank will focus on and this may differ from one country to another. The message is the most visible part of communication. Islamic banks generally opt for the safe approach by enhancing Islamic values in advertisements, but it can happen that they also engage in borderline advertisements with contrasting outcomes. Taking a risk is a necessity because of the competition, but not every risk is worth taking it.

---

[24] The advertisement is available on https://joads.wordpress.com/tag/publicis.

References

Books

HOFSTEDE, G., HOFSTEDE, G.V., & MINKOV, M., *Cultures and Organizations: Software of the Mind*, 3rd edition, McGraw Hill Education, 2014.

JAIN, S.C., *Marketing, Planning and Strategy*, South-Western Publishing Co., 1993.

KOTLER, P., *Marketing Management Analysis, Planning, Implementation, and Control*. Prentice Hall International, 1997.

KOTLER, P., & ARMSTRONG, G., *Principles of Marketing*, 17th edition, Pearson, 2017.

NESTOROVIC, C., *Islamic Marketing: Understanding the Socio-Economic, Cultural, and Politico-Legal Environment*, Springer, 2016.

Articles

ALAM, I., & SEIFZADEH, P., *Marketing Islamic Financial services: A Review, Critique and Agenda for Further Research*, in Journal of Risk and Financial Management, 13, 12 (January 2020), 1–20.

ALI, M.M., *Unleashing the Potential of Cash Waqf*, in The New Straits Times, (June 9, 2017).

ANG, B., *Indonesia Makes Progress in Islamic Finance*, in IPE Magazine, (November 2020).

ANSOFF, I.H., *A Model for Diversification*, in Management Science, 4, 4 (July 1958), 392–414.

KAMARULZAMAN, Y., & MADUN, A., *Marketing Islamic Banking Products: Malaysian Perspective*, in Business Strategy Series, 14, 2-3 (March 2013), 60–66.

KIM, J., GUTTER, M., & SPRANGLER, T., *Review of Family Financial Decision Making: Suggestions for Future Research and Implications for Financial Education*, in Journal of Financial Counseling and Planning, 28, 2 (November 2017), 253–267.

Muslims Forbidden from Extending Xmas Greetings, says PAS Youth, in The Malaysian Insight, (December 24, 2018).

ORHAN, Z.H., *Mit Ghamr Savings Bank: A Role Model or an Irreplicable Utopia?* in The Journal of Humanity and Society, 8, 2 (June 2018), 85–102.

RUSLAN, S.M.M., *The Financial Performance of Islamic Real Estate Invest-*

ment Trusts (REITs) in Malaysia, in Asian Academy of Management Journal of Accounting and Finance, 15, 1 (August 2019), 191–220.
SANDER, R., *George Clooney Will Continue Boycotting Brunei Hotels Over LGBTQ Death Penalty*, in Forbes (May 6, 2019).
SCHOTTMANN, S.A., *From Duty to Choice: Marketing Islamic Banking in Malaysia*, in South East Asia Research, 22, 1 (March 2014), 57–72.

Chapter 9

ISLAMIC FINANCE TO ENHANCE BUSINESS OPPORTUNITIES:

PRIVATE INVESTMENT

Michael J.T. McMillen

SUMMARY: 1. Introduction. – 2. Considerations at Inception. – 3. *Murabaha*. – 4. Lease (*Ijara*) in Real Estate Investments. – 5. Lease (*Ijara*) in Private Equity. – 6. Opportunities. – References.

1. Introduction

Conceptions of the practice of Islamic finance tend to be associated primarily with Muslims and countries with predominantly Muslim populations.[1] Approximately 30% of the world's population is Muslim and is largely concentrated in countries in the Middle East, Southeast Asia, South Asia, and Africa. Many of those countries incorporate principles of Islamic Shari'ah into their secular law to some extent and are referred to as "Shari'ah-Incorporated Jurisdictions". More importantly, the legal, regulatory, financial, economic, tax, and socio-cultural institutions within these countries take cognisance of the Shari'ah, often as being dominant.

This chapter focuses on the potential of Islamic finance to enhance private investment business opportunities in, principally, countries that do not incorporate the principles of Islamic Shari'ah into the secular law and do not afford Shari'ah principles dominance in legal, regulatory, financial, economic, tax, and socio-cultural institutions and practices. These are referred to as "Secular Jurisdictions" and include countries in Europe and North America. Secular Jurisdictions permit Shari'ah-based institutions and practices, including commercial and financial transactions, to the extent it does not conflict with dominant institutions and practices.

This chapter will consider two frequently used Islamic finance contracts. Both are sale contracts. They are the *murabaha* or cost-plus sale or sale at a mark-up; and the lease (*ijara*). The context is financings which could use interest-based loans as an alternative. The lease is considered in

[1] Islamic finance is comprised of four overlapping areas of activity: banking; finance; investment; and insurance.

two types of investment transactions: real estate and private equity.[2] In most Secular Jurisdictions, these types present significant private investment opportunities. Others amenable to lease financings relate to equipment (including aircraft, railcars, medical, industrial, and other equipment) and projects (including electricity, mining, petrochemical, and industrial projects). The structural discussions are indicative, not comprehensive. The intention is to indicate the types of issues and structural considerations encountered when attempting to realise upon business opportunities using Islamic finance structures.[3]

2. Considerations at Inception

Shariʿah principles and requirements are the same for transactions in both Secular or Shariʿah-Incorporated Jurisdictions. As are the basic contractual structures. There are differences in the institutional parameters, such as tax, legal, and regulatory regimes, and thus in transactional structures.[4] As a generalisation, tax, legal, and regulatory regimes in Secular Jurisdictions are based on interest concepts. A few examples are indicative. Interest income is taxed. Interest payments are deductible expenses. Principal repayments on a loan are not taxed. Rental income is taxed. The entire amount of a rent payment is usually deductible against income for tax determinations. Whether a financing transaction is acceptable for bank regulatory purposes often depends upon its classification as a loan. Whether a transaction constitutes a loan afforded the benefits and protections of the tax, legal, and regulatory regimes is often determined by whether a market rate of interest is charged. The examples are myriad. In short, interest principles are at the core of dominant institutions and practices in Secular Jurisdictions.[5]

[2] Chapter 10 considers capital markets transactions, focusing on equity investing and *sukuk* (inaccurately called Islamic bonds; more accurately thought of as securitisations). The lease is a fundamental structure underlying *sukuk*, especially international issuances.

[3] For more detailed treatment of the contracts and structures discussed in this chapter see MICHAEL J.T. MCMILLEN, *Islamic Finance and the Shariah: The Dow Jones Fatwa and Permissible Variance as Studies in Letheanism and Legal Change* (2013) ("McMillen 2013"), with citations and treatment of related matters, such as the composition and functioning of Shariah boards, which are discussed at 125–153.

[4] In addition, under applicable international law and treaties, the Shariʿah is not accepted as a law that may govern contracts in most Secular Jurisdictions. The law of a country must be chosen to govern contracts.

[5] The leading cases on the Shariah as governing law in Secular Jurisdictions are *Shamil Bank of Bahrain v. Beximco Pharmaceuticals Ltd and others*, [2004] EWCA CIV

An interest-based systemic orientation is usually not preclusive of, or even significantly disruptive of, Shari'ah-compliant arrangements. An important consideration in assessing the use of Shari'ah-compliant arrangements in a Secular Jurisdiction is the extent to which the tax regime (for example) is based on economic substance, rather than form. The implementation of Shari'ah-compliant transactional arrangements is easiest in jurisdictions employing a substance-over-form perspective. Interpretation of the Shari'ah is itself a matter of substance over form, although it is frequently not presented in that manner in the popular press. [6]

In considering Islamic finance in Secular Jurisdictions, it is constructive to shed preconceptions and adopt the view that the commonalities between contracts and structures used in Islamic finance and those used in interest-based finance far exceed the differences. The lease is a good example, especially because of its prominence in Islamic finance. There are relatively few differences between secular and Shari'ah-compliant financing leases. The differences are important, and must be accommodated, but they are minimal.

Two other aspects of Islamic finance are informative. Islamic investing is ethical investing and Islamic finance is ethical finance. Comparison of the investment parameters and principles of ethical investment funds with Shari'ah-compliant funds reveal few differences. The principal differences relate to Shari'ah prohibitions on (a) interest-based activities and (b) activities involving the production or distribution of alcohol or pork for human consumption. [7] Second, Islamic finance is "structured finance". Cash flows and collateral security arrangements are structured for transactional purposes. The reference is not to derivative financial instruments, which are largely prohibited under the Shari'ah for their failure to involve a tangible asset or the involvement of an interest-based element.

Most Secular Jurisdictions have not licensed Islamic banks, England being an exception. Implementation of Islamic finance in private investment transactions does not require the existence of Islamic banks. Islamic finance can be fully implemented by interest-based banks and financial institutions and other business practitioners. Islamic finance is the conduct of

---

19, [2004] All ER (D) 280 (Jan), issued 28 January 2004, and *Musawai v. R E International (UK) Ltd and others*, [2007] EWHS 2981 (Ch), [2007] All ER (D) 222 (Dec), issued 14 December 2007.

[6] Tax and bankruptcy principles in the United States are examples of regimes that are predominantly substance over form.

[7] The "human consumption" qualifier is illustrative of the care that must be taken in interpreting Shariah principles. Generalisations are inadequate. For example, many, if not most, Shariah scholars do not prohibit activities relating to alcohol as a medical or industrial cleaning agent.

commercial and financial activities in compliance with Shariʿah principles. It is activity-based – transactionally based – and can be conducted within the parameters and constraints of the dominant interest-based secular legal, tax, and institutional regimes. Some Secular Jurisdictions have encouraged this transactional practice of Islamic finance. Herein lie enormous opportunities for business practitioners. For example, to access capital held by Muslim investors, to serve Muslim communities within Secular Jurisdictions as well as those in Shariʿah-Incorporated Jurisdictions, to support diversity through encouragement of transactional arrangements that promote unity of objectives and methods, and to enhance cooperation and understanding across religious and cultural divergences, among many others.

Another set of considerations in implementing Islamic finance pertains to the market that is accessed and the predominant interpretation of the Shariʿah within that market. The market may be a group of Muslim investors within the relevant Secular Jurisdiction. Or it may be investors in a Shariʿah-Incorporated Jurisdiction from which funds are derived. There are different schools of Islamic jurisprudence, the best known being the Hanbali, Hanafi, Shafiʿi, and Maliki schools. Different schools predominate in different populations or geographic areas. Each school tends to interpret relevant Shariʿah principles somewhat differently, although for commonly used contracts and structures many of those differences have been resolved in previous transactions. Interpretive differences are due to many factors, including (a) the diversity that is, and is encouraged by, Islam, (b) the nature of the Shariʿah as a set of principles, with relatively few specific injunctions, and (c) the oral tradition of the Shariʿah. Nonetheless, the practitioner in a Secular Jurisdiction should seek the guidance of a Shariʿah scholar or board early in the transactional process to ensure that the product (security, investment) will be acceptable in the target market. [8]

3. *Murabaha*

A *murabaha* is a cost-plus-profit sale in which essentially all transactional elements, including the cost of the object that is sold and purchased, the

---

[8] For introductions to the Sunni schools of Islamic jurisprudence, see McMillen 2013, *supra* note 1, at 113, WAEL B. HALLAQ, *Sharīʿa: Theory, Practice, Transformations* (2009), at 60–71, JOSEPH SCHACHT, *The Schools of Law and Later Developments of Jurisprudence*, following upon JOSEPH SCHACHT, *Pre-Islamic Background and Early Development of Jurisprudence*, each in *Law in the Middle East, Volume I, Origins and Development of Islamic Law*, MAJID KHADDURI and HERBERT J. LIEBESNY, eds. (1955), at 57 and 28, respectively, NOEL J. COULSON, *A History of Islamic Law* (1964), and KNUT S. VIKØR, *Between God and the Sultan: A History of Islamic Law* (2005), at 89–184.

transactional profit, and most transaction expenses, are disclosed fully to both the purchaser and seller. The price (cost plus profit plus certain expenses) is established at the inception of the transaction and may not thereafter be changed. The object of sale is a permissible commodity or property. A few objects, including gold and silver, may not be the subject of *murabaha* transactions due to Quranic prohibitions. The purchaser must acquire certain ownership risks pertaining to the object (such as the risk of "spoilage") and usually must acquire actual or constructive possession of the object. A seller may not sell an unowned object.[9]

Two formulations are used in contemporary Islamic finance. Both involve an intermediary between the ultimate seller and the ultimate purchaser. In each, the intermediary provides financing for the transaction, usually by purchasing the object from the ultimate seller and selling the object to the ultimate purchaser on a deferred payment basis. The *murabaha* contract is between the intermediary and the ultimate purchaser. The seller may take collateral security to secure the purchaser's payment obligation.

The difference between the two formulations relates to the purchaser's intent regarding the object: specifically, whether the purchaser has a genuine interest in the substance of that object. One formulation is used to acquire an object desired by the acquiror, either to hold or to use in the acquiror's business. This formulation is depicted in Figure 9.1 and is referred to as a "true *murabaha*". In the other formulation the purchaser has no interest in the substance of the object other than as a vector to generate cash for the acquiror and creation of a deferred payment obligation for the purchase price. This formulation is depicted in Figure 9.2 and is referred to as

[9] For the *murabaha*, see McMillen 2013, *supra* note 1, at 247, MICHAEL J.T. MCMILLEN, *Trends in Islamic Project and Infrastructure Finance in the Middle East: Re-Emergence of the Murabaha*, available at http://papers.ssrn.com/sol3/papers.cfm?abstract_id=1753252, WAHBAH AL-ZUHAYLĪ, *Al-Fiqh Al-Islāmī wa-Adillatuh (Islamic Jurisprudence and its Proofs, Financial Transactions in Islamic Jurisprudence* (4th edition, 1997), Mahmoud El-Gamal, translator, Muhammad S. Eissa, revisor (2002) ("al-Zuhayli"), Volume 2, at 353–366, MUHAMMAD TAQI USMANI, AN INTRODUCTION TO ISLAMIC FINANCE (2002), at 37–68, MUHAMMAD TAQI USMANI, *Murabahah*, available at www.accountancy.com.pk/docs/islam_murabahah.pdf, *Shari'a Standard No. (8), Murabaha to the Purchase Order*, issued 1 Dhul Qada 10427H corresponding to May 16, 2002, in AAOIFI Standards, *id.*, *Shari'a Standard No. 30, Monetization (Tawarruq),* issued 4 Rabi al-Awaal corresponding to May 16, 2002, in AAOIFI *Shari'a Standards of the Accounting and Auditing Organization for Islamic Financial Institutions* (2010) ("AAOIFI Standards"), *Shariah Opinions (Fatwa) on Murabaha*, Ahmed Mohiedden Ahmed, compiler, Abdul Sattar Abu Ghuddah, reviewer, Dallah Al-Baraka Group, available at www.albaraka.com/media/pdf/Research-Studies/RSIS-200706201-EN.pdf, and YUSUF TALAL DELORENZO, *Murabaha, Sales of Trust, and Money-value of Time*, in *Proceedings of the Second Harvard University Forum on Islamic Finance: Islamic Finance in the 21st Century* (1998), at 145. A *musawamma* is essentially identical to a *murabaha* except that the cost need not be disclosed.

a "vector *murabaha*". Each formulation is a multi-step series of transactions in the sequences noted in Figures 9.1 and 9.2.

Figure 9.1 Generic true *murabaha* transaction

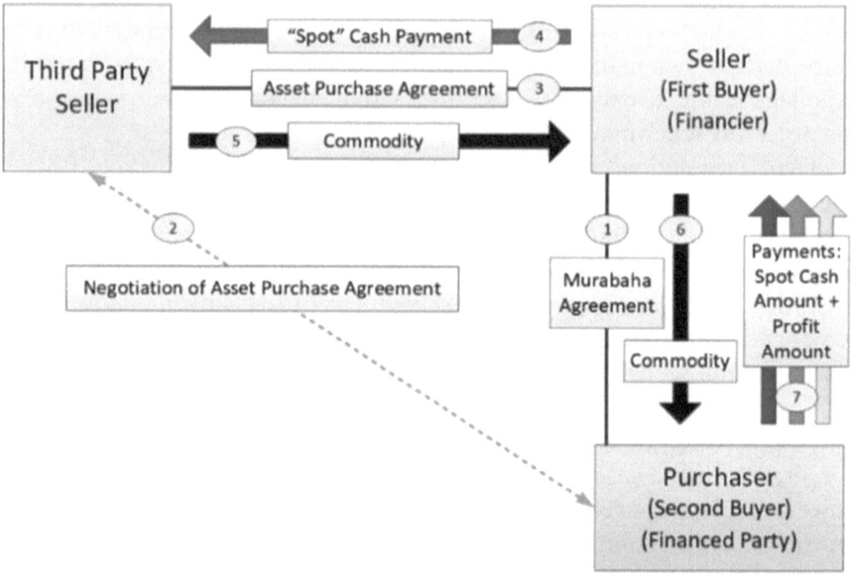

Consider, first, Figure 9.1. ① The Purchaser and Seller enter into a *Murabaha* Agreement. ② The Purchaser negotiates the terms of the Asset Purchase Agreement with the Third Party Seller but does not execute the agreement. ③④⑤ The Seller executes the Asset Purchase Agreement and makes a spot purchase payment for the object, which is transferred by the Third Party Seller to the Seller-Financier. ⑥ The Seller-Financier then sells the commodity to the Purchaser. ⑦ The Purchaser makes instalment payments to the Seller for the price (principal plus profit plus, possibly, certain expenses). Profit is often determined at rate equal to the interest rate that would be paid on a loan to the Purchaser if a loan had been used to finance the purchase from the Third Party Seller. The Purchaser acquires, owns, and holds the commodity. True *murabaha* arrangements are used to finance acquisitions of diverse objects, including sesame seeds, fruits, vegetables, cars, buses, homes, other commodities, and other assets. An owner of a grocery store or an automobile or truck dealer may use this arrangement to acquire inventory. A baker may acquire flour in this manner. [10]

[10] Although not here discussed, and less acceptable, are "*tawarruq*" arrangements involving a pre-arranged resale of the object by the ultimate purchaser. See the AAOIFI

Figure 9.2 Generic vector (metals) *murabaha* transaction

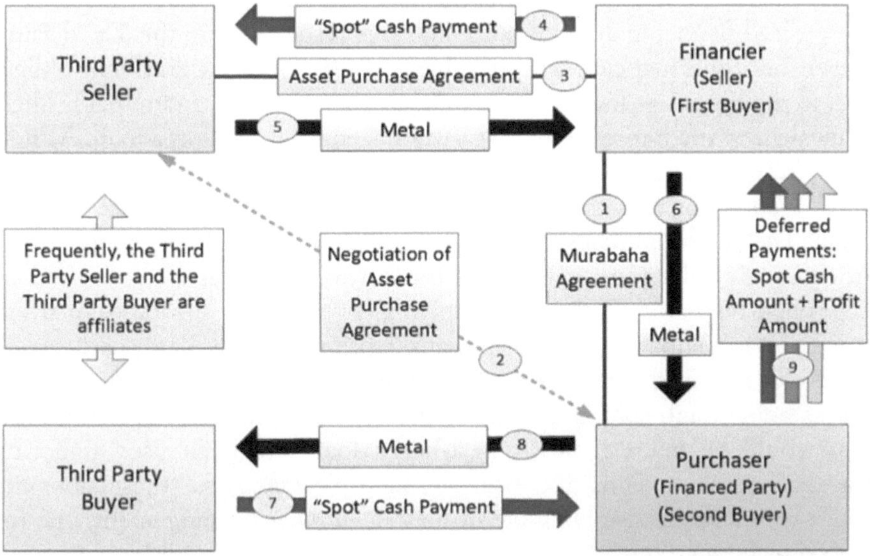

Steps ① through ⑥ are the same as in a true *murabaha* transaction. Step ⑨ in Figure 9.2 is the same as step ⑦ in Figure 9.1. The difference between the two formulations is the sale by the Purchaser to the Third Party Buyer in steps ⑦ and ⑧ in Figure9. 2. In those steps, the Purchaser disposes of the commodity (the metal) for cash.

The vector *murabaha* is used where the purchaser desires cash, not ownership of the transactional object.[11] To that end, the purchaser will resell the object for cash almost immediately upon its purchase. In contemporary practice, the object sold and purchased is often platinum or palm oil or a similar commodity that does not spoil and does not move during the transaction (it remains in a vault or warehouse). These and related characteristics allow compliance with all Shari'ah requirements while minimizing the risks associated with those requirements. It is the vector *murabaha* that has earned a characterisation as the most frequently used and most frequently abused structure in Islamic finance.

In net, the Financier has paid out an amount of cash equal to the

---

Monetization Standard, *id.*, *Shari'a Standard No. (30), Monetization (Tawarruq)*, issued 1 Dhul Qada 1427H corresponding to May 16, 2002, in AAOIFI Standards, *id.*, and MAHMOUD EL-GAMAL, *Limits and Dangers of Shari'a Arbitrage*, in Islamic Finance: Current Legal and Regulatory Issues, S. Nazim Ali, ed. (2005), at 125–126.

[11] Unfortunately, and confusingly, in contemporary discussions vector *murabaha* transactions are often referred to as "commodity *murabaha*" transactions. A true *murabaha* is, and historically was, often to acquire a commodity. It would be more accurate to describe a true *murabaha* as a commodity *murabaha*.

amount of financing desired by the Purchaser, although it is paid to the Third Party Seller. The Purchaser has received an amount of cash equal to the desired financing amount, although it is received from the Third Party Buyer, not the Financier. The Purchaser owes a deferred payment obligation to the Financier for the desired financing amount at a rate that is likely equivalent to the interest rate that would have been paid on a loan. As noted in Figure 9.2, the Third Party Seller and Third Party Buyer may be affiliates. Transaction fees and costs are ignored in Figures 9.1 and 9.2: they are small. The vector *murabaha* is used in all manner of financing transactions. In economic substance, it is little different to a loan, as is recognised by U.S. bank regulatory authorities applying an economic substance analysis. It is used as a substitute for term loans, working capital loans, and revolving credit arrangements. In each case, the amount of platinum or palm oil that is bought and sold in a transaction is equal to the amount of the draw that would be made if an interest-based loan had been used (ignoring transaction costs). Thus, for example, multiple *murabaha* transactions are run within a single revolving credit master *murabaha* arrangement, one for each drawdown. [12]

Structural adjustments to the loan formulation to ensure Shariʿah compliance is rather easily addressed. An example is the requirement that the price may not be changed after inception of the *murabaha* contract. The term or tenor is appropriately established and profit, like interest, is determined daily.

In some instances, however, Shariʿah principles make it difficult to structure a *murabaha* as a loan substitute. An example is a commitment fee in a loan arrangement. A commitment fee is essentially an interest payment on amounts of a loan commitment that are undrawn during a period. The commitment fee cannot be determined until the end of the period. Because it is unknown at the inception of a period, it cannot be accommodated in a *murabaha* for that period. The commitment fee determined at the end of a period can be the subject of a *murabaha* obligation for the next succeeding period. That will ensure an obligation to pay the commitment fee, but also entail some risk of non-payment and result in delayed payment. Similar difficulties exist whenever amounts are determinable only after inception of the *murabaha*, such as profit participations.

---

[12] See Office of the Comptroller of the Currency of the United States of America, *Office of the Comptroller of the Currency Interpretive Letter #867* (November 1999), characterizing the *murabaha* as a loan for bank regulator purposes.

4. Lease (*Ijara*) in Real Estate Investments

Figure 9.3 Generic lease (*ijara*) structure

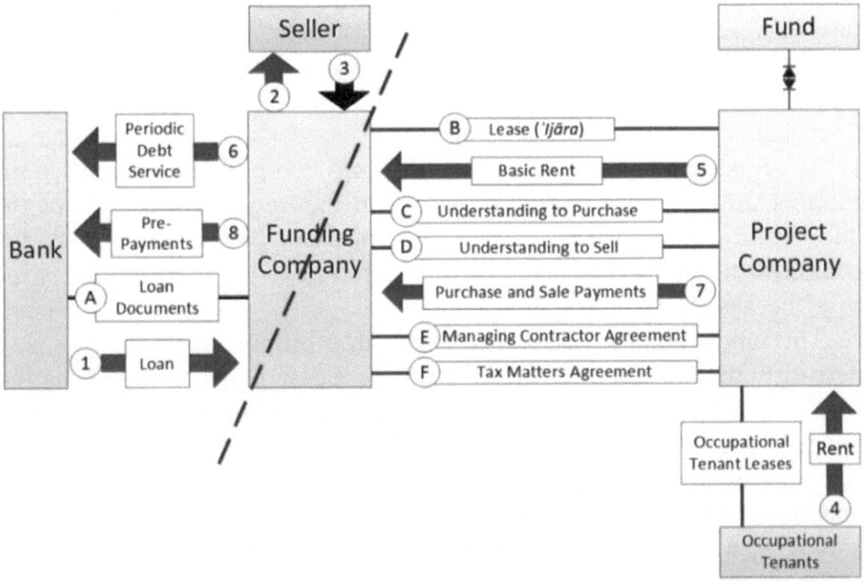

Source: Copyright ©2009–2020: Michael J.T. McMillen.

Real estate is, and has long been, a preferred investment class for many Middle Eastern investors. That induced business professionals in the United States to establish Shari'ah compliant real estate investment funds in the United States, Canada, and many European countries in the late 1990s and early 2000s. Subsequently, Shari'ah-compliant real estate investments have multiplied. The most widely used structure for effecting Shari'ah-compliant real estate investments is the lease (*ijara*), which is accepted by all schools of Islamic jurisprudence. The lease has been used in thousands of real estate investment transactions throughout the world since 2000. While the structure varies somewhat by jurisdiction to accommodate real estate and tax laws, there is a basic structural form. That structure is illustrated in Figure 9.3. [13]

---

[13] See McMillen 2013, *supra* note 1, at 189–227 and 233–235, Michael J.T. McMillen, *Islamic Shari'ah-Compliant Project Finance: Collateral Security and Financing Structure Case Studies*, 24 Fordham International Law Journal, 1184 (2001) (discussing some of the first *ijara* structures of this type), al-Zuhaylī, *supra* note 5, at 381–434, Ibn Rushd, *The Distinguished Jurist's Primer, Bidayat al-Mujtahid wa Nihayat al-Muqtasid* (1996), Volume II, Book 30, 264–281, Judge C.A. Hooper, transla-

The *ijara* structure was developed to allow financing by interest-based as well as Shariʿah-compliant financiers. It permits interest-based loans and, as necessary, accommodates the myriad tax, legal, and regulatory requirements of Secular Jurisdictions. This section discusses the *ijara* structure in a Secular Jurisdiction using interest-based financing. Chapter 10 discusses the same *ijara* structure in transactions involving no interest-based financier, substituting a Shariʿah-compliant *sukuk* issuance for bank financing.

The transactional structure is divided into two parts by the dashed line running through the Funding Company in Figure 9.3. To the left of that line, the arrangements are not Shariʿah compliant. To the right are Shariʿah compliant arrangements. This is often referred to as a "bifurcated structure" because of this division.

The fundamental structural principle in a bifurcated transaction is, of necessity, that risks be allocated, to the greatest possible extent, as they would in a loan transaction, in terms of whether the financier or the financed party bears a risk. The necessity is mandated by the nature and structure of the tax, legal, and regulatory regimes in Secular Jurisdictions and the institutionalised practices of transactional participants regarding, among many other matters, underwriting procedures and determinations and transactional and administrative roles. The relatively standardised doc-

tor, MAJALAT AL-AHKAM AL-ADLIYAH (an English language translation prepared by Judge C.A. Hooper as *The Civil Law of Palestine and Trans-Jordan*, Volumes I and II (1933), which has been reprinted in various issues of 4 Arab Law Quarterly (1968), and C. R., TYSER, D. G. DEMETRIADES, and ISMAIL HAQQI EFFENDI, translators, *The Majelle: Being an English Translation of* Majallah El-Ahkam-I-Adliya *and a Complete Code on Islamic Civil Law* (2001), at Book II, Articles 404–611, ALI IBN ABI BAKR BURHAN AL-DIN AL-MARGHINANI, *The Hedàya, or Guide: a Commentary on the Mussulman Laws: Translated by Order of the Governor-General and Council of Bengal, by Charles Hamilton* (1791) (digital scan edition of ECCO Publications), at Volume 3, Book XXXI, 312–375, MUHAMMAD TAQI USMANI, *Ijarah*, available at www.accountancy.com.pk/frameit.asp?link=docs/islam_ijarah.pdf, MICHAEL J.T. MCMILLEN, *Islamic Project Finance*, in Handbook of Islamic Banking, M. KABIR HASSAN and MERVYN K. LEWIS, eds. (2007), at 200, MICHAEL J.T. MCMILLEN, *Islamic Project Finance: An Introduction to Principles and Structures*, III Global Infrastructure 1 (2009), *Shariʿah-Compliant Infrastructure and Project Finance*, in Infrastructure Finance: Trends and Techniques, HENRY A. DAVIS, ed. (2008), at 374, *Shariʿa Standard No. (9), Ijarah and Ijarah Muntahiah Bitamleek*, issued 4 Rabi al-Awaal 1423H corresponding to May 16, 2002, in AAOIFI Standards, *supra* note 5, *Office of the Comptroller of the Currency Interpretive Letter # 806 (December 1997)*, the date of the original letter being October 17, 1997, reprinted at [1997–1998 Transfer Binder] Federal Banking Law Reports (CCH) 81,253 (October 17, 1997), and *New York State Department of Taxation and Finance, Office of Tax Policy Analysis, Taxpayer Guidance Division, Advisory Opinion TSB-A-08(2)R, Petition No. M071001A, April 28,* 2008.

umentation reflecting those practices, allocations, procedures, determinations, and roles functions to preclude variances. All these matters were established prior to the development of contemporary Islamic finance and will not be modified by the requisites of Islamic finance. That said, Shari'ah documents that precisely mirror risk allocations under loan documents are not achievable. Methods have been developed to address the variances to the satisfaction of both interest-based banks and Shari'ah-compliant investors. The consequence of that principle in the documentation is that the Shari'ah documentation is a mirror image of the Loan Documents (as nearly as possible).

The Loan Documents are customary documents for an interest-based loan for the type of transaction being considered. These include a loan or credit agreement, a promissory note, and collateral security documents (a mortgage and grants of security interests). They also include other documents appropriate for the specific transaction given its nature, circumstances, and credit considerations, including completion undertakings, guarantees, environmental indemnity agreements, and others. The Shari'ah documentation is comprised of the Lease (*Ijara*), the Understanding to Purchase, the Understanding to Sell, and the Managing Contractor Agreement. It may include a Tax Matters Agreement.

Shari'ah-compliant investors enter the transaction through the Fund, which owns the Project Company (often jointly with a host-country sponsor). The Project Company is a newly formed special purpose entity that is responsible for the operation of the relevant property. It is often the tax owner, although it does not hold title to the property. Title is held by the Funding Company, a special purpose entity established expressly for the transaction. The Funding Company is not Shari'ah compliant. It is the borrower under an interest-based loan that funds the purchase of the property from the Seller (Steps ①, ②, and ③).

After acquiring the property, the Funding Company leases it to the Project Company pursuant to the Lease (*Ijara*). The Lease (*Ijara*) contains the covenants governing the operation of the asset (such as maintenance and insurance) as well as the payment provisions that operate to ensure loan repayment. Those provisions mirror the loan agreement provisions, although they are drafted as obligations to the Funding Company as landlord. Basic Rent is the principal rental obligation of the Project Company as tenant and is structured to ensure that the Funding Company receives exactly as much money as it needs to pay its Bank loan. In terms of transactional cash flows, periodic rent from the Occupational Tenant is first paid to the Project Company (step ④). Those funds are then used, in part, by the Project Company to pay Basic Rent to the Funding Company (step ⑤). The Funding Company uses those funds to pay the debt service on the interest-bearing loan (step ⑥).[14]

From this sequence, it is determinable that the amount of Basic Rent should be equal, exactly, to the debt service due on the interest-bearing loan. In jurisdictions that recognise *ijara* transactions as economically equivalent to loan transactions, such as the United States, that equality is achievable. In Secular Jurisdictions that do not recognise *ijara* transactions as economically equivalent to loan transactions, or do not give effect to that recognition in the tax structure, the Basic Rent may be taxed as rental income to the recipient Funding Company. Because the Basic Rent is economically equivalent to the debt service, it is comprised of both interest and, to the extent of debt amortisation under the Loan Documents, principal. In that case, the system discriminates against Islamic finance by taxing the principal amount in circumstances where it does not tax the principal amount of a loan repayment. This exemplifies an issue encountered in implementing Shariʿah-compliant financings in Secular Jurisdictions: achieving non-discriminatory parity with interest-based finance (achieving a level playing field). Tax discrimination of this type is commonplace in Secular Jurisdictions.

If there is discrimination of this sort regarding rental payments, it is a near certainty that there will be similar discrimination in the treatment of amounts paid through the Understanding to Purchase and the Understanding to Sell. Those two documents address, respectively, mandatory prepayments (including in defaults) and voluntary prepayments, and are illustrated by steps ⑦ and ⑧. These two documents mirror the mandatory and voluntary prepayment provisions of the Loan Documents for both total and partial prepayments. The qualification is that the Understanding to Purchase and Understanding to Sell do not include any amounts that correspond to interest payable by the Funding Company under the Loan Documents. All interest equivalents are paid under the Lease (*Ijara*) as part of Basic Rent. Which is to say that all amounts under the Understanding to Purchase and Understanding to Sell are equivalents only to principal amounts due under the Loan Documents. If those amounts are taxed as rent or purchase payments, the tax regime discriminates against Islamic finance in jurisdictions where repayment of the principal amount of a loan is not taxed or is not taxed at like rates.

---

[14] Other portions of the Occupational Tenant Rent are used to pay operating expenses and to fund insurance, tax, maintenance, and capital expenditure reserves. Amounts remaining after expenses and reserves are distributed to the investors through the Fund.

The necessity of the Understanding to Purchase and Understanding to Sell derives from various Shari'ah principles, including the nature of a lease as a sale. For example, a tenant under a Shari'ah-compliant lease (*ijara*) cannot be compelled to pay future rents before their due dates. A Shari'ah-compliant lease is a sale of usufruct and the tenant must be afforded use of the leased asset in order for a rental obligation to be enforceable. To take one example, if there is a tenant default and the tenant is to be removed prior to the end of the lease term, the lease will usually have to be terminated. All future rents will then be uncollectible under the Shari'ah principles. In a financing lease arrangement, most or all the outstanding principal constitutes future rent that would be collected through future Basic Rent payments absent a lease termination.

The Understanding to Purchase is the economic equivalent (though not a Shari'ah equivalent) of a put option on the leased asset. The Bank causes the Funding Company to put the asset to the Project Company for an amount (a strike price) equivalent to the total outstanding principal amount of the loan. That price is immediately payable. Which has the effect of accelerating the loan amount equivalent down to the Project Company. Without the Understanding to Purchase, amounts due in the future, which constitute the principal to be repaid to the financier, would not be collectible. Conversely, the Understanding to Sell allows the Project Company to repay the financing prior to the due date. For example, in circumstances where the asset is sold prior to the maturity date of the financing. It is the economic equivalent of a call option on the asset (although not a call option for Shari'ah purposes). Again, the strike price is equal to the outstanding principal amount of the financing. It is apparent in each case that economic and financial equivalency, and equivalency of related risks, is the structural principle embodied in the structure and documents. [15]

The Managing Contractor Agreement also derives from Shari'ah principles. Under the Shari'ah, a tenant cannot be made mandatorily responsible for structural maintenance of the leased asset. Half or more of the real estate lease financings in the global markets are triple-net leases in which

---

[15] Both the Understanding to Purchase and the Understanding to Sell also provide for partial prepayments. Examples under the Understanding to Purchase include circumstances in which adjustments must be made to the outstanding principal amount of the financing due to financial ratio changes. For example, where the value of the leased asset decreases and it is necessary to readjust the outstanding principal to the value of the asset (the rent-to-value ratio, which is equivalent to a loan-to-value ratio). An example under the Understanding to Sell is where individual condominiums or lots are sold and some or all of the sale proceeds are applied in reduction of the outstanding principal amount of the financing.

the tenant is responsible for all maintenance (including structural maintenance) as well as insurance, taxes, and other amounts. In equipment financing arrangements, say for aircraft, essentially all leases are triple-net leases. Without a correction to the structure, Shari'ah compliant investors would be at a competitive disadvantage in the markets for properties that are lease financed. The structure makes use of a separate Shari'ah principle to adjust this aspect of the transaction. The principle is that a lessor may retain others to take maintenance risks (and certain other risks). Pursuant to the Managing Contractor Agreement, the lessor hires the lessee, for a fee, to take maintenance risks and perform all maintenance (and to procure insurance). This has the effect of conforming the Shari'ah compliant transaction to market practices.

The Managing Contractor Agreement performs a second function. It removes the Funding Company from all decision making in the transaction. Decisions are all made by either the Bank or the Project Company, which are the only parties with an economic interest in the transaction. The Funding Company is relegated to its pure structural roles: holding title to the asset; taking an interest-bearing loan; leasing the asset to the Project Company; ensuring that all economic benefits are allocated only to the Bank and the Project Company; and providing bankruptcy-remoteness protections (the Funding Company will have only a single creditor, the Bank, and will be structured to protect it from other competing claims).

The Tax Matters Agreement is not present in every transaction. Its only substantive purpose is to ensure that tax filings are consistent with the intention of the parties. That is, to ensure that the Project Company is treated as the tax owner of the asset even though it is not the title holder and to ensure that the Basic Rent payments and payments under the Understanding to Sell and Understanding to Purchase are treated on an equivalent basis with the tax treatment afforded to interest-based loans. The tax authority is not bound by this agreement, of course. Only the transactional parties are bound. The role of the Tax Matters Agreement vis-à-vis the taxing authority is informational. It explains, with total transparency, why the structure was necessary from a Shari'ah perspective and how the structure works.

The lease (*ijara*) structure involves two special purpose entities, some structural complexity, and a good deal of care in mirroring and harmonizing the Loan Documents and the Shari'ah documents. As compared with a leveraged (or similar) lease financing of the same asset, the transactional costs are comparable. But they are greater than a direct loan financing from a bank to the Project Company.

Additionally, there are Shari'ah considerations that restrict the pool of available tenants for commercial real estate properties financed using

Shari'ah-compliant structures. Under the Shari'ah, tenants in such a commercial property must be in businesses that are not prohibited by the Shari'ah. The types of businesses that are prohibited include companies that sell or distribute alcohol or pork for human consumption, are engaged in pornography or gambling activities, or are engaged in interest-based finance (among others). The last category limits the number of available tenants for these properties because such a high percentage of tenants in commercial properties are engaged in interest-based financial services. That said, Shari'ah scholars are sensitive to situations where it is permissible to have tenants that are engaged in some activities that are not compliant with the Shari'ah. For example, if an interest-based bank is conducting only check sorting activities or some other activity not related to interest-based banking, Shari'ah scholars may permit the tenancy. And not all alcohol-related activities are impermissible, even where human consumption is involved. For example, the presence in a commercial office building of a restaurant serving alcohol may not be disqualifying if the restaurant is not the primary tenant and if a portion of the rent that correlates with impure income from alcohol sales can be donated to charity to "purify" the arrangement.

The lease (*ijara*) structure is accepted throughout the world, from both a Shari'ah perspective and a secular perspective, which renders it an enormously powerful tool for realizing business opportunities. It should be thoroughly understood by anyone contemplating the use of Islamic financing techniques. As a cautionary note, there are many other intricacies to the lease (*ijara*) structure that are not discussed in this chapter. These also need to be mastered. Given the power of the tool, and its wide acceptance, the effort will be rewarded.

5. Lease (*Ijara*) in Private Equity

The *ijara* structure used in private equity transactions varies little from real estate and equipment financings. Figure 9.4 depicts a generic private equity *ijara* arrangement in which a business is acquired from a Seller. The critical difference is that the economic party in interest is not a newly formed entity like the Project Company in Figure 3. It is an entity with on-going operations, such as the manufacture and sale of products (to use an example). It is referred to as the Operating Company in Figure 9.4. The Operating Company is acquired as an on-going business.

Figure 9.4 Generic private equity lease (*ijara*) structure

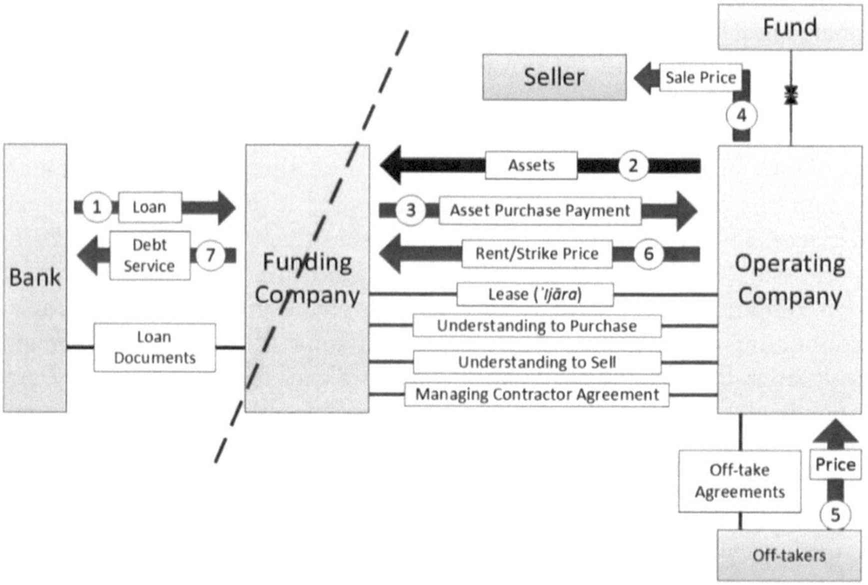

Source: Copyright © 2009–2020: Michael J.T. McMillen.

The documentary structure of the private equity lease financing is the same as was discussed in connection with Figure 3, for both the Loan Documents and the Shari'ah documents. One additional document in the private equity transaction, which is not shown in Figure 9.4, is an asset sale and purchase agreement for the assets of the Operating Company that are transferred to the Funding Company in steps ② and ③).

As with the generic lease described in Figure 9.3, a Funding Company will be established as a newly formed special purpose entity. Its purposes are the same as those of the Funding Company in the Figure 9.3 transaction: holding title to some assets; taking an interest-bearing loan; leasing the assets to the Project Company; ensuring that all economic benefits are allocated only to the Bank and the Project Company; and providing bankruptcy-remoteness protections.

In the private equity context, all assets necessary for operation of the business are already held by the Operating Company at the time it is acquired. In order to make use of a Shari'ah-compliant lease, some assets need to be lodged in the Funding Company to allow the Funding Company to lease those assets to the Operating Company for an amount of Basic Rent sufficient to pay the debt service due to the Bank under the Loan Documents. This is accomplished by using the proceeds of the Bank loan (step ①) to acquire those assets from the Operating Company (in steps ② and ③). Some or all of the loan proceeds transferred to the Operating Company in step ③ are paid to the Seller as part of the purchase price (step ④), allowing the Seller a profit on the sale of the Operating Company.

A real estate acquisition financing is different in concept from an acquisition financing for an operating company. The amount of financing made available in a real estate transaction is closely correlated with the market value of the real estate, both at the inception of, and throughout the term of, the financing. Thus, the importance of a loan-to-value or rent-to-value ratio and related concepts in the financing documents. A private equity financing is quite different. The financing amount is not closely related to the value of the assets of the Operating Company. Often those assets have small values relative to the amount of the financing. Cash flows from operations and operational parameters are more important considerations.

This has implications for the asset transfer described in steps ② and ③ of Figure 9.4. What assets should be transferred to the Funding Company to enable leasing? Some asset transfers will attract taxation, both upon the transfer to the Funding Company at the inception of the financing and when transferred back to the Operating Company after payment of the financing. It is optimal to avoid these tax events where possible. Dividing the assets into two entities (the Funding Company and the Operating Company) introduces structural and tax complexities and increases transaction costs. That asset division may also introduce undesirable legal and regulatory complexities. An additional category of considerations relates to branding and reputation, which may be adversely affected by the asset division. In short, there is no universal formula for determining which assets are transferred to the Funding Company. A determination will be made based upon all relevant considerations. One notable Shari'ah parameter is that the value of the transferred assets must be adequate to support a Basic Rent payment that is large enough to ensure payment of the loan made by the Bank.

After transfer of the assets to the Funding Company, those assets are leased back to the Operating Company. The Basic Rent payments and payments under the Understanding to Purchase and Understanding to Sell are structured in the same manner as in the Figure 9.3 transaction. As are the mirroring of Shari'ah documents and Loan Documents and other matters.

The generic lease structure presented in Figure 9.4 has been used successfully in a wide range of Shari'ah-compliant private equity transactions. The generic structure is adjusted to local tax, legal, and regulatory parameters. As a cautionary note, some jurisdictions prohibit the use of acquired assets as collateral for a financing for the acquisition of those assets.

6. Opportunities

This chapter touches upon how fundamental Shari'ah-compliant contracts can be used to effect private investment transactions (and related financing) in Secular Jurisdictions in accordance with existing tax, legal, and regulatory regimes. Two contracts serve as examples, from the many that are used in Islamic finance.

Each of the true *murabaha* and the *ijara* can be used to finance the acquisition and/or operation of most Shari'ah-compliant assets for the short, medium, or long term. Acquisitions of produce, meat, other foodstuffs, raw materials, cars, trucks, equipment, homes, and even entire projects are financed using the *murabaha*. The limitations are few and relate to the relatively small number of business activities that are impermissible. Those limitations are discussed in Chapter 10.

The vector *murabaha* can also be used as a loan substitute for most, though not all, types of loans. Term loans, working capital facilities, and revolving credit facilities are all amenable to financing through the vector *murabaha*. With only a few limitations, the vector *murabaha* can be used to provide funds as a loan substitute, allowing the financed party to use the funds as he, she, or it desires. To repair a home or conduct industrial maintenance, or to acquire an asset.

Islamic financing in Secular Jurisdictions is widespread, though difficult to track or quantify with precision. Private investment transactions are, by design and intention, private. For the business practitioner intent on realizing new opportunities, new sources of capital, new client bases, what is required is a will to explore, learn, and implement with rigor and sensitivity to a set of legal, ethical, and moral principles of ancient lineage and fundamental importance to almost a third of the world's population. The task is not as daunting as first appears. Islamic and secular contracts are more alike than different. The financial, cultural, social, and intellectual rewards will redound both to the individuals that undertake the journey and the greater cause of human understanding.

References

ACCOUNTING AND AUDITING ORGANISATION FOR ISLAMIC FINANCIAL INSTITUTIONS, *Shari'a Standard No. (8), Murabaha to the Purchase Order*, issued 1 Dhul Qada 10427H corresponding to May 16, 2002, in *AAOIFI Shari'a Standards of the Accounting and Auditing Organization for Islamic Financial Institutions* (2010).

ACCOUNTING AND AUDITING ORGANISATION FOR ISLAMIC FINANCIAL INSTITUTIONS, *Shari'a Standard No. (9), Ijarah and Ijarah Muntahiah Bitamleek*, issued 4 Rabi al-Awaal 1423H corresponding to May 16, 2002, in *AAOIFI Shari'a Standards of the Accounting and Auditing Organization for Islamic Financial Institutions* (2010).

ACCOUNTING AND AUDITING ORGANISATION FOR ISLAMIC FINANCIAL INSTITUTIONS, *Shari'a Standard No. 30, Monetization (Tawarruq),* issued 4 Rabi al-Awaal corresponding to May 16, 2002, in *AAOIFI Shari'a Standards of the Accounting and Auditing Organization for Islamic Financial Institutions* (2010).

AHMED, A.M. (compiler), ABU GHUDDAH, A.S. (reviewer), & DALLAH AL-BARAKA GROUP, *Shariah Opinions (Fatwa) on Murabaha*, available at http://www.albaraka.com/media/pdf/Research-Studies/RSIS-200706201-EN.pdf.

COULSON, N.J., *A History of Islamic Law* (1964).

DELORENZO, Y.T., *Murabaha, Sales of Trust, and Money-value of Time*, in Harvard Islamic Finance Information Program, *Proceedings of the Second Harvard University Forum on Islamic Finance: Islamic Finance in the 21st Century* (1998).

DOW JONES ISLAMIC MARKET INDEX, *The Dow Jones Islamic Market Index: Statement by the Shariah Supervisory Board* (undated; issued in 1998) (copy on file with the author).

EL-GAMAL, M., *Limits and Dangers of Shari'a Arbitrage*, in ALI, N. (ed.), *Islamic Finance: Current Legal and Regulatory Issues* (2005).

HALLAQ, W.B., *Sharī'a: Theory, Practice, Transformations* (2009).

HOOPER, C.A. (translator), *Majalat Al-Ahkam Al-Adliyah, prepared as The Civil Law of Palestine and Trans-Jordan,* Volumes I and II (1933) (reprinted in various issues of 4 Arab Law Quarterly (1968)).

IBN RUSHD, *The Distinguished Jurist's Primer, Bidayat al-Mujtahid wa Nihayat al-Muqtasid*, Volume II (1996).

AL-MARGHINANI, A.I.B.B.D., *The Hedàya, or Guide: a Commentary on the Mussulman Laws: Translated by Order of the Governor-General and Council of Bengal, by Charles Hamilton* (1791) (digital scan edition of ECCO Publications).

MCMILLEN, M.J.T., *Trends in Islamic Project and Infrastructure Finance in the Middle East: Re-Emergence of the Murabaha,* available at http://papers.ssrn.com/sol3/papers.cfm?abstract_id=1753252.

MCMILLEN, M.J.T., *Islamic Shari'ah-Compliant Project Finance: Collateral Security and Financing Structure Case Studies*, in 24 Fordham International Law Journal 1184 ff. (2001).

McMillen, M.J.T., *Islamic Project Finance, in Handbook of Islamic Banking*, Hassan, M.K. & Lewis, M.K. (eds.) (2007).

McMillen, M.J.T., *Shari'ah-Compliant Infrastructure and Project Finance*, in Davis, H.A. (ed.), *Infrastructure Finance: Trends and Techniques* (2008).

McMillen, M.J.T., *Islamic Project Finance: An Introduction to Principles and Structures*, in III *Global Infrastructure*, 1 (entire issue) (2009).

McMillen, M.J.T., *Islamic Finance and the Shariah: The Dow Jones Fatwa and Permissible Variance as Studies in Letheanism and Legal Change* (2013).

Musawai v. R E International (UK) Ltd and others, [2007] EWHS 2981 (Ch), [2007] All ER (D) 222 (Dec), issued 14 December 2007.

New York State Department of Taxation and Finance, *New York State Department of Taxation and Finance, Office of Tax Policy Analysis, Taxpayer Guidance Division, Advisory Opinion TSB-A-08(2)R, Petition No. M071001A, April 28,* 2008.

Office of the Comptroller of the Currency of the United States of America, *Office of the Comptroller of the Currency Interpretive Letter # 806* (October 17, 1997), Federal Banking Law Reporter ¶ 81–253, reprinted at [1997–1998 Transfer Binder] Federal Banking Law Reports (CCH) ¶ 81,253 (October 17, 1997).

Office of the Comptroller of the Currency of the United States of America, *Office of the Comptroller of the Currency Interpretive Letter # 867* (June 1, 1999), Federal Banking Law Reporter, ¶ 81–361, reprinted in [1999–2000 Transfer Binder] Federal Banking Law Reports (CCH) ¶ 81–361 (June 1, 1999).

Schacht, J., *Pre-Islamic Background and Early Development of Jurisprudence*, in Khadduri, M., & Liebesny, H.J. (eds.), *Law in the Middle East, Volume I, Origins and Development of Islamic Law* (1955), at 28 ff.

Schacht, J., *The Schools of Law and Later Developments of Jurisprudence*, in Khadduri, M., & Liebesny, H.J. (eds.), *Law in the Middle East, Volume I, Origins and Development of Islamic Law* (1955), at 57 ff.

Shamil Bank of Bahrain v. Beximco Pharmaceuticals Ltd and others, [2004] EWCA CIV 19, [2004] All ER (D) 280 (Jan), issued 28 January 2004.

Tyser, C.R., Demetriades, D.G., & Effendi, I. (translators), *The Majelle: Being an English Translation of Majallah El-Ahkam-I-Adliya and a Complete Code on Islamic Civil Law* (2001).

Usmani, M.T., *Ijarah,* available at www.cba.edu.kw/elsakka/islam_ijarah.pdf.

Usmani, M.T., *Murabahah*, available at www.accountancy.com.pk/docs/islam_murabahah.pdf.

Usmani, M.T., An Introduction to Islamic Finance (2002), also available at www.muftitaqiusmani.com/en/books/PDF/An%20Introduction%20To%20Islamic%20Finance/An_Introduction%20_to_Islamic_Finance.pdf.

VIKØR, K.S., *Between God and the Sultan: A History of Islamic Law* (2005), at 89–184.

AL-ZUHAYLĪ, W., *Al-Fiqh Al-Islāmī wa-Adillatuh* [Islamic Jurisprudence and its Proofs, Financial Transactions in Islamic Jurisprudence] (4th edition, 1997), Mahmoud El-Gamal, M., translator, Eissa, M.S., revisor (2002).

Chapter 10

ISLAMIC FINANCE TO ENHANCE BUSINESS OPPORTUNITIES:

CAPITAL MARKETS

Michael J.T. McMillen

SUMMARY: 1. Introduction. – 2. The Dow Jones Fatwa. – 2.1. Principles. – 2.2. Tests. – 3. *Sukuk*. – 3.1. Basics. – 3.2. Market Issuances. – 4. Opportunities. – References.

1. Introduction

Two of the most notable developments in modern Islamic finance relate to the Shari'ah-compliant capital markets. Without developed capital markets Islamic finance could never be global or serve more than niche markets. The monumental *fatwa* issued in 1998 to Dow Jones & Company, Inc. in connection with the establishment of the Dow Jones Islamic Market Index opened and defined the equity side of the Islamic capital markets. The development of *sukuk* in 2002 opened and defined the debt side of those markets. These two developments have come to define principles of contemporary Islamic finance applicable across industries and practices. The business opportunities made available by the Dow Jones Fatwa and the development of *sukuk* extend well beyond buying and selling securities. These two developments and the opportunities that they afford are the subject of this chapter. [1]

2. The Dow Jones Fatwa

2.1. Principles

In 1993, Dow Jones undertook to establish an Islamic equity benchmark index as part of its family of equity indices. The approach was to develop and apply "screens" to identify Shari'ah-compliant equity securities on a

---

[1] The Dow Jones Fatwa is *The Dow Jones Islamic Market Index: Statement by the Shariah Supervisory Board* (undated; issued in 1998) (copy on file with the author).

global basis. The result was the Dow Jones Islamic Market Index and a related group of indices.[2]

The reality was that nearly every company had (and most still have) some impermissible interest income or expense from, among other activities, direct or indirect deposits, investments, or indebtedness. Some companies engage primarily in permissible business activities, but also have limited involvement in impermissible activities. Examples include credit companies associated with vehicle or engine manufacturers, grocery purveyors that sell pork products or beer, and conglomerates.

The critical inquiries encompassed both indices' formulations and a broader goal of identifying circumstances in which a *non-controlling* investment[3] could be made in equity securities of an entity that has some degree of (i) impermissible interest income or expense and/or (ii) engagement in impermissible business activities.[4]

The framework of the *fatwa* is comprised of a series of tests. The tests acknowledge, and sanction, on a conditional and temporary basis, a degree of variance from or impurity relative to absolute standards. Recognition of permissible variance led to institutionalisation of "cleansing" or "purification" mechanisms that are operative upon and after the investment and are designed to address impure consequences (such as receipt of interest income). An example of purification is donation to charity by a Shari'ah-compliant investor of interest income received by that investor to the ex-

---

[2] This was not the first such effort. See MICHAEL J.T. MCMILLEN, *Islamic Finance and the Shariah: The Dow Jones Fatwa and Permissible Variance as Studies in Letheanism and Legal Change* (2013) ("McMillen 2013"), at 161–164, and MICHAEL J.T. MCMILLEN, *Islamic Capital Markets: Market Developments and Conceptual Evolution in the First Thirteen Years*, available at https://papers.ssrn.com/sol3/papers.cfm?abstract_id=1781112 ("McMillen 2011"), and sources cited in each. This section draws from McMillen 2013. For development of the Dow Jones Fatwa, Rushdi Siddiqui, Shari'ah *Compliance, Performance and Conversion: The Case of the Dow Jones Islamic Market Index*^{SM}, 7 Chicago Journal of International Law 495 (2007) ("Siddiqui 2007"), at 496.

[3] If an investment is controlling, all aspects of the business must be Shari'ah compliant.

[4] The equity indices are described at http://www.djindexes.com/islamicmarket/. See, also, Siddiqui 2007, *id.*, RUSHDI SIDDIQUI, *Islamic indexes: the DJIM framework*, in Sohail Jaffr, ed., *Islamic Asset Management: Forming the Future for Shariah-Compliant Investment Strategies* (2004) ("Jaffer 2004"), at 46–58, Nizam Yaquby, *Trading in Equities: A Sharia Perspective*, available at www.djindexes.com/mdsidxlindex.cfm?event=showlslamicArticles, Wilson, *Screening Criteria for Islamic Equity Funds*, in Jaffer 2004, at 38, DAVID E. MORAN, *The Role of the Dow Jones Islamic Market Index in Islamic Finance*, in The Proceedings of the Third Harvard University Forum on Islamic Finance: Local Challenges, Global Opportunities 111 (2000), at 257–258, and MICHAEL J.T. MCMILLEN, *Asset Securitization Sukuk and Islamic Capital Markets: Structural Issues in these Formative Years*, 25 Wisconsin International Law Journal 703 (2008) ("MCMILLEN 2008a").

tent that income is reflected in a dividend or other distribution. Understanding the tests is fundamental to assessing possible business opportunities arising from the Dow Jones Fatwa (and similar formulations). Of even greater importance, however, is how the permissible variance principle is interpreted and applied in different contexts and factual situations, including, but extending beyond, equity investing.

2.2. Tests

Generally stated, two levels of screening were established to determine the permissibility of an equity investment or includability of an equity security in an index of Shariʿah-compliant securities. The first level has two branches: (a) whether the equity security is itself impermissible; and (b) whether the "primary" or "basic" business activities of the subject entity are *haram* (impermissible) The second level considers whether the entity has sufficient impure income that investment in that entity is precluded. The screens for each level and branch are applied sequentially, in the order presented.

The first branch prohibits transactions in "fixed-income securities, preferred shares, convertible notes, and the like". The stated reason for the prohibition is that these instruments stipulate a predetermined return, essentially guaranteeing return of principal. Predetermined returns violate fundamental principles of profit and loss sharing and related risk-reward principles. There is also a concern about impermissible preferential returns (evidenced in the prohibition on preferred shares). Applications of this level of screening will preclude investments in securities and instruments that provide for a fixed return in situations in which there is no permissible fixed profitability of the relevant entity.

Applications of this test involve careful analysis and are not subject to simple formulas. Consider a generic example of a structured financing involving an equity instrument in an entity that (a) owns only one asset, a commercial office building, (b) leases that building to a single tenant at a fixed rent pursuant to a Shariʿah-compliant lease, (c) has fixed operating costs, and (d) has fixed capital costs. The profit of this entity will be fixed, and the equity return will then be fixed as a factual matter, even though the equity instrument itself does not provide for a fixed return (or any return). In this case, the equity instrument is a *de facto* fixed income instrument. The fixed income depends not on the terms of the instrument, but on the fixed rental and expenses. In the real estate investment realm, equipment leasing, and some similar areas, transactions of this type are not infrequent. Different types of Shariʿah-compliant transactions involving structured *de facto* fixed returns have been developed since the Dow Jones Fatwa was issued. As have different convertible notes, including convertible *sukuk*. Some of these transactions involve permissible variance; some do not. The literal statement belies the relevant principles, and the principles will prevail.

The second branch of the first level screen focuses on impermissible business activities. If the entity in which the investment is to be made is engaged in a single prohibited business activity, the equity investment is impermissible. The more complicated situation is where the entity conducts multiple business activities, some permissible and some impermissible. The Dow Jones Fatwa specifies a non-exclusive list of impermissible activities. It identifies alcohol, tobacco, pork products, conventional financial services (banking, insurance, etc.), defense, weapons, and entertainment (hotels, casinos, gambling, cinema, pornography, music, etc.).

The Dow Jones Fatwa then observes, and industry practice confirms, that unanimity does not exist with respect to what constitutes a prohibited industry or prohibited business activity. Tobacco, defense, and weapons are examples. Shari'ah scholars hold a range of different opinions. Some scholars take the position that defense and weapons are permissible so long as they do not include weapons of mass destruction. Others take the position that not all entertainment and not all cinema is offensive and impermissible, only those involving pornography or indecency. Some opine that not all hotel equities are impermissible, only those in entities that sell alcohol for human consumption. Some scholars allow investments in hotels that sell alcohol if the purification is adequate.[5]

Caution should be exercised in considering and applying lists of prohibited industries or activities. Transactional experience reveals that Shari'ah scholars are more discerning than is suggested by the sweeping statements of prohibited securities and activities. The statements of prohibitions set forth in tests are attributable to different types of factors, including the level of inquiry, practicality considerations, and establishment of the burden of proof with respect to permissibility.

The level of inquiry for a Shari'ah board considering prohibitions for an index is on business sectors. Each of the entertainment sector, the alcohol category, and the pork category includes impermissible and permissible elements, despite the blanket prohibition. Broad prohibitions set forth in

---

[5] Dow Jones Fatwa, *supra* note 1, at 3. See, e.g., Oxford Islamic Finance – Dar Al Istithmar, *A Universal Platform for Shari'a Compliant Equity Screening* (2009), at 12, noting differences of opinion with respect to insurance, weapons, defense, night clubs, cinema, contraception, and massage parlours and categorization issues based upon whether an activity is "direct" or "indirect" and secondary. The latter group includes hotels, media, food, restaurants, advertising, and airlines.

formulations governing index criteria are often by industry or sector. More detailed screening may be undertaken where individual stocks are being considered and the game is worth the candle. For example, index or fund criteria may prohibit investments in equity securities of hotels. However, the Shari'ah scholars may determine that investment in a specific hotel stock is permissible because, for example, the hotels are road-side hotels that do not serve alcohol in a bar or minibar. The general statement may yield to microscopic inquiry.

The practicality factor is related. At the index level, it is impractical, in terms of time, cost, and effort, to evaluate every alcohol or pork usage and every entertainment entity in microscopic detail. It is more efficient to preclude the entire industry or sector and leave detailed inquiry to the relevant Shari'ah board as and when detailed inquiry is necessary. The role of the board for an investment fund or an individual investor is to examine specific investments, where time and cost incurrences are more refined, directed, and acceptable. The board, at the request of management, with undertake microscopic examinations of each entity in which an investment is considered with respect to direct and indirect business activities, including those relating to alcohol, pork, entertainment, interest-based finance, and other activities.

It is here that the burden of proof factor becomes relevant. A generalised prohibition puts the burden of proof on the investment fund, company, or other party desiring an exception to the prohibition to demonstrate why, in a particular instance, the prohibition should not be applicable.

Consider, for example, prohibitions on alcohol. The usual intention is a prohibition relating to intoxication effects. Alcohol is a chemical compound in which the hydroxyl functional group (-OH) is bound to a carbon atom (-C-OH). There are many different types of alcohols, one being ethanol in beverages for human consumption. Other uses of alcohol are many and varied. It is used in antiseptics and disinfectants and as a base for liquid soaps and hand sanitisers. Ethanol and methanol are used as fuel additives. Alcohols are used as preservatives in medicine and science and as solvents in industrial applications, medicines, perfumes, and vegetable essences. Or, consider pork products, even those for human consumption. Pork components and derivatives are ubiquitous in foodstuff offerings, including, among many others, lard, fry fats, cooking oils, cookies, marshmallows, gelatine, and many flavours of potato chips. Ascertaining involvements with pork is not always easy or straightforward. As another example, consider the Dow Jones Fatwa exclusion of "entertainment" activities. Most Shari'ah scholars agree that none of Mickey Mouse, Tom and Jerry, and Popeye the Sailor, or their cartoons, are violative of fundamental Shari'ah principles. Yet, these entertainment activities, and businesses engaged in those activities and their equities, are prohibited under the literal formulations of the Dow Jones Fatwa tests. In a particular instance, a fund manager or other investor may shoulder the burden of demonstrating to the Shari'ah board that the generally stated prohibition should not apply to a specific equity investment.

In short, each transaction, instrument, and undertaking must be carefully examined with the relevant Shari'ah board, *de novo*, on a case-by-case basis, taking into consideration the precise facts of that transaction. This examination should be undertaken with full disclosure and complete transparency. Not unexpectedly, these inquiries entail incremental transaction costs not encountered in most conventional counterpart transactions, although they are encountered in comparable transactions that incorporate ethical investing principles.

If those threshold tests do not preclude investment, the inquiry turns to whether the entity has an *impermissible degree* of *riba* or *haram* income as determined pursuant to a series of financial tests. The concern is with *haram* income that incidentally becomes part of the entity's total income. The relevant tests in the Dow Jones Fatwa are based upon balance sheet information because that was the financial information generally available in the markets in the 1993–1998 time frame.[6] Specifically, the Dow Jones Fatwa permits investment in the equity security of a subject company if:

- total interest-bearing debt (long-term and short-term) to market capitalisation of that company is less than 33%;
- the accounts receivable of that company do not exceed 45% (subsequently amended to 33%) of its market capitalisation;[7] and
- cash (including cash equivalents) and interest-bearing securities owned or held by that company do not exceed 33% of its market capitalisation.[8]

[6] Other tests have been developed subsequent to issuance of the Dow Jones Fatwa. Some are variations on the tests set forth in the Dow Jones Fatwa, some take a slightly different approach, and some consider factors other than (usually in addition to) those considered in the Dow Jones Fatwa. Some include a separate 5% threshold test for impure income from all sources. For present purposes, the principles embodied in the tests, rather than the exact tests, are the relevant focus.

[7] This test recognizes that instalment payments are commonplace and that most of the world does not adhere to the Shari'ah rules prohibiting interest-based payment structures and interest-based discounting.

[8] This test is responsive to the global realities that monies are usually deposited into interest-bearing accounts, invested in interest-bearing securities, or invested in principle guaranteed instruments.

In each case in which market capitalisation, a 12-month (subsequently amended to 24-month) trailing average is adopted to address volatility issues.[9]

Market capitalisation was chosen over total assets as the denominator in these equations because: (a) it was thought to provide a more precise value of a company (including factors such as goodwill) in real time than book value or assets; (b) it was thought to be more sensitive to debt incurrence events (such as rating agency adjustments); (c) stock exchanges have minimum market capitalisation requirements; and (d) it was thought to be more transparent, and less amenable to manipulation, than asset values, particularly for small-cap and mid-cap companies and emerging market companies. With respect to a particular entity, industry, and/or equity security, market capitalisation may not be the best denominator. Here, again, the burden of proof rests with the investor seeking to use an alternative.

If an investment is permissible and the entity in which the investment is made has some degree of impurity, the Dow Jones Fatwa requires "purification" of the impurity, if possible. The concept of purification or cleansing was institutionalised by the Dow Jones Fatwa (it existed prior to the Dow Jones Fatwa). It is an essential correlative of the permissible variance principles. The purification principle is that income from impure sources must not inure to the benefit of the Shari'ah-compliant party (investor). Thus, expenses related to impure sources cannot be netted against income from impure sources. The most common purification technique is donation of the impure income to charity. Identifying impure income is not always easy or precise in non-controlling investments. For example, most public companies do not identify the portion of a dividend or distribution that is attributable to interest or other impure income. Identification of the contribution of impure income is more precise in private equity transactions where control is achieved.

Purification processes are also operative in real estate investment transactions. A couple examples provide a flavour of the dynamic. Assume an approved investment by an investment fund in a commercial office building with two tenants that is located in a metropolitan area. The business activities of one of the tenants are entirely Shari'ah compliant. The other ten-

[9] See MCMILLEN 2013, *supra* note 2, at 175–188, *Sharia Standard No. (21), Financing Paper (Shares and Bonds)*, in Shari'a Standards of the Accounting and Auditing Organisation for Islamic Financial Institutions (2010) ("AAOIFI Standards"), and two "fact sheets, for the Hijrah Index, available at www.ftse.com/Indices/FTSE_Bursa_Malaysia_Index_Series/Downloads/FTSE_Bursa_Malaysia_Hijrah_Shari'ah_Factsheet.pdf, and the EMAS Index, available at www.ftse.com/Indices/FTSE_Bursa_Malaysia_Index_Series/Downloads/FTSE_Bursa_Malaysia_Emas_Shari'ah_Index_Factsheet.pdf.

ant, occupying 2% of the total space, is an ATM owned and operated by an interest-based bank. What is the purification obligation in this circumstance? As a general description of one customary procedure, the total revenue from the rental of the ATM space will be compared with the total rental revenue of the entire building. Assume it to be 2%. That ratio will be applied to the net distributable income, and the Shari'ah-compliant investor is notified that 2% of its dividend or distributed income is attributable to *haram* income. Either the fund will donate the 2%, and deduct it from the dividend or distribution, or the investor will receive the gross amount and have the purification obligation. A simple concept, and a simple calculation.

As another example involves a grocery store tenant that sells pork products and alcohol (beer and wine). The total rent of that tenant may be, say, 10% of the aggregate rent of all tenants in the building, but the portion of the rent from that tenant that is attributable to *haram* sources will likely not be 10%. The grocery store sells many non-*haram* foods, paper products, light bulbs, personal hygiene products, clothing, school supplies, hardware, and a raft of other products. It may also sell products that include pork derivatives (e.g., lard, cookies). How can one determine the portion of the rent of that store that is attributable to *haram* products (which is the necessary starting point in making the calculations)? It is likely that the store will be unwilling to disclose that information or provide detail of that type. Various tools are available to estimate the impure income. For example, industry trade groups and large multi-store purveyors often have information from similarly situated stores that can be used as a starting point and be refined for local circumstances.

Two conclusions are important. Purification is required where there is impure income. The purification process is closely tied to the specific facts and circumstances of the investment or business being considered and those facts and circumstances must be carefully analysed.

3. *Sukuk*

3.1. Basics

Few aspects of Islamic finance have received as much publicity as *sukuk* (plural; *sakk* is the singular). *Sukuk* are hailed as the fastest growing segment of Islamic finance and the backbone of contemporary Islamic finance. The first assertion is likely true, if dollar volume is the measure. It is certainly true if the referential base is the Islamic capital markets. The second assertion is subject to qualification, if not direct challenge. *Sukuk* issuances have increased markedly since 2002, for governments and government-related issuers. Outside of Malaysia, the potential of *sukuk* in assisting the private sector is almost totally untapped, whatever the benefits to the government and quasi-government sector. Each market segment provides enormous business opportunities, the latter far greater than the former. [10]

Both in the popular press and much of the Islamic finance literature, *sukuk* are described as "Islamic bonds". That is a convenient and catchy description which does denote the linkage to the financing side of the capital markets. But it is inaccurate. *Sukuk* are not bonds. They are not dependent upon the credit of the issuing entity. There have been concerted efforts to structure *sukuk* as bonds. Those efforts were rejected by Shari'ah scholars, including the Shari'ah board of the Accounting and Auditing Organisation for Islamic Financial Institutions (AAOIFI). [11]

The *sukuk* standard issued by AAOIFI in 2003, although voluntary, has assumed a prominent, almost definitive, role in the structuring of *sukuk*. The AAOIFI Sukuk Standard defines *sukuk* as certificates of equal value put to use as common shares and rights in tangible assets, usufructs, and services or as equity in a project or investment activity. The standard carefully distinguishes *sukuk* from equity, notes, and bonds. It emphasises that *sukuk* are not debts of the issuer; [12] and that they are fractional or propor-

---

[10] This chapter draws on McMillen 2011, *supra* note 2, especially at 16–36, McMillen 2008a, *supra* note 3, and Michael J.T. McMillen, *Contractual Enforceability Issues: Sukuk and Capital Markets Development*, 7 Chicago Journal of International Law 427 (2007) ("McMillen 2007"). For the early history of *sukuk* and fundamental principles, Abdulkader Thomas, *Securitization in Islamic Finance*, in Islamic Finance: The Regulatory, Challenge, Simon Archer and Rifaat Ahmed Abdel Karim, eds. (2007), at 259 *et seq.*, Mohamed Rafe Md. Haneef, *Recent Trends and Innovations in Islamic Debt Securities: Prospects for Islamic Profit and Loss Sharing Securities*, in Islamic Finance: Current Legal and Regulatory Issues, S. Nizam Ali, ed. (2005), at 29–60, *Islamic Bonds: Your Guide to Issuing, Structuring and Investing in Sukuk*, Nathif J. Adam and Abdulkader Thomas, eds. (2004), Nathif J. Adam, & Abdulkader Thomas, *Islamic fixed-income securities: sukuk*, in Jaffer 2004, *supra* note 3, at 72–81, Michael J.T. McMillen & John A. Crawford, *Sukuk in the First Decade: By the Numbers*, Dow Jones Islamic Market Indexes: Quarterly Newsletter, December 2008, available at https://papers.ssrn.com/sol3/papers.cfm?abstract_id=2293690 ("McMillen & Crawford"), and Michael J.T. McMillen, *Sukuk in Its Infancy: Misstep and Sequel*, Dow Jones Islamic Market Indexes: Quarterly Newsletter, May 2008, available at http://now.eloqua.com/e/er.aspx?s=812&lid=33&elq=0F71972189AB4B799F291CA4BD1F5909 ("McMillen 2008b").

[11] McMillen 2011, *supra* note 2, 25–29, and McMillen 2008b, *id.*, each discussing the "clarification" of fundamental *sukuk* principles that was issued by Taqi Usmani, chairman of the AAOIFI Shariah board, in March 2008 as *sukuk* structures became more bond like. The clarification is undated (copy on file with the author).

[12] This assertion may conflict with the relevant secular legal definition of "debt", especially where debt is defined as an obligation to pay money. Some Shari'ah scholars

tional interests in underlying Shari'ah compliant assets, usufructs, services, projects, or activities.[13] The standard provides that *sukuk* may not be issued on a pool of receivables.[14]

Sukuk are defined relative to the assets (including usufructs and services) generating cash flows that are used to make payments on the *sukuk* certificates. That is, *sukuk* are securitisations. The following is a working definition of securitisation:[15]

> the sale of equity or debt instruments, representing ownership interests in, or secured by, a segregated, income producing asset or pool of assets, in a transaction structured to reduce or reallocate certain risks inherent in owning or lending against the underlying assets and to ensure that such interests are more readily marketable and, thus, more liquid than ownership interests in and loans against the underlying assets.

A principal purpose of asset securitisation is to lower the cost of funding for identified assets. The assets are segregated from the originator of those assets. Risks associated with the segregated assets are divorced from other risks associated with the asset originator, especially bankruptcy and insolvency risks. The assets are placed in a new vehicle (often a trust) that issues certificates representing interests in the segregated assets (or the new vehicle, whose only assets are the segregated assets). The new vehicle – the

---

note that this formulation in the AAOIFI Sukuk Standard should be read to mean "*sukuk* are not an obligation to pay money where the issuer has not generated a distributable profit from the relevant assets", acknowledging that *sukuk* are obligations to pay distributable profits of this type.

[13] The Dow Jones Fatwa is relevant in determining whether the underlying assets, usufructs, services, projects, or investment activities are Shari'ah compliant.

[14] This statement is also subject to some qualification. For example, *sukuk* may be and are issued on receivables constituting rent under Shari'ah-compliant obligation, such as an *ijara*.

[15] JOSEPH C. SHENKER, & ANTHONY J. COLLETTA, *Asset Securitization: Evolution, Current Issues and New Frontiers*, 69 Texas Law Review 1369 (1990–1991), at 1374–1375. The literature on asset securitizations is voluminous. A sampling of introductions to concepts, structures, and issues includes JAMES A. ROSENTHAL, & JUAN M. OCAMPO, *Analyzing the Economic Benefits of Securitized Credit*, 1 Journal of Applied Corporate Finance 32 (1992), STEVEN L. SCHWARCZ, *The Alchemy of Asset Securitization*, 1 Stanford Journal of Law, Business & Finance 133 (1994–1995), ROBERT DEAN ELLIS, *Securitization Vehicles, Fiduciary Duties, and Bondholder's Rights*, 24 Journal of Corporate Law 295 (1998–1999), STEVEN L. SCHWARCZ, *The Universal Language of International Asset Securitizations*, 12 Duke Journal of International & Comparative Law 285 (2002), and FRANK J. FABOZZI, ed. *The Handbook of Mortgage-Backed Securities*, (2001), which should be compared with the 1985 edition of the same book: pre-1985 structures (such as pass-through certificates) had greater similarity to *sukuk* structures.

issuer of the certificates – has a low likelihood of becoming involved in a bankruptcy or insolvency, usually because it has no creditors other than holders of its certificates and it is constrained by requirements designed to maintain bankruptcy remoteness.[16] All of which works to lower the cost of funding. Cash flows from the segregated assets are the primary source of payment for the securitisation or *sukuk* certificates that are issued in respect of the segregated assets. Those cash flows may be lease rental payments, royalty payments, services payments, receivables, sales proceeds, or of some other type. In a *sukuk* issuance, the cash flows must derive from Shari'ah compliant assets and processes.

The AAOIFI Sukuk Standard provides for 14 eligible assets classes. In broad summary, they are securitisations: (a) of an existing or to-be-acquired tangible asset (*ijara*); (b) of an existing or to-be-acquired leasehold estate (*ijara*); (c) of presales of services (*ijara*); (d) of presales of the production of goods or commodities at a future date (*salam* or forward sale); (e) to fund construction (*istisna'a* or construction/manufacture contract); (f) to fund the acquisition of goods for future sale (*murabaha* or sale at a markup); (g) to fund capital participation in a business or investment activity (*mudaraba* or *musharaka*, which are types of partnerships); and (h) to fund various asset acquisition and agency management (*wakala* or agency), agricultural land cultivation, land management, and orchard management activities. Notably, five of the 14 categories pertain to leases.

3.2 Market Issuances

Total global *sukuk* issuances have grown dramatically since the first issuance in 2002, as illustrated by gross issuance data. Beyond gross issuance data, the data is confusing, and often misleading. Three tables are presented to give an overview of the *sukuk* markets and to emphasise some cautionary notes in interpreting available *sukuk* data.

---

[16] Frequently the transfer of assets into the new vehicle (issuer) is structured to constitute a "true sale". A true sale is a sale that is sufficient under relevant bankruptcy and insolvency laws to remove the assets from the bankruptcy estate of the asset originator. If a true sale has been effectuated, the investor in the newly issued certificates has relatively little concern with the asset originator (unless that originator has a continuing role in the transaction as, say, a servicer). Preservation of the bankruptcy remoteness of the issuer is maintained by limiting the issuer to a single business purpose and requiring various formalities in the conduct of business by the issuer.

Table 10.1 Total global *sukuk* issuances

(US$, billions)			Issuer type	2014	2016
Year(s)	Global	International	(% of total global issuances)		
2002–11/7/2008	88				
2009	37.9	7.0	Sovereign	67	58
2014	107.3	26.7	Quasi-Sovereign	16	6
2016	87.8	31.2	Corporate	22	32
2017	116.7	37.6	Financial Institutions	–	4
2018	123.2	33.0			
2019	145.7	38.5			

Table 10.1 illustrates the growth pattern, total global issuances, and total international issuances for select years, and the types of issuers for two years. [17] The difference between the International column and the Global column for any year indicates domestic issuances for that year. [18]

The categories of issuers set forth in Table 10.1 obfuscate the influence of sovereigns on the *sukuk* markets. For example, some question the distinctiveness, and even the appropriateness, of the category of "quasi-sovereign" issuers. These are entities controlled by, and often largely owned by, sovereigns. The category includes telecommunications companies, investment companies that operate almost entirely for the benefit of sovereigns, and similar entities. Prior to 2011 most issuances in this category were by Islamic Development Bank and the Malaysian finance ministry's Khazanah Nasional Berhad. Examples in more recent times include Saudi Electricity Company, Saudi Arabian Oil Company (Saudi Aramco), Saudi Arabian Mining Co., PLUS Malaysia Berhad (PLUS Expressways Berhad), Tenaga Nasional Berhad, DP World PLC, Arab Petroleum Investments Corporation, and similar entities. [19] The dependency of "corporate" entities on contracts with sovereigns and quasi-

---

[17] The pattern for types of issuers is not materially different for other years.

[18] Sources: For dollar volumes from 2002–2008, MCMILLEN & CRAWFORD, *supra* note 5, and IIFM SUKUK REPORT, July 2019, 8th edition, International Islamic Finance Market, at 21 for other years, 25–26 for domestic issuances, and 32–35 for types of issuers, and IIFM SUKUK REPORT, July 2020, 9th edition, International Islamic Finance Market, at 28 and 31, for 2019.

[19] An important consideration is the small size of the total *sukuk* market (the denominator in the percentage calculations). A large issuance by a sovereign or quasi-sovereign significantly distorts percentage determinations.

sovereigns also obscures the dominance of sovereign influence for those entities. The revenue base of these corporates is dependent upon providing goods and services to sovereigns and quasi-sovereigns. It should be noted corporate issuers that are not dependent upon sovereign and quasi-sovereign business are largely concentrated in Malaysia.[20]

Table 10.2 Infrastructure issuances in 2013 (percentages, rounded)

Governmental	46
Financial Services	18
Transport	12
Telecommunications	10
Power and Utilities	5
Construction	4
Real Estate	4
Other	2

Table 10.2 illustrates the categorisation of *sukuk* issuances by sector for a representative quarter year (fourth quarter, 2013). The purpose of Table 10.2 is to illustrate some interpretive difficulties with available data, especially in understanding how categories are differentiated and how and why any given issuance is allocated to a particular category. The data in this table pertains almost entirely to infrastructure. How the categories are differentiated in this data set is unclear. Transport, telecommunications, and power and utilities are almost always governmental (or quasi-governmental) functions in the countries included in the database. Some financial services, construction, and real estate issuances are also governmental (or quasi-governmental) and it is not possible to determine the extent to which non-governmental issuances are included in this data set.

[20] IIFM Report, *supra* note 9, at 35. Consider the categorization 2002–2008: 35% of all issuances were categorized as sovereign and 65% as corporate. See McMillen & Crawford, *supra* note 5, at 3, which includes issuances by category of issuer.

Table 10.3. Shari'ah structures in 2013 (percentages, rounded)

Murabaha	59
Murabaha – Mudaraba	3
Murabaha – Musharaka	1
Total *Murabaha*	63
Ijara	11
Musharaka	10
Bai Bithaman Ajil	8
Wakala	3
Al-Istithmar	4
Wakala-Bel-Istithmar	1
Salam	1
Mudaraba	1

Table 10.3 summarises *sukuk* issuances by Shari'ah structure in the same quarter, using the same data as Table 10.2. *Murabaha* structures had become widely used by 2013.[21] That was historically atypical but illustrates a trend among sovereign issuers that began around 2009. That type of trend is an important consideration in assessing how to structure and use *sukuk*. The trend has continued to the present.[22]

With some regional variances attributable to varying Shari'ah interpretations, certain structures are not tradeable above or below par value (face amount) because they represent debt obligations. *Sukuk al-murabaha* are one such structure. Why then were significant issuances of non-tradable *sukuk* and why has the trend continued?

---

[21] For domestic *sukuk* issuances in 2018, approximately 66.71% of sovereign, 59.25% of quasi-sovereign, and 22.53% of corporate issuances were *murabaha*-based. Up to 2008, approximately 75% of all globally issued *sukuk* were *ijara* and *musharaka* structures and *murabaha*-based issuances were minimal outside Malaysia and 9.2% of all issuances (domestic and international). The *musharaka* structures were criticized in a clarification by the AAOIFI Shariah board after a series of hearings and their use diminished radically. The usage of *murabaha* structures then increased, led by sovereign and quasi-sovereign issuances from Saudi Arabia.

[22] Source: *Zawya Islamic Sukuk Quarterly Bulletin*, Issue 20, 4Q 2013. For 2007, see *Ratings Direct*, Standard & Poor's Corporation (March 11, 2008), at 5. For the AAOIFI criticism, see note 7, *supra*. For *murabaha* during 2002–2008, MCMILLEN & CRAWFORD, *id.*, at 4–7. For increased use of *murabaha*, see MICHAEL J.T. MCMILLEN, *Trends in Islamic Project and Infrastructure Finance in the Middle East: Re-Emergence of the Murabaha* (November 17, 2012), available at https://papers.ssrn.com/sol3/papers.cfm?abstract_id=1753252.

The answers pertain to fundamental aspects of the Islamic capital markets of relevance to anyone considering use of *sukuk* to realise business opportunities. Secondary markets for Shari'ah-compliant debt instruments are exceptionally thin and illiquid. There is some trading, mostly between major financial institutions. And the secondary markets in Malaysia are better developed than elsewhere in the world. But, generally stated, secondary markets are almost non-existent. Thus, some issuers are not concerned that a given *sukuk* issuance is not tradeable.

Another factor is the dearth of available Shari'ah-compliant instruments. Often, an investor that acquires a desirable Shari'ah-compliant instrument will be reluctant to dispose of that instrument because of the difficulties of acquiring an alternative instrument. The issue is particularly acute for Islamic banks that are subject to tier capital requirements of bank regulators (such as under the Basel Accords). The supply of Shari'ah-compliant instruments that constitute tier 1 or tier 2 capital is especially limited. An Islamic bank that obtains such an instrument will not relinquish that instrument. Alternative tier-qualifying instruments are interest-bearing. Which means the Islamic bank is prohibited, under Shari'ah principles, from investing in those alternative instruments.[23]

The strength of a rating for a sovereign and quasi-sovereign issuer may induce that issuer to be unconcerned with the tradability of a *sukuk* issuance, at least as a relative matter, because of the identities of the *sukuk* purchasers. Highly rated sovereign and quasi-sovereign issuances are often sold, in both domestic and international markets, to insurance companies and pension funds. Many of those entities, especially in non-Muslim jurisdictions, care little about Shari'ah compliance. They purchase the *sukuk* because of its rating, high quality, and longer term. Their objective is often to use the *sukuk* instruments to match fund pension and similar obligations. In such cases, tradability is of limited concern, both to the purchaser and, as a result, to the issuing sovereign or quasi-sovereign. If the insurance company or pension fund is not a Shari'ah-compliant institution and needs to trade the *sukuk*, it will look to secondary markets that are unconcerned with Shari'ah prohibitions on tradability.

[23] For the Basel Accords, see the web site of the Bank for International Settlements at www.bis.org/bcbs/index.htm?m=3%7C14 and www.bis.org/bcbs/history.htm and links from those pages.

Figure 10.1 Generic lease (*ijara*) *sukuk* structure

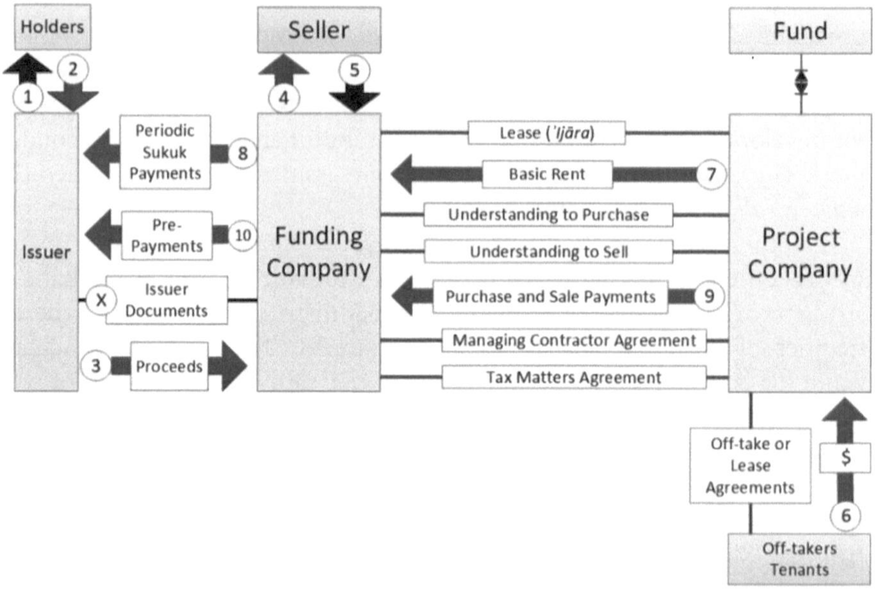

Source: Copyright © 2009–2020: Michael J.T. McMillen.

Historically, *ijara* based *sukuk* have predominated international issuances. For international issuances in the 2002–2008 period, the *ijara* was used in 53.59% of sovereign issuances, 12.11% of quasi-sovereign issuances, and 46% of corporate issuances. The lease structure is widely accepted by all schools of Islamic jurisprudence and lease-based *sukuk* are tradable above and below par in the primary and secondary markets.[24]

Figure 10.1 illustrates an *ijara sukuk* structure. Figure 10.1 should be compared with Figure 9.3 in Chapter 9. Figure 10.1 has been modified slightly to emphasise that the structure is the same whether used to finance an industrial or infrastructure project where a product is sold to off-takers or a real estate project where rent is paid by tenants.

The structure described in Chapter 9 is unchanged when introduced into a *sukuk*, with one exception. Rather than a bank providing an interest-based loan to finance the acquisition of the asset, the financing is provided by selling *sukuk* to a group of holders in steps ① (issuance of *sukuk* certificates) and ② (issuance proceeds). That results in removal of the dashed line of bifurcation from Figure 9.3. The transaction is no longer bifurcated. It is entirely Shari'ah compliant. In all other respects the structure is identi-

[24] IIFM Report, *supra* note 9, at 48–58.

cal, including with respect to how payments by an occupational tenant (or off-taker), through Basic Rent, fund periodic *sukuk* payments or payments under the Understanding to Purchase or Understanding to Sell fund pre-payments of the *sukuk* certificates. The bifurcated private equity financing illustrated in Figure 9.4 (private equity) can be made entirely Shariʿah compliant in the same manner as shown in Figure 10.1 through use of a *sukuk* issuance rather than a bank loan.

4. Opportunities

Business opportunities on the equity side of the Islamic capital markets are of two general types. One relates to investments in equity securities and related activities, such as brokerage. These are straight forward in concept and, despite considerable growth in the Islamic equity capital markets, still underutilised in practice. The other set of opportunities derive from the principles established in the Dow Jones Fatwa, most notably the "permissible variance" concepts. These principles are applicable in a broad range of situations and provide enhanced flexibility to those sensitive to their use in pursuing business opportunities. They allow non-controlling investments in businesses that are not entirely Shariʿah compliant. With respect to real estate investments, they work to expand the pool of permissible tenants, thereby significantly enhancing the ability of Shariʿah-compliant investors to compete and successfully realise on investments. Mastery of the screens, and the purposes of the screens, facilitates identification and realisation of acquisition and investment opportunities that may be perceived as precluded. Consider, for example, entertainment opportunities. The criteria of the Dow Jones Fatwa, literally stated, preclude these investments. But that is not the purpose or structure of the Dow Jones Fatwa. If an investor or entrepreneur is willing to take up the burden of proof and approach the relevant Shariʿah scholars, there are many entertainment business opportunities that are not pornographic or obscene and will be permissible.

Few areas of Islamic finance present as many opportunities as *sukuk* issuance. European and North American jurisdictions are particularly well situated to realise these opportunities. And it is an edifying circumstance that realisation of these opportunities will benefit each of the business practitioners sponsoring *sukuk* issuances out of these jurisdictions, the Islamic finance industry and its constituent elements, and the global capital markets. For example, successful issuances from European and Northern American jurisdictions will significantly increase the pool of Shariʿah-compliant securities, especially if the issuances are rated. There is a significantly greater likelihood of being able to issue rated Shariʿah-compliant *sukuk* from European and North American jurisdictions than from other jurisdictions. The increased pool of Shariʿah-compliant securities will, in turn, enhance the development of Islamic secondary markets. That will both strengthen Islamic finance and work to integrate Islamic finance into the global capital markets. In almost all cases, the securities issued will be desirable for both Muslim and non-Muslim investors. If these issuances are structured to qualify as tier 1 and tier 2 capital under the Basel Accords, the Shariʿah compliance, viability, and economic soundness of Islamic banks, and the stability of the Islamic banking system, will be notably enhanced.

The principal requisites for realizing upon these opportunities are (a) experience with asset securitisations, (b) a fulsome supply of Shariʿah-compliant assets that can be securitised, (c) stable and sophisticated legal systems that allow predictability regarding issues that are critical to securitisation and ratings, and (d) the ability to obtain ratings for the certificates issued off the securitised assets. With respect to each of these matters, European and North American jurisdictions are better situated than most of the jurisdictions from which *sukuk* are currently issued. European and North American jurisdictions lead the world in terms of securitisation experience, including institutional infrastructure. Similarly, the pool of Shariʿah-compliant assets in these jurisdictions, from a practical perspective, is almost limitless. The legal systems of European and North American jurisdictions are sophisticated and stable, with strong and tested regimes pertaining to bankruptcy and insolvency, securities, collateral security regimes, true sales, non-consolidation of entities, and all other concepts that underlie successful securitisation (and thus *sukuk*) issuances. Rated securitisations from European and North American jurisdictions are commonplace.

The dearth of corporate *sukuk* outside Malaysia is directly attributable to the inability of obtaining ratings. Ratings are only available for sovereigns and quasi-sovereigns, in each case based upon the country rating rather than the transactional structure and assets. The inability to obtain ratings for other issuances (such as corporate issuances), in turn, is directly attributable to the lack of development of legal regimes pertaining to bankruptcy, insolvency, securities, collateral security, true sale, non-consolidation, and similar concepts, and the inability of lawyers to render the legal opinions necessary to obtain the ratings. None of these impediments exist in European and North American jurisdictions. On the contrary, securitisation issuances from European and North American jurisdiction have been extensively tested in the courts. Outcomes are known and predictable. Which means legal opinions and ratings are routinely issued. The potential to issue *sukuk* from Europe and North America, based upon assets from those jurisdictions, is untapped, and, for all practical purposes, essentially limitless.

References

ACCOUNTING AND AUDITING ORGANISATION FOR ISLAMIC FINANCE INSTITUTIONS, *Sharia Standard No. (21), Financing Paper (Shares and Bonds)*, in *Shari'a Standards of the Accounting and Auditing Organisation for Islamic Financial Institutions* (2010).

ADAM, N.J., & THOMAS, A. (eds.), *Islamic Bonds: Your Guide to Issuing, Structuring and Investing in Sukuk* (2004).

ADAM, N.J., & THOMAS, A., *Islamic Fixed-Income Securities: Sukuk*, in Jaffer, S. (ed.), *Islamic Asset Management: Forming the Future for Shariah-Compliant Investment Strategies* (2004).

DOW JONES ISLAMIC MARKET INDEX, *The Dow Jones Islamic Market Index: Statement by the Shariah Supervisory Board* (undated; issued in 1998) (copy on file with the author.)

ELLIS, R.D., *Securitization Vehicles, Fiduciary Duties, and Bondholder's Rights*, in 24 *Journal of Corporate Law* 295 ff. (1998–1999).

EMAS Index, available at www.ftse.com/Indices/FTSE_Bursa_Malaysia_Index_Series/Downloads/FTSE_Bursa_Malaysia_Emas_Shari'ah_Index_Factsheet.pdf.

FABOZZI, F.J. (ed.), *The Handbook of Mortgage-Backed Securities* (2001).

HANEEF, M.R.M., *Recent Trends and Innovations in Islamic Debt Securities: Prospects for Islamic Profit and Loss Sharing Securities*, in ALI, S. N. (ed.), *Islamic Finance: Current Legal and Regulatory Issues* (2005).

Hijrah Index, fact sheets, available at www.ftse.com/Indices/FTSE_Bursa_Malaysia_Index_Series/Downloads/FTSE_Bursa_Malaysia.

INTERNATIONAL ISLAMIC FINANCE MARKET, IIFM Sukuk Report, July 2020, 9th edition (2020).

INTERNATIONAL ISLAMIC FINANCE MARKET, IIFM Sukuk Report, July 2019, 8th edition (2019).

JAFFER, S. (ed.), *Islamic Asset Management: Forming the Future for Shariah-Compliant Investment Strategies* (2004).

MCMILLEN, M.J.T., *Contractual Enforceability Issues: Sukuk and Capital Markets Development*, in 7 Chicago Journal of International Law 427 ff. (2007).

MCMILLEN, M.J.T., *Asset Securitization Sukuk and Islamic Capital Markets: Structural Issues in these Formative Years*, in 25 Wisconsin International Law Journal 703 ff. (2008).

MCMILLEN, M.J.T., *Sukuk in Its Infancy: Misstep and Sequel, in Dow Jones Islamic Market Indexes: Quarterly Newsletter*, May 2008, available at http://now.eloqua.com/e/er.aspx?s=812&lid=33&elq=0F71972189AB4B799F291CA4BD1F5909.

McMillen, M.J.T., *Islamic Capital Markets: Market Developments and Conceptual Evolution in the First Thirteen Years* (May 5, 2011), available at https://papers.ssrn.com/sol3/papers.cfm?abstract_id=1781112.

McMillen, M.J.T., *Trends in Islamic Project and Infrastructure Finance in the Middle East: Re-Emergence of the Murabaha* (November 17, 2012), available at https://papers.ssrn.com/sol3/papers.cfm?abstract_id=1753252.

McMillen, M.J.T., *Islamic Finance and the Shariah: The Dow Jones Fatwa and Permissible Variance as Studies in Letheanism and Legal Change* (2013).

McMillen, M.J.T., & Crawford, J., *Sukuk in the First Decade: By the Numbers, in Dow Jones Islamic Market Indexes: Quarterly Newsletter*, December 2008, available at https://papers.ssrn.com/sol3/papers.cfm?abstract_id=2293690.

Moran, D.E., *The Role of the Dow Jones Islamic Market Index in Islamic Finance*, in *Harvard Islamic Finance Information Program*, The Proceedings of the Third Harvard University Forum on Islamic Finance: Local Challenges, Global Opportunities 111 ff. (2000).

Oxford Islamic Finance, & Dar Al Istithmar, *A Universal Platform for Shariʿa Compliant Equity Screening* (2009).

Rosenthal, J.A., & Ocampo, J.M., *Analyzing the Economic Benefits of Securitized Credit*, in 1 Journal of Applied Corporate Finance 32 ff. (1992).

Schwarcz, S.L., *The Alchemy of Asset Securitization*, in 1 Stanford Journal of Law, Business & Finance 133 ff. (1994–1995).

Schwarcz, S.L., *The Universal Language of International Asset Securitizations*, in 12 Duke Journal of International & Comparative Law 285 ff. (2002).

Shenker, J.C., & Colletta, A.J., *Asset Securitization: Evolution, Current Issues and New Frontiers*, in 69 Texas Law Review 1369 ff. (1990–1991.

Siddiqui, R., *Islamic indexes: the DJIM framework*, in Jaffer, S. (ed.), *Islamic Asset Management: Forming the Future for Shariah-Compliant Investment Strategies* (2004).

Siddiqui, R., *Shariʿah Compliance, Performance and Conversion: The Case of the Dow Jones Islamic Market Index^{SM}*, in 7 Chicago Journal of International Law 495 ff. (2007).

Standard and Poor's Corporation, *Ratings Direct* (March 11, 2008).

Thomas, A., *Securitization in Islamic Finance*, in Archer, S., & Karim, R.A.A. (eds.), *Islamic Finance: The Regulatory Challenge* (2007).

Wilson, R., *Screening Criteria for Islamic Equity Funds*, in Jaffer, S. (ed.),

Islamic Asset Management: Forming the Future for Shariah-Compliant Investment Strategies (2004).

YAQUBY, N., *Trading in Equities: A Sharia Perspective*, available at www.djindexes.com/mdsidxlindex.cfm?event=showlslamicArticles.

ZAWYA, *Zawya Islamic Sukuk Quarterly Bulletin*, Issue 20, 4Q 2013.

Chapter 11
APPLICATION OF THE LEGAL PRINCIPLES OF ISLAMIC FINANCE TO OUR LEGAL SYSTEM

Fabrizio Vismara

SUMMARY: 1. Implementation of Shari'ah Principles as a Result of Recourse to Foreign Law. – 2. Comparative Aspects between the Principles of Islamic Finance and Italian Law. – 3. Islamic Financial Products: Hints of Consistency with Italian Law. – 4. The Italian Offer of Islamic Financial Products. – References.

1. Implementation of Shari'ah Principles as a Result of Recourse to Foreign Law

If chosen by the parties, Islamic finance principles can be applied to financial contracts. In this regard, it should be remembered that parties may include in contracts choice of law clauses that expressly refer to Shari'ah principles in contracts. [1]

Almost all legal systems recognise the freedom for the parties to choose the applicable law for their contracts. [2] This choice is not conditioned by the fact that the contract has international elements, even though in some cases, if the contract is entirely related to a specific legal system, the mandatory rules of that system may still be applicable. [3] Furthermore, it does not

---

[1] See ZAHID A., & MOHD ALI H., *Shari'ah as a Choice of Law in international Islamic finance contracts: Shamil Bank of Bahrain case revisited*, in US-China Law Review, 2013, 27 ff.

[2] According to GIULIANO M., *La loi applicable aux contrats: problèmes choisis*, in Recueil des cours, 1977, 5, 199, "une règle de droit international privé de ce contenu se retrouve, à l'heure actuelle, dans presque tous les systèmes juridiques nationaux". See also VON OVERBECK A.E., *L'irrésistible extension de l'autonomie en droit international privé*, in Hommage à François Rigaux, Bruxelles (1993), 619.

[3] With regard to this aspect, see Article 3, paragraph 3 of EU Regulation No. 593/2008, according to which "Where all other elements relevant to the situation at the time of the choice are located in a country other than the country whose law has been chosen, the choice of the parties shall not prejudice the application of provisions of the law of that other country which cannot be derogated from by agreement.". On this topic, see: MOSCONI F., & CAMPIGLIO C., *Diritto internazionale privato e processuale*, Vol. I, *Parte generale e obbligazioni,* 7th ed., Torino (2015), 402.

seem necessary that the law chosen by the parties expresses an effective link between a specific legal system and the contract at issue.[4]

In this regard, reference should be made to Article 2, paragraph 1, of the 1991 Resolution of the *Institut de Droit International* on "l'autonomie de la volonté des parties dans les contrats internationaux entre personnes privées", where it is pointed out that parties, in the consensual determination of the applicable rules, "peuvent convenir de l'application de tout droit étatique".[5]

The application of Shariʿah to financial contracts must also consider public order principles.[6]

Article 16 of Italian Law 218/95 provides in fact that "foreign law is not applied if its effects are contrary to public order". Public order aims at ensuring the respect, in any given situation, of the fundamental principles of the internal order in a given historical period, grounded upon the necessary protection of fundamental human rights shared by different legal systems and which may be inferred from the protection granted by a legislation which takes precedence. Moreover, Article 17 of Law 218/95 should be considered a mandatory rule.[7] Article 17 in fact states that the prevailing importance of "Italian rules that, in consideration of their object and purpose, must be applied despite references to foreign law" is uncontested. Therefore, mandatory rules, identified through an interpretative process, always prevail despite recourse to foreign law, in light of their object and purpose.

---

[4] See ICC interim award No. 4145/1983, according to which "the principle of autonomy – widely recognised – allows the parties to choose any law to rule their contract, even if not obviously related with. This is what the parties have done in mentioning Swiss law, although at first sight less related with the agreement than the law of the country X", published in Year. Comm. Arb., 1987, 101.

[5] Please find the text at: http://www.idi-iil.org/app/uploads/2017/06/1991_bal_02_fr.pdf. With regard to that resolution, see Kohler C., *L'autonomie* de la volonté en droit international privé: un principe universel entre libéralisme et étatisme, in Recueil des cours, 2013, 359, 62 ff.

[6] See MOSCONI F., *Exceptions to the operations of choice of law rules*, in *Rec. des cours*, 1989, 217.

[7] See SPERDUTI G.; *Les lois d'application nécessaire en tant que lois d'ordre public*, in Rev. crit., 1977, 258 ff.; id, *Norme di applicazione necessaria e ordine pubblico*, in Riv. dir. int. priv. proc., 1976, 469 ff.; FRANCESCAKIS P., *Lois d'application immédiate et droit du travail*, ibidem, 1974, 273 ff.; MOSCONI F., *Norme di applicazione necessaria e norme di conflitto di origine convenzionale*, in Riv. dir. int. priv. proc., 1967, 730 ff.; POCAR F., *Norme di applicazione necessaria e conflitti di leggi in tema di rapporti di lavoro*, 734 ff.

2. Comparative Aspects between the Principles of Islamic Finance and Italian Law

Comparison between Shari'ah and Italian law with reference to agreements of a financial nature, highlights a series of significant differences.[8]

First of all, it should be remembered that the Shari'ah prohibits the accrual of interest on loans (*riba*).[9] The reason for this prohibition is to exclude the possibility of a purely speculative financial benefit situation. Furthermore, Shari'ah prohibits the possibility of financial gains without the bearing of the risk associated with the investment. The elements characterizing interest on loans or *riba* can be summarised as: (i) the presence of an interest rate with respect to a certain capital, (ii) the ex-ante determination of such interest rate, (iii) the fact that the accrual of interest is linked to a time element and (iv) the fact, of primary importance, that the payment of interest is due by the borrower regardless of the economic results of the loan.

On the other hand, Article 1815 of the Italian Civil Code provides that loans are presumed to be onerous.[10] Thus, interest on loans is always due, unless otherwise agreed by the parties. Agreements of the parties may also be implicit when, due to specific circumstances and the nature of the contracting parties involved, the intention to exclude compensation may be automatically inferred.[11]

Furthermore according to Italian case law, failure to enter into a loan agreement cannot be inferred from the mere absence of an agreement on interest and a deadline for repayment of borrowed amounts, since these are not essential elements for the existence of the contract.[12] However, there is still the obligation to indicate in writing the conventional interest rate in excess of the legal interest rate.[13]

As a result, the agreement of the parties on a higher interest rate than the legal interest rate, as well as the specific agreed interest rate,[14] must be

[8] See ALVARO S., *La finanza islamica nel contesto giuridico ed economico italiano*, Quaderni giuridici CONSOB, No. 6, luglio 2016. See also BIANCONE P., SECINARO S., & RADWAN M., *Compatibilità della finanza islamica alla normativa italiana*, in Rivista telematica (www.statoechiese.it), 9, 2020.

[9] BORRONI A., *A Comparative Survey on Islamic Riba and Western Usury*, in Rivista telematica (www.statoechiese.it), 4, 2019.

[10] SIMONETTO E., *Mutuo*, in Enc. Giur., XX, Roma (1992).

[11] FRAGALI M., *Del mutuo*, in *Comm. Scialoja, Branca, artt. 1813–1822*, Bologna-Roma (1966), 347 ff.

[12] Cass., 3/12/1991, No. 12926.

[13] See art. 1284 Italian Civil Code.

[14] Cass., 3017/2014.

indicated in writing. This agreement is valid even if reference is made to contractual elements that do not indicate in figures the extent of the agreed interest rate, but that indicate the pre-established criteria and elements, external to the negotiating document and objectively identifiable, that allow the concrete determination of the conventional interest rate without leaving it to the discretion of the creditor. [15]

In any case usury, i.e., the agreement of an interest rate higher than that established by law, is forbidden. Italian law identifies objective parameters beyond which an interest rate is always usurious. In addition, if the rate of interest exceeds the thresholds provided by law, the creditor's right to receive payment of any interest is denied. [16]

Interest is deemed to be not usurious when it corresponds to the average global effective interest rates periodically determined.

In the case of Shari'ah, since the profit and loss sharing principle is of key importance in Islamic finance, cooperation forms are mainly characterized by sharing both profits and risks. The main characteristic stemming from this principle is that people contributing to the capital can receive a return that is proportionate to the actual value of the investment and not to a predetermined amount. [17]

This sharing principle affects both the owner of the capital and the individual who uses such capital for business purposes.

On the other hand, the above-mentioned aspect has a minor applicability within the Italian legal system. Article 2265 of the Italian Civil Code is particularly relevant in this regard, stating in fact that any agreement excluding shareholders from participation in profits or losses is null and void. [18]

This provision lies upon the principle that an agreement to exclude someone from profits is in contrast with the functioning of companies, characterised by the sharing of economic results, but also, that an agreement to exclude someone from losses is contrary to moral and political considerations. [19] In this way it is highlighted that shareholders must be in-

---

[15] Cass., 3480/2016.

[16] The thresholds established on the basis of legal provisions are determined not simply by reference to the interest rate, but by reference to the average overall effective interest rate, including commissions, remuneration for any reason and expenses, excluding those for taxes and duties per year. This average global effective interest rate, identified taking into account the nature, object, amount, duration, risks and guarantees, is calculated on a quarterly basis.

[17] ALVARO S., *La finanza islamica nel contesto giuridico ed economico italiano*, 11.

[18] ABRIANI N., *Il divieto del patto leonino. Vicende storiche e prospettive applicative*, Milano (1994).

[19] FERRI G., *Delle società*, in *Comm. Scialoja, Branca, artt. 2247–2324*, Bologna-Roma (1981), 199.

volved in the enterprise risk for economic policy reasons: if, in fact, a shareholder only participated in the company's profits and not in its losses, such shareholder would not have the same interest in the development of the social will as much as the other shareholders, but he/she could be induced to prefer risky businesses that offer greater possibilities of loss but also greater possibilities for profits. [20]

An additional element of Shari'ah that should be taken into consideration is the prohibition of introducing elements of uncertainty into contractual relations (*ghàrar*). This prohibition makes the presence of uncertainty unlawful with regard to the essential elements of a contract, such as object and price. The result is the prohibition of random contracts, that are, on the other hand, admitted by Italian law. In this regard, it should be remembered that random contracts, distinguished and opposed to commutative contracts, are characterised by an original uncertainty regarding the economic result pursued by the parties. [21] Therefore, according to Italian law, the risk borne by one or more parties must characterise the entire contractual relationship and render the economic advantage proposed by the parties completely uncertain. [22] However, in case of a random contract, Italian law does not allow resort to the remedy of excessive onerousness. [23]

3. Islamic Financial Products: Hints of Consistency with Italian Law

Interesting profiles of comparison between Italian law and the Islamic finance discipline emerge from an analysis of financial products. Reference is made, in particular, to mutual funds, Sukuk and shares. In relation to these Islamic financial products, it should be remembered that Article 1 of Legislative Decree No. 58 of 1998 provides three relevant definitions: "financial products", consisting of financial instruments and every other form of financial investment; bank or postal deposits without the issue of financial instruments do not constitute "financial products"; in addition, it is considered "financial instrument" any instrument shown in Section C of An-

---

[20] SIMONETTO E., *Responsabilità e garanzia nel diritto societario italiano*, Padova (1959), 137.

[21] CAPALDO G., *Contratto aleatorio e alea*, Milano (2004).

[22] Cass., No. 6452, 1991. In order for a contract to be considered uncertain it is necessary that the uncertainty on the economic result of the deal concluded by the parties is objective and depends on the occurrence or not of a future event considered as a source of uncertainty. See Cass., No. 10 del 1993.

[23] See Article 1469 of the Italian civil code.

nex I.[24] Payment instruments are not "financial instruments"; "transferable securities" are those categories of security that can be traded in capital markets, such as for example: a) company shares and other titles equivalent to company shares, of partnership or of other parties and share deposit receipts; b) bonds and other debt titles including the deposit receipts relative to said shares; c) any other transferable security that permits buying or selling transferable securities indicated in letters a) and b) or that involve spot settlement determined with reference to transferable securities, foreign exchange, interest rates or rates of return, commodities or other indices or measurements".[25]

As far as Islamic mutual funds are concerned, it is believed that there is full equivalence between Islamic investment funds and mutual funds as regulated by European Union regulations and the Italian regulations that have implemented them.[26] With reference to Sukuk it should be remembered that, according to the definition given by the *Accounting and Auditing Organization for Islamic Finance*[27] they are characterised by the pres-

---

[24] Section C of Annex I – Financial instruments: (1) Transferable securities; (2) Money-market instruments; (3) Units in collective investment undertakings; (4) Options, futures, swaps, forward rate agreements and any other derivative contracts relating to securities, currencies, interest rates or yields, emission allowances or other derivatives instruments, financial indices or financial measures which may be settled physically or in cash; (5) Options, futures, swaps, forwards and any other derivative contracts relating to commodities that must be settled in cash or may be settled in cash at the option of one of the parties other than by reason of default or other termination event; (6) Options, futures, swaps, and any other derivative contract relating to commodities that can be physically settled provided that they are traded on a regulated market, an MTF, or an OTF, except for wholesale energy products traded on an OTF that must be physically settled; (7) Options, futures, swaps, forwards and any other derivative contracts relating to commodities, that can be physically settled not otherwise mentioned in [point 6 of this Section] and not being for commercial purposes, which have the characteristics of other derivative financial instruments; (8) Derivative instruments for the transfer of credit risk; (9) Financial contracts for differences; (10) Options, futures, swaps, forward rate agreements and any other derivative contracts relating to climatic variables, freight rates or inflation rates or other official economic statistics that must be settled in cash or may be settled in cash at the option of one of the parties other than by reason of default or other termination event, as well as any other derivative contracts relating to assets, rights, obligations, indices and measures not otherwise mentioned in this Section, which have the characteristics of other derivative financial instruments, having regard to whether, inter alia, they are traded on a regulated market, OTF, or an MTF; (11) Emission allowances consisting of any units recognised for compliance with the requirements of Directive 2003/87/EC (Emissions Trading Scheme).

[25] COSTI R., *I prodotti finanziari emessi dalle banche e dalle imprese di assicurazione*, in *I prodotti finanziari, bancari e assicurativi*, Milano (2008), 11.

[26] ALVARO S., *La finanza islamica nel contesto giuridico ed economico italiano*, 38.

[27] "Certificates of equal value representing undivided shares in ownership of tangible assets, usufruct and services or (in the ownership of) the assets of particular projects or special investment activity".

ence of some very specific elements, i.e., the fact that the owner possesses a share of the underlying assets, the fact that the price depends on the expected return on the financed project and in relation to the circumstance that, alongside the issuance contract, there is a commitment of administration and management based on the investors' recommendations. These do not present characteristics incompatible with internal regulations and reflect, in substance, the above-mentioned principle of profit and loss sharing.

With regard to shares, it should be noted that pursuant to Islamic law, by virtue of the above-mentioned principles, shares must respect certain principles. First, preferred shares are not acceptable, as they would be incompatible with the principle of profit and loss sharing. Second, and in light of the same fundamental principle, shares must represent an undivided part of the assets of the company to which the investment of the shareholder refers.

Furthermore, it is not in accordance with the principles of the Shari'ah to invest in over-indebted companies, which operate on a speculative basis, given that in such a case a significant part of the profits would derive from the payment of interest.[28] An investment in companies that carry out lawful activities is therefore admitted, but it must be such as not to result in mere speculation, which is not allowed by the Shari'ah; the pursuit of the economic ends, through the search for profit, must be combined with participation in economic activity. With reference to shares issued by foreign companies, it must be considered that Article 25 of Italian Law 218/95 establishes that companies, associations, foundations and any other body, public or private, even if not of an associative nature, are governed by the law of the State in whose territory the incorporation procedure has been completed. However, Italian law applies if the administrative headquarters are located in Italy, i.e., if the main object of such entities is located in Italy.[29] As a consequence of this principle and on the basis of the *lex loci incorporationis*, foreign law can be applied to financial products issued by a company based in an Islamic state and marketed in Italy.[30] This is without

---

[28] ALVARO S., *La finanza islamica nel contesto giuridico ed economico italiano*, 26.

[29] It is also provided that the following are governed by the law governing the entity: a) the legal nature; b) the name or corporate name; c) the constitution, transformation and extinction; d) the capacity; e) the formation, powers and operating procedures of the bodies; f) the representation of the entity; g) the procedures for the acquisition and loss of the status of associate or partner, as well as the rights and obligations inherent to such status; h) the liability for the obligations of the entity; i) the consequences of violations of law or of the deed of incorporation.

[30] On legislation applicable to companies see BENEDETTELLI M., *Brussels I, Rome I and issues of company law*, in MEUSEN J., PERTEGÁS M., & STRAETMANS G. (eds.) *Enforcement of International Contracts in the European Union* (2004), 225 ff.; CARBONE S. M.,

prejudice to the prevalence of Italian mandatory rules, i.e., those rules that are in any case applied in the Italian legal system despite recourse to foreign law as a result of the rules of private international law.

4. The Italian Offer of Islamic Financial Products

In principle, Islamic financial products are compatible with Italian law. More in general, it has been observed by the *International Organization of Securities Commissions*[31] that "there are no concerns with respect to the compatibility of the IOSCO Core Principles with the Islamic securities market. However, there are certain aspects pertaining to implementation in which further work may be beneficial, and these are detailed in the recommendations". This does not result in the absence of regulatory differences, reflecting the different perspectives of Shari'ah regulation as well as its principles. The issue, highlighted by the *International Organization of Securities Commissions* is rather to facilitate the understanding and knowledge of Islamic financial products, in order to ensure investors' awareness of the reasons for investing in such products.[32] In this regard, there is a need for securities regulators to verify the effectiveness of their disclosure regimes in relation to Islamic products and services to ensure that purchasers of Shari'ah compliant products are able to access the information necessary to make informed decisions. It should also be noted that accounting transparency should be based on generally accepted international standards (such

La riforma societaria tra conflitti di leggi e principi di diritto comunitario, *DCI*, 2003, 97 ff.; DAMASCELLI D., *I conflitti di legge in materia di società*, Bari (2004); KINDLER P., *Aspetti essenziali di un futuro regolamento comunitario sulla legge applicabile alle società*, RDIPP, 2006, 658 ff.; KOZYRIS P. J., *Corporate Wars and Choice of Law*, DukeLJ., 1985, 1 ff.; LOUSSOUARN Y., TROCHU M., *Conflits de lois en matière* de sociétés, in Editions du Juris-Classeur, 1997, 1 ff.; LUZZATTO R., & AZZOLINI C., *Società (nazionalità e legge regolatrice)*, Dig. Comm., XIV, Torino, 1997, 136 ff.

[31] INTERNATIONAL ORGANIZATION OF SECURITIES COMMISSIONS, *Analysis of The Application of IOSCO's Objectives and Principles of Securities Regulation for Islamic Securities Products,* September 2008, 32.

[32] See INTERNATIONAL ORGANIZATION OF SECURITIES COMMISSION, *op. cit.*, 32: "The differences in approach to Islamic capital markets regulations are not in themselves problematic; regulation of conventional financial markets also differs between jurisdictions. There are some existing initiatives in this area [see section 1.3] but in general there is a lack of information exchange, and awareness of the products and practices of Islamic finance. In general, IOSCO could facilitate the understanding of accounting and risk management standards by encouraging further information exchange and co-operation between regulators. Thematic work on disclosure standards for Islamic funds and Sukuk is recommended".

as IFRS) and markets that intend to deal with Islamic financial products should report them to investors with appropriate indicators.[33]

The public offer in Italy of Islamic financial products, with respect to terms and conditions, will be subject to local regulations, as well as the European Union regulations implemented in the Italian legal system. In particular, reference should be made to local legislation regarding the public offer process, disclosure requirements and the offer prospectus. The provisions contained from Articles 94 of Legislative Decree 58/1998 are relevant in this regard. In particular, consideration should be given to provisions concerning the offer prospectus, its publication and mandatory minimum disclosure requirements, also for the protection of the investor and the requirements relating to the approval of the prospectus, concerning the powers of the supervisory authority (CONSOB) and subjecting the issuer and the offeror to such powers. The same shall apply with regard to the prescribed responsibilities, in particular, of the issuer, the offeror and the persons responsible for the information contained in the prospectus.[34]

References

ABRIANI, N., *Il divieto del patto leonino. Vicende storiche e prospettive applicative*, Milano (1994).

ALVARO, S., *La finanza islamica nel contesto giuridico ed economico italiano*, in Quaderni giuridici CONSOB, 6, July 2016.

BENEDETTELLI, M., *Brussels I, Rome I and issues of company law*, in J. MEUSEN, PERTEGÁS, M., & STRAETMANS, G. (eds.), *Enforcement of International Contracts in the European Union* (2004), 225 ff.

BIANCONE, P., SECINARO, S., & RADWAN, M., *Compatibilità della finanza islamica alla normativa italiana*, in Rivista telematica (www.statoechiese.it), 9, 2020.

BORRONI, A., *A Comparative Survey on Islamic Riba and Western Usury,* in Rivista telematica (www.statoechiese.it), 4, 2019.

CAPALDO, G., *Contratto aleatorio e alea*, Milano (2004).

CARBONE, S.M., *La riforma societaria tra conflitti di leggi e principi di diritto comunitario*, in Dir. comm. int., 2003, 97 ff.

COSTI, A., *I prodotti finanziari emessi dalle banche e dalle imprese di assicurazione*, in *I prodotti finanziari, bancari e assicurativi*, Milano (2008), 11 ff.

DAMASCELLI, D., *I conflitti di legge in materia di società*, Bari (2004).

[33] ALVARO S., *La finanza islamica nel contesto giuridico ed economico italiano*, 34.

[34] See Article 94 d.lgs. No. 58, 1998.

FERRI, G., *Delle società*, in *Comm. Scialoja, Branca*, artt. 2247–2324, Bologna-Roma (1981), 199.

FRAGALI, M., *Del mutuo*, in *Comm. Scialoja, Branca, artt. 1813–1822*, Bologna-Roma (1966), 347 ff.

FRANCESCAKIS, P., *Lois d'application immédiate et droit du travail*, in Rev. crit. dr. int. priv., 1974, 273 ff.

GIULIANO, M., *La loi applicable aux contrats: problèmes choisis*, in Recueil des cours, 1977, 158.

INTERNATIONAL ORGANIZATION OF SECURITIES COMMISSIONS, *Analysis of The Application of IOSCO's Objectives and Principles of Securities Regulation for Islamic Securities Products,* September 2008.

KINDLER, P., *Aspetti essenziali di un futuro regolamento comunitario sulla legge applicabile alle società*, in Riv. dir. int. priv. proc., 2006, 658 ff.

KOHLER, C., *L'autonomie de la volonté en droit international privé: un principe universel entre libéralisme et étatisme*, in Recueil des cours, 2013, 359.

KOZYRIS, P.J., *Corporate Wars and Choice of Law*, in Duke Law Jour., 1985, 1 ff.

LOUSSOUARN, Y., & TROCHU, M., *Conflits de lois en matière* de sociétés, in Editions du Juris-Classeur, 1997, 1 ff.

LUZZATTO, R., & AZZOLINI, C., *Società (nazionalità e legge regolatrice)*, in *Dig. Comm.*, XIV, Torino (1997), 136 ff.

MOSCONI, F., *Norme di applicazione necessaria e norme di conflitto di origine convenzionale*, in Riv. dir. int. priv. proc., 1967, 730 ff.

MOSCONI, F., *Exceptions to the operations of choice of law rules*, in Rec. des cours, 1989, 217.

MOSCONI, F., & CAMPIGLIO, C., *Diritto internazionale privato e processuale*, Vol. I, *Parte generale e obbligazioni,* 7th ed., Torino (2015).

POCAR, F., *Norme di applicazione necessaria e conflitti di leggi in tema di rapporti di lavoro*, in Riv. dir. int. priv. proc., 1967, 734 ff.

SIMONETTO, E., *Responsabilità e garanzia nel diritto societario italiano*, Padova (1959).

SIMONETTO, E., *Mutuo*, in *Enc. Giur.*, XX, Roma (1992).

SPERDUTI, G., *Norme di applicazione necessaria e ordine pubblico*, in Riv. dir. int. priv. proc., 1976, 469 ff.

SPERDUTI, G., *Les lois d'application nécessaire en tant que lois d'ordre public*, in Rev. crit. dr. int. priv., 1977, 258 ff.

VON OVERBECK, A.E., *L'irrésistible extension de l'autonomie en droit international privé*, in Hommage à François Rigaux, Bruxelles (1993), 619 ff.

ZAHID, A., & MOHD ALI, H., *Shari'ah as a Choice of Law in international Islamic finance contracts: Shamil Bank of Bahrain case revisited*, in US-China Law Review, 2013, 27 ff.

INDEX

T

U

V

W

Y

Z